Schools Council
Research Studies

The Effects of Environmental Factors on Secondary Educational Attainment in Manchester: a Plowden Follow-up

A report from the Schools Council Project on the Effect of Environmental and Social Factors in Educational Attainment based at the Manchester University School of Education

Schools Council
Research Studies

The Effects of Environmental Factors on Secondary Educational Attainment in Manchester: a Plowden Follow-up

Marjorie E. Ainsworth and
Eric J. Batten

Macmillan

First published 1974

SBN 333 15996 9

Published by MACMILLAN EDUCATION LTD
London and Basingstoke

Associated Companies and representatives throughout the world

Printed in Great Britain by
Hazell Watson & Viney Ltd
Aylesbury, Bucks

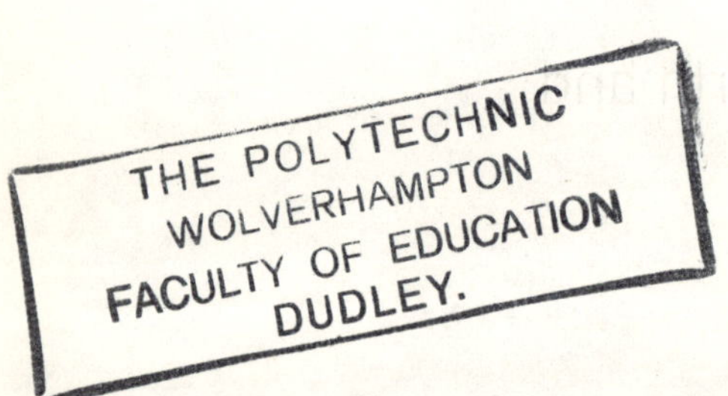

Contents

Tables and figures

Tables

Figures

Preface

The aim of this inquiry was to investigate the educational attainment of a special sample of Manchester secondary school pupils in relation to social and environmental factors. The pupils to be studied were those 2348 primary school children who had been the experimental sample for the Manchester Survey undertaken on behalf of the Plowden Committee by the late Stephen Wiseman, and about whom a report has been published. (Plowden Report, *Children and their Primary Schools*, Volume 2, Appendix 9.) In October 1965, Professor Wiseman, then the Director of the School of Education at the University of Manchester, approached the Schools Council with a proposal for a follow-up study of these same children. His intention was to continue and extend his research into the effects of environment on educational attainment, at least until these pupils left secondary school. Permission and facilities to undertake the follow-up study were granted by the Schools Council and the Department of Education and Science in the summer of 1966. Two research associates—the present authors—were appointed from September 1st 1966, Mrs M. E. Ainsworth, M.Ed., as educational psychologist to look mainly at the school environment of these children, and Mr E. J. Batten, M.A., as educational sociologist to investigate their home circumstances.

The children who formed the Plowden sample had transferred from primary to secondary school in September 1964, just two years before the present investigation could begin. They were then about to become third-formers in the secondary school, being between 13 and 14 years of age. Most of them left school and did not embark on a course of sixth-form study; those who did took the A-level examinations of the General Certificate of Education in 1971. Our Plowden pupils have obviously not all had an equal or similar educational experience during their school careers, and we have been concerned to find out what environmental factors have been associated with their differential ability to extract the maximum advantage from the school system as it exists. The following report is therefore concerned with the second stage of a longitudinal study, the first phase of which was completed with the publication of the Manchester Survey in the Plowden Report.

We are indebted to many hundreds of people without whom the completion of this report would not have been possible. First and foremost we are grateful to the late Chief Education Officer in Manchester, Mr J. K. Elliot, who gave us permission to initiate our study of Manchester schools, and to his successor, Mr D. A. Fiske, for allowing us to complete it. In the initial stages of the research the headteachers and staffs of one hundred and twelve secondary schools in the area assisted us in tracing our sample pupils and finally, when we required the active assistance, co-operation and advice of fifty-three of these schools, the amount of help and support we were given over a long period was not stinted. Our thanks are also due to the parents of 114 of our sample pupils who received us into their homes and answered our questions.

We also wish to thank the Schools Council for initiating the investigation and Mr F. Sparrow, Senior Educational Researcher, for his continued interest and support. The late Dr Stephen Wiseman, who directed the research in its early important stages, laid firm definitive foundations for the study. His untimely death, before he was able to see his results in publication, was both a great personal and professional loss. The sadly brief help we received from our succeeding director, the late Professor Frank Warburton was also invaluable, and his guidance was very much missed during the later stages of the research.

1 Background to the project

The design of our experiment was controlled by three major considerations: (a) the fact that this was to be a follow-up study with a pre-selected sample; (b) the pressure of time due to the advancing age of the sample pupils, and (c) that secondary education within the jurisdiction of the Manchester Local Education Authority was to be reorganized on comprehensive lines in September 1967, just twelve months from our starting date. These factors did not represent three separate problems to be resolved singly by simple strategies or methods of approach. They interacted to produce a background climate to the research, interesting in itself, which was obviously going to set limits to both the range and type of data we should be able to collect. It was clear from the beginning that all the problems inherent in follow-up studies were going to be encountered in one form or another.

In the time lag of over two full years between the completion of data collection for the Plowden Survey and the commencement of the next phase of the research, circumstances had overtaken us. Some of the secondary schools in Manchester were to be reorganized and some were not. Within both these categories there were those schools which would have many pupils leaving school at the statutory leaving age as soon as Easter 1968, and those which would have few. Until we had been able to trace the Plowden pupils to their secondary schools it was not possible to predict how these circumstances were going to affect our experiment. It was clear that we would not have had an overabundance of time for the collection of data even if reorganization had not been envisaged, but the fact that it was due to be implemented in so short a time made it obvious that our criteria of school attainment would have to be restricted to those three years in the secondary school before the effects of reorganization could complicate the issue. It was known, for example, that three of the secondary schools to which Plowden pupils were likely to have transferred would be closing down completely in July 1967, and that twenty-nine of the remaining schools would be changing their nature. Considerable movement between schools of headteachers, teachers and pupils would be inevitable, and—from September 1967—the composition, organization and ethos of most of the secondary schools would be radically altered.

As it was part of our brief to study the effect of secondary school environment on educational attainment, it was clear that any data we required on school characteristics would have to be collected before the school year September 1966 to July 1967, when reorganization became effective. Thus, attainment in the first three years of secondary school would have to be the main criterion of educational achievement. Also, on a very practical level, there was no certainty that records of the attainment of individual pupils would be easily available from many of our schools after that date.

This narrowing of horizons was not simply the result of the pressure of time. The atmosphere prevailing in the schools during this last year of the 'old system' had to be considered. It was a particularly difficult period for headteachers and staff, many of whom were uncertain of their professional placement in the newly organized schools. Timetables and normal routines were frequently disrupted so that teachers and principals could attend the necessary meetings and interviews. It was therefore clear that elaborate testing sessions would be far from welcome and, when we held a meeting to explain the research to headteachers, the Teachers Unions and the representatives of the Manchester Education Authority, definite promises were extracted from us to keep our requirements in this respect to an absolute minimum. Equally importantly, we felt that any attempt to make assessments on the quality of teachers or teaching in those schools to be reorganized would be grossly unfair if not impossible, and this was a serious restriction when we were looking for the concomitants of good educational attainment.

It was clear, also, that in the time available it would be impossible for us to construct and administer specially designed measures of school attainment, and that we should have to rely on existing measures. Similar considerations of urgency had applied to the Manchester Survey for the Plowden Report, but the situation in secondary schools was even more difficult as, unlike the primary schools, they had no standardized test scores available which were directly comparable school with school. The idea of using existing standardized tests was discarded because, even if we had been able to find tests covering a wide range of subjects—which was unlikely, we did not feel the schools would be able to complete them in the time available. More importantly, since our sample of schools was so varied, it could not be assumed that all the pupils would have had an equal opportunity of assimilating the material. Thus, the only possible course open to us was to collect all the marks obtained in internal school examinations during the first three years in the secondary school and to apply to them scaling techniques which would render them grossly comparable school with school.

All these facts had to be borne in mind when devising an experimental plan. As this was to be a follow-up study, we knew our design would have to enable us to draw comparisons with the main findings of the primary school survey. Originally Plowden had been primarily interested in *school* environment and had therefore followed a school based plan with the schools as the units of study. This had been seen at the time as the main inquiry, to be supported by a more detailed and intensive study of individual children and their home environment. The supportive study, however, had emerged as the more interesting. The schools study had shown that, at the primary stage, the major loadings on attainment factors were concentrated among home variables, and that school and neighbourhood together had contributed only 38% of the educational test variance. The supportive individual research had thrown much more light on those aspects of the home which were concerned with attainment effects. For our secondary school survey it was decided to replicate the primary school plan in so far as there would be both school based and pupil based analyses but, from the outset, the latter was expected to produce the more important findings.

Broadly stated, our experimental hypothesis was that, as children grow into adolescence, they become less home orientated and are more likely to be susceptible to extra-familial influences than primary school children, and that this will in turn affect school performance. In the school based study these influences are represented by the school variables. In a tripartite system of secondary education, such as existed in the first three years of our sample's secondary schooling, institutions show greater dissimilarity than primary schools in their composition, organization, aims and ethos. It was hypothesized that, by their very nature, these dissimilarities—in so far as they reflect the educational attitudes of those responsible for their existence—would produce attainment differentials. The study of individuals in the primary inquiry had shown that the heaviest loadings on attainment were for those variables indicating parental attitudes towards education and the standards of literacy in the home background. The individual study at the secondary stage was designed not only to replicate the primary investigation in similar but more refined variables—to see if there was any change of effect at later ages—but also to include variables to calculate the effect of the pupils' own perceptions of their schools. It was also hoped that significant interactions would be found that would help to throw light on the processes involved in the formation of home-school relationships and to calculate any effect they might have on educational progress.

It was obvious from the outset that simple correlation analyses for the sample of schools and the individual sample would not be adequate to uncover the nature of such complex interactions, and that separate analyses of such sub-groups as the data revealed would be necessary. It was felt to be particularly important that individual pupils could be identified as 'improvers' or 'deteriorators', since it was for them that a study of the interaction of school, parents and pupils would be most revealing.

2 The experimental samples

The sample of secondary schools

The subjects for the present investigation represent a sizeable proportion of those pupils selected for study in the Manchester Survey for the Plowden Report. The representativeness of the present sample can only be inferred from a study of the sampling techniques adopted for the primary survey. As in most follow-up studies it was not possible to reproduce the original sample of pupils in its entirety for reasons that will be explained later. The original subjects, however, were of necessity the same individuals from whom the present sample had to be drawn, and it could not follow that, after transfer at eleven-plus, the distribution of secondary schools would be as satisfactory on sampling criteria as that of the primary schools. Table 2.1 shows the sample of forty-four primary schools which provided our secondary sample, broken down by school type and geographical area.

Table 2.1 Sample of contributing primary schools—Plowden Report

	County	C of E	RC	TOTALS
Northern	5	1	2	8
Central	10	7	6	23
Southern	5	1	2	8
Wythenshawe	4	—	1	5
TOTALS	24	9	11	44

These forty-four primary schools provided a sample of 2348 ten-year-old pupils with a complete set of standardized test scores covering the age range seven-plus to ten-plus. They were the primary school children to be followed up in the present study, and our first task was to trace whereabouts in the Manchester school system they were now third form secondary school pupils.

Nominal rolls had been sent to the headteachers of the relevant primary schools in June 1964 when the children were nearing the end of their primary education. In anticipation of a possible follow-up study the headteachers had been asked to insert the name of the secondary school to which it was expected each pupil would transfer after the summer holidays. In September 1966, over two years later, these lists were sifted and new nominal rolls prepared for each of the secondary schools named. We found that the 2348 pupils from forty-four primary schools had dispersed among a total of one hundred and twelve secondary schools of all types. These secondary schools were asked to return the nominal rolls after checking whether the pupils were actually on the school roll and, if not, for any information they could give about removals and transfers. From this preliminary exercise it was possible to identify 2017 pupils with their present secondary schools. The remaining 331 pupils had to be discarded from the sample for the reasons given in Table 2.2.

Table 2.2 Pupils excluded from first sampling selection

Reason for exclusion	No. of pupils
Removal outside Manchester boundary	223
Emigrated	25
Sent to approved school	13
Entered seminaries	2
Killed in road accident	1
Error in date of birth—pupil now working	7
Unable to trace	60
TOTAL	331

It was decided to confine the study to schools within the Manchester County Borough boundary. Most of the 223 children who had moved away during the period July 1964 to September 1966 had gone to live in overspill estates within reasonable distance of Manchester as a result of the extensive slum clearance that had taken place during this period, but they did not have three years' continuous records in the same school. The children who had been sent to approved schools would have made an interesting subsample, but they were widely scattered over the country. The 7 pupils, who should not have been in the original Plowden sample because they were over ten years of age at the time, were pupils in an all-age school who had apparently been kept back in junior classes and the discrepancy in their age had been overlooked. It was regretted that no information about 60 of the pupils could be obtained in spite of the active co-operation in the search of all secondary school headteachers, Education Office staff and school welfare officers. Most of these children had never appeared at the secondary school named by their primary school headteachers and, although school welfare officers scrutinized the third year registers in all Manchester secondary schools, their names were not to be found. It was interesting to note that several headteachers considered it possible that pupils might escape from the educational system for considerable periods as a result of the mass removal of households from clearance areas at that particular time.

In September 1966 there were, in all, one hundred and thirty-two schools within the Manchester boundary which theoretically could have received pupils from the forty-four primary schools after transfer at eleven-plus. These are classified in Table 2.3, which also shows the number of schools of each type which did, in fact, receive pupils from the Plowden sample, and the distribution of the 2017 pupils amongst them. It will be seen that the pupils from 25% of the primary schools in Manchester had been distributed among one hundred and twelve schools taking pupils of secondary age, i.e., to 85% of such schools.

The largest number of Plowden pupils to go to any one secondary school was 90. At the other extreme, nine secondary schools each received only one

Table 2.3 Distribution of primary school sample over existing secondary schools

Type of school	No. of existing schools	No. of schools receiving Plowden pupils	No. of Plowden pupils	Percentage of Plowden pupils
County schools				
Grammar	9	9	228	11
Technical High	10	10	235	12
Comprehensive	2	2	77	4
Secondary Modern	40	35	793	39
Voluntary schools				
Grammar/Technical	2	2	20	1
Technical High	4	4	86	4
Secondary Modern	23	23	453	22
Unreorganized all-age	7	6	25	1
Direct Grant schools				
Grammar	9	9	79	4
Independent schools				
Grammar	2	2	4	1
Special schools	24	10	17	1
TOTALS	132	112	2017	100

pupil from the Plowden sample. It was clearly not feasible to retain in the sample those secondary schools to which a very small number had transferred, as it would not be possible to calculate the effects of school environment variables on the attainment of a very small number of pupils not necessarily representative of a particular school's population. It was therefore decided initially to eliminate all those secondary schools with fewer than 20 of the Plowden subjects. This left us with a total of forty-nine schools. Six other schools containing fewer than 20 Plowden subjects were later added—two because they had nevertheless received a number of pupils from the individual subsample, which we wanted to retain as far as possible, and four Direct Grant grammar schools, in order that this type of school should be represented. This total of fifty-five schools was then reduced to fifty-three, because one school had been in operation in a new building for only one year and had not held any internal examinations, and it was later found that one of the Direct Grant grammar schools kept records of pupils' attainment which were inadequate for our purposes. The breakdown of the final sample by type and number of Plowden pupils is shown in Table 2.4.

Table 2.4 Final sample of schools and distribution of Plowden pupils

Type of school	No. of schools	No. of Plowden pupils
County schools		
Grammar	9	225
Technical High	7	191
Comprehensive	2	75
Secondary Modern	19	593
Voluntary schools		
RC Technical High	2	75
Secondary Modern	10	341
Unreorganized all-age	1	10
Direct Grant schools		
Grammar	3	34
TOTALS	53	1544

The total of 1544 pupils represents those members of the sample in the fifty-three chosen schools for whom a full set of school examination data was available.

Socio-economic stratification, using the same criteria as for the primary school sample was neither possible nor desirable when considering the same pupils distributed over a range of secondary schools. These last are not neighbourhood schools in the same sense as primary schools—their pupils travel widely from their home bases. It will be seen from Table 2.5 that the central area, designated as profoundly 'black' on all the Plowden socio-economic criteria, contains four grammar schools and five technical high schools, all of which had pupils living in 'white' areas. The secondary modern schools are more nearly neighbourhood based in their intake, but even here considerable numbers of children travel to school as a result of parental choice or because the nearest school to home did not provide the secondary modern GCE courses for which a number of pupils were selected at eleven-plus. However, stratification by geographical area does reflect differences in the actual physical environment of the school buildings, and Table 2.5 shows how these are represented.

Table 2.5 Sample of schools by geographical area

Area	Grammar	Technical High	Compre-hensive	Secondary Modern	All-age	TOTALS
Northern	2	1	1	4	—	8
Central	4	5	—	14	1	24
Southern	5	1	—	4	—	10
Wythenshawe	1	2	1	7	—	11

The final sample of fifty-three secondary schools was considered to have stratified itself adequately in terms of school type and geographical area. School size was not controlled but in actuality a full range of school sizes is represented.

The subsample of individuals

The Plowden primary study of individual children had related finally to 186 subjects from twenty-two primary schools. It was possible to identify 151 of these pupils with their secondary schools. Of the remainder, 26 had removed outside Manchester, 4 had emigrated, 2 were in approved schools, one in a seminary, and the remaining 2 had proved impossible to track down. The largest number of subsample pupils in any one secondary school was 10 and nineteen schools had received only one Plowden subject each. It was decided to retain for study all those subsample subjects who attended one of the fifty-three schools selected for the schools analysis, as for these pupils we would have a very definite personal impression of their school environment and so the pupils' reactions to school would be more significant. In this way, a further 25 pupils attending twenty-two schools not selected for the school-based study were eliminated. One other pupil was discarded because of her very chequered school career, which had resulted in inadequate records of attainment. This left us with a sample of 125 pupils in forty-one schools.

The study of these 125 subjects was divided into two main areas for the purpose of data collection. One research officer interviewed all the pupils individually and administered two questionnaires relating to the pupils' own perceptions of school and details of their secondary school careers. The parents of 114 of these pupils were interviewed by the other research officer, who made assessments on home variables hypothetically assumed to bear on the school attainment of their children. Parents of 11 children refused to be interviewed or repeatedly failed to keep appointments. The final total of 114 pupils represents those members of the Plowden individual subsample for whom a full set of data on all variables was available, and a breakdown of their distribution under school type and sex is given in Table 2.6.

Table 2.6 Individual subsample by school type and sex

Type of school	Boys	Girls	TOTALS
County schools			
Boys' grammar	4	—	4
Girls' grammar	—	8	8
Boys' technical high	2	—	2
Girls' technical high	—	2	2
Mixed technical high	3	2	5
Mixed comprehensive	3	5	8
Girls' secondary modern	—	7	7
Mixed secondary modern	18	28	46
Voluntary schools			
Boys' technical high	3	—	3
Girls' technical high	—	4	4
Boys' secondary modern	1	—	1
Girls' secondary modern	—	7	7
Mixed secondary modern	7	5	12
Boys' unreorganized all-age	2	—	2
Direct grant schools			
Boys' grammar	2	—	2
Girls' grammar	—	1	1
TOTAL	45	69	114

3 The variables

School-based study—attainment criteria

For the reasons given previously our criteria of secondary school attainment had to be the marks obtained by individual pupils in internal school examinations taken during the first three years of secondary schooling. Once this decision had been made a meeting was arranged for the headteachers of our sample schools, representatives of the local authority, and the teachers' unions. The aims of the research were explained and an outline given of the procedures we hoped to follow in the collection of data. Following this meeting a questionnaire was sent to each headteacher requesting details of internal examinations and the policies adopted in streaming and subject setting. A copy of this questionnaire will be found in Appendix 1.

It was apparent from the returned questionnaires that there would be no easy solution to the problem of selecting subjects from school curricula to be criterion measures, as it would be necessary to isolate subjects for which a mark was available for every pupil in the year group in every one of the fifty-three schools for each of the first three years. It emerged, not surprisingly, that English and Mathematics were the only subjects to meet these requirements. Even here the marks obtained could not be regarded as representing the same circumstances in all the schools. They reflected such factors as the academic standing of the school, the amount of time allocated to the subjects in the timetable, and the subdivisions under which they were studied. Results in English, for example, were variously recorded as a single mark or as separate marks for a range of activities which included language, literature, essay, comprehension, spelling, reading, oral work, poetry and handwriting. Mathematics marks covered arithmetic, algebra and geometry, with subdivisions such as mechanical, problem, mental and practical. It was decided to extract single marks representing English and Mathematical abilities by adding the marks recorded under subdivisions where this was applicable.

The other subjects mentioned on the questionnaires as appearing in timetables at some time over the first three years included French, German, Spanish, Russian, Latin, Greek, general science, combined sciences, biology, chemistry, physics, geology, rural science, hygiene, history, geography, social studies, woodwork, metalwork, technical drawing, domestic science, needlework, art, craft, music, drama, speech training, physical education, games, dancing, swimming, religious education, shorthand, typing, commerce and book-keeping. In none of these subjects was a mark available for every pupil in the age group for each of the three years in question. The various combinations of subjects presented resulted from policies of pupil choice, grouping of subjects to fit the exigencies of timetabling and staffing, the range of ability in different streams and, of course, the academic standing of the school, tradition, and what might be called 'philosophical' concepts of the relative importance of certain subject areas in the content of any educational course. These inferences could be drawn from the remarks made by headteachers on the returned questionnaires, of which the following are typical examples.

'All second year pupils have a choice between needlework and domestic science. In the third year, the three top streams (having started a second language) choose between art, needlework and domestic science. The two bottom streams continue with needlework or domestic science and also have art.'

'Not all forms study needlework and domestic science in the third year.'

'Art and craft become options in the second year, and geography and biology become options in the third year.'

'We have a strong physics tradition in this school, but we were unable to include it in the second and third years as we had no teacher.'

'This school offers options in all subjects except English and mathematics after the second year.'

'French and needlework were dropped in the third year because of loss of staff. Boys start metalwork in the third year in place of woodwork.'

'Music and housecraft omitted because of shortage of staff in second and third years. French taken only by top stream as we have only one part-time teacher.'

'French taken by top stream only. Rural science taken by bottom stream only.'

We wanted to measure as many school activities as possible, not just tool subjects. Wiseman, in the Plowden Report, particularly stressed that such measures are a necessary part of any criterion of school attainment but that they give a far from balanced picture. They take no account of the many other activities which go on in school, in art and craft, music, science, history and geography, and in many other pursuits which often cannot be classified under traditional subject labels, but are assumed to be of great importance and significance educationally.

However, it became obvious when we analysed the returned questionnaires that subjects other than English and mathematics would have to be clustered under 'subject area' headings, and the marks in any subdivisions regarded as equivalent. For example, a mark for 'the sciences' would be a general science mark or the summated marks for any combination of biology, chemistry or physics. Similarly, a mark for 'the social sciences' would be the mark for history or geography or social studies, or the summated marks of any combination of these. The non-academic subjects such as art, craft, woodwork, metalwork, needlework and music were regarded as subdivisions under the general heading of 'non-academic subjects', and the vagueness of this measure would have to be borne in mind when interpreting any apparently significant findings. The remaining subjects—religious education, physical education, games, drama, etc., could not be included at all, as in many cases performance had not been recorded in any way, or had been the subject of unquantifiable comment. Foreign and classical languages had been taken consistently over all three years by only a very small number of the Plowden pupils and for this reason were not considered as criteria measures.

Finally five subject areas were decided upon—English, mathematics, the sciences, the social sciences and non-academic subjects. While these obviously did not represent the same content or level of instruction in all the schools, they could yield scores which would be adequately comparable and provide sufficient indicators of gross differences between schools and types of school, if suitable scaling techniques were employed.

The amount of clerical work likely to be involved in the extraction of the necessary marks from school records, and their tabulation, was a task we could not reasonably ask the schools to do for us. A try-out procedure was undertaken by the two research officers, who visited a school of average size and copied marks by hand from school files. It was found to take the better part of two days and was clearly impracticable. We knew that, of the fifty-three schools involved, forty-three would not be setting their third year annual examinations until June or early July 1967 and, of these, thirty-two were to be closed or reorganized in September. There was no guarantee that records would be available to us after that date. It was thus essential to collect all examination data between the last examination and the school holidays in July—at least in the thirty-two changing schools. After much discussion and experiment a method of photocopying was adopted.

The research officers visited each school with a 35 mm reflex camera and a copying stand with lighting equipment. Negatives were obtained on microfilm loaded into empty cassettes by the photocopying department staff of the Manchester University library. As school records variously took the form of class lists, individual record cards, carbon copies of reports and report books, the number of exposures per school varied enormously. In a small school with one class in each year and mark lists only three exposures were required. In our largest school with 207 pupils in the third year and records in the form of carbon copies of annual reports 621 exposures, i.e., 30 rolls of film were expended. In all, several hundred rolls of exposed film were developed for us.

All the school examination data had been collected by this method by December 1967 and, in the meantime, the task of transcription from film to data sheets had been proceeding. A microfilm reading machine was used to investigate the negative film and the necessary marks were transcribed by hand. This work took several months of concentrated and eyestraining effort, as there were fifteen scores to be extracted for more than 6000 pupils in the thirteen to fourteen year old age range in the fifty-three schools. The marks from the raw data sheets had then to be scaled to make them comparable school with school.

It was recognized that a pupil's school attainment scores, as extracted from school records, would be meaningless unless they could be related to his ability level. It is equally possible to obtain a mark of 50% for English in the 'A' stream of a grammar school and in the remedial stream of a secondary modern school, but they have no comparative meaning except in so far as they are relative to the scores obtained by other individuals in the same class or English set. We were required to establish the relativity of such marks to those obtained by all other individuals in the total sample of 1544 pupils in fifty-three schools of all types. The marks of these 1544 pupils would of course be relative to those obtained by all the pupils in their particular classes or sets, which made it necessary for us to obtain scores for the whole year group in all schools before extracting the scaled marks of the sample pupils.

A necessary first step was to administer a single test of general ability to all pupils in the year group in the fifty-three schools. The scores derived from this would establish the range of ability in each class, stream or set, and these ranges could be used as scales against which to plot raw attainment scores in school subjects. Thus, raw attainment scores could be scaled to reflect the ability level at which each pupil was working.

A general ability test in both verbal and non-verbal forms had been constructed at the University of Manchester as part of a Guidance Programme for Secondary Schools, standardized on the thirteen to fourteen year old age group. Although national norms for the test had not been completed at the time, it was considered that the range of difficulty they encompassed was adequate for our purposes. Both the verbal and non-verbal forms were administered, the verbal form being used as the basis of scaling the school marks. The research officers administered the tests personally at twelve schools at the request of headteachers, and the remaining schools made their own arrangements. When the 12 000 completed scripts were returned to us, raw scores were derived and the scoring checked for accuracy.

The Verbal General Ability Test is scored from 0 to 44. For each class or set these scores were given a rank order. In one class, position one might have a score of 43 and position thirty a score of 19, whereas in another class position one might have a score of 19 and position thirty a score of nought. This procedure established the score from the class ability range which would be allotted to the equivalent class position in any of the school subjects for the same group of pupils. The normality of the distributions could be easily assessed. Any very extreme scores at the head or tail of a distribution were adjusted to avoid the distortion of school means by atypical individuals.

In this way we derived eighteen criteria measures for each pupil—scaled scores in English, mathematics, the sciences, the social sciences and non-academic subjects, plus a year total score for each of the first, second and third years in the secondary school. A further criterion measure—of success in external examinations at sixteen-plus (GCE, O-level or CSE)—was added later. When all the raw scores had been scaled, the scaled marks appertaining to the 1544 Plowden pupils were extracted from those for the whole year group. A preliminary investigation of the resulting distributions of scores revealed an amount of positive skew only to be expected from the constitution of the sample and the nature of the variables.

In order to diminish the distorting effect of this on subsequent correlations the criteria scores were normalized and standardized to have a mean of 50 and a standard deviation of 10, the normalizing sample being the 1544 pupils from the fifty-three schools. The scores obtained by these pupils in the six eleven-plus selection tests were also normalized and standardized in the same way, as were the scores obtained on the verbal and non-verbal general ability tests taken at fourteen-plus. For the school-based study these marks were converted into mean scores for each school separately to indicate the quality of intake of each school and the level of subject attainment relative to the standard of ability. All the school environment variable scores were also normalized and standardized to a mean of 50 and a standard deviation of 10.

School-based study—environment variables

Wiseman (1964), when discussing the effect of school environment on educational progress, expresses astonishment at the small amount of research designed to investigate this problem. One reason for this state of affairs may be that because educational institutions, by their very nature and existence, are seen to be the main agents of intellectual development, their ostensible primacy has led to their neglect as a field of study. As it is difficult to envisage how intellectual development can take place without them, their effect on intellectual progress may have been prejudged. It would be easy to suppose that because schools appear to be fairly homogeneous with respect to their aims and functions they could not be responsible for differential results in individuals. That individuals do not each respond to schooling in exactly the same way is only too evident, and researchers have tended to look outside the school and concentrate on extra-school factors in an attempt to explain differences in educational outcome.

There appear to have been two main avenues of approach to the problem of studying the effects of social and physical environment on school progress. The first method has been to look at one aspect of environment at a time—

either home, neighbourhood or school—and within these specific areas to describe and evaluate those aspects which appear to be associated with intellectual development. The second method has been to study a number of aspects of all three environmental areas and analyse the collective data for their relative effects on educational attainment. Both methods have produced fairly conclusive results. From the great number of studies using the first method it has been shown that certain home environment factors correlate highly with school attainment, and results show a high degree of consensus as to what the crucial concomitants of attainment are likely to be. The studies following the second method, which have attempted to quantify the relative effects of home, neighbourhood and school environments, have tended to show that extra-school factors do indeed play the predominant part in influencing the effects of schooling. Thus, both methods of inquiry have tended to support the premise that children import into schools qualities associated with their out-of-school background that strongly influence their reaction to the instruction purveyed by the school. Furthermore, these imported qualities do not seem, by and large, to be transformed by qualities in the school environment. The question of what, if any, are the qualities of school environment which maximize the effectiveness of instruction is still largely unanswered. Even though, as the researches show, the effects of home and neighbourhood are of major importance, the dissimilarities existing between schools still need to be described and their effect, if any, on the attainment of their pupils evaluated. Many of the differences between schools are the result of deliberate conscious choice and action on the part of governments, local authorities, headteachers and staffs of schools, and the results of these choices need to be evaluated, though their effects on educational attainment may be minimal compared with the influences of society at large. It would appear to be an easier matter, in the short term, to change a school in the direction of maximum effectiveness than to change the home background and family experience of pupils or the physical and social aspects of a neighbourhood. The possibility also exists that schools may be instrumental in ameliorating those home and neighbourhood conditions most related to poor school achievement, once ameliorating factors can be identified. There is no doubt that, in the long term, the transformation of adverse social conditions is the effective answer.

The very few studies that have specifically looked for school environment factors in isolation for their effect on educational attainment have produced results which are far from conclusive. There appear to have been only three major studies in this field, and their results are not strictly comparable because their experimental samples have been drawn from different populations. Mollenkopf (1956) in the United States, tested 17 957 ninth- and twelfth-grade pupils in two hundred and six high schools. He included thirty-four variables including the number of school facilities, size of school, attendance and size of class. Size of class was found to influence the prediction of attainment. Kemp (1955) broke the ground in this country with his study of fifty junior mixed schools in London. He collected data on forty-two variables grouped under the headings of school atmosphere and organization, size of school and size of class, site and buildings, type of neighbourhood, attainment of the children, etc. Size of school was the only variable to correlate significantly with attainment. Much of Kemp's work was replicated by Warburton (1964) with a sample of forty-eight secondary modern and all-age schools in Salford. He found that the three main factors affecting scholastic attainment and intelligence test scores were socio-economic level showing chiefly as good school neighbourhood, progressiveness, good teaching conditions based mainly on small classes, and good attendance. Griffin (1968) studied the differential effect of school organization (secondary modern, comprehensive or grammar) on the development of intelligence and attainment in English, and found no one type of school emerged as superior to the other two. It appears that there has been no study previous to this investigation which has used a multivariate approach on a sample of secondary schools of all types, and it is for this reason that many school environment variables have been included that individually have been found to have little or no significant effect on attainment either in primary schools or secondary modern schools.

As comparisons were to be made between the results of the present study and those of the Plowden primary school survey, it was decided to retain from the latter work such variables as appeared, prima facie, to be applicable to secondary schools also. Information on the more objective variables was provided by headteachers' replies to questionnaires. Ratings on the more subjective variables were made by the research associates, based on the responses of the headteachers in lengthy interview, and on an observation visit to each school in the sample. The variables which also appeared in the primary school survey are discussed below.

(i) SIZE OF SCHOOL

The findings of the primary school survey revealed a positive correlation (0·315) between school size and attainment, supporting the results of Kemp (1955) and Morris (1966). The National Survey in Appendix 4 of the Plowden Report has also shown that HMIs (Her Majesty's Inspectors) had more often rated larger schools than smaller schools as average or above average. Warburton (1964) had also deduced that the larger schools in his sample of secondary modern schools were more efficient. This was clearly a variable to be looked at again in relation to secondary schools of all types, particularly as Wiseman (1967) had shown that the size of the school had an increasing effect with age.

(ii) SIZE OF CLASS

Wiseman (1967) had found a positive correlation of 0·316 between class size and attainment in those primary schools attended by pupils in the present sample, this association being further supported by the appearance of the variable in the most important educational factor emerging from his factor analysis. A similar result had been reported by Mollenkopf (1956) in the United States high schools. The National Survey (1967) also reported an association between better work and larger classes. Morris (1966) found that reading attainment was better in the larger classes of primary schools. These findings are inconclusive because of discrepant samples and controversial in that they appear to fly in the face of common sense. Warburton (1964), on the other hand, had come to the conclusion that optimum attainment was shown in the middle-sized classes of secondary modern schools, but that in general the results—particularly in arithmetic—tended to show higher attainment in smaller classes. It is obvious that class size is an important variable, and that not enough is known of the other factors that contribute to its correlation with attainment.

(iii) PUPIL/TEACHER RATIO

It could be hypothesized that the correlation between this variable and size of class should be close to unity because one assumes that large classes exist because of shortage of teachers. The primary school survey, however, showed results that are puzzling. The correlation between size of class and pupil/teacher ratio was 0·859 but, although the first had a high loading in the major attainment factor, the latter did not. This effect may have been due to a statistical artefact produced by assumptions applied to the Varimax analysis, or it may have been due to real influences arising from the distribution of available staff because of the number of classrooms available, the presence of specialist teachers for certain subjects, or the temporary overstaffing of schools due to rapid migration to slum clearance estates, etc. As larger classes appear to be correlated with high attainment in the primary schools, it may be that teachers with a number of free periods are more effective than those with none, even if their classes are larger in number as a consequence. Pupil/teacher ratio is clearly a variable with greater complexity than is immediately apparent. Its inclusion in a secondary school study is clearly justified where small sixth forms and examination groups are contributing differences, where small remedial classes are often organized, and where—in Manchester at any rate—practical subjects are conventionally taught in groups limited to twenty pupils.

(iv) PERCENTAGE ATTENDANCE

In the primary school study this variable correlated 0·414 with attainment measures, and also contributed to the major attainment factor derived from the factor analysis. Kemp (1955) also found a significant relationship (0·45) between school morale (which included regularity of attendance) and attainment. Warburton (1964) found that this was the only variable for which the average correlation with the school environment was lower for intelligence than for attainment. His hypothesis that high attendance would show beneficial effects chiefly in arithmetic was confirmed, the average correlation between attendance and arithmetic being 0·34 compared with 0·27 for reading. Morris (1966) found that, in the primary schools, the good readers had a significantly better attendance record than the poor readers. On the other hand, Mollenkopf (1956) found very low and even negative correlations with reading in the United States. The English results are therefore in line with what is to be expected. The inclusion of this variable in the present research was in order to investigate whether it had any differential effects with age, school subject and type of secondary school.

(v) PERCENTAGE OF PUPILS RECEIVING FREE MEALS AND FREE CLOTHING

Free meals and free clothing had proved to be two important variables in the primary survey, where they were included as 'home' variables and had correlated negatively and significantly with attainment measures at −0·471 and −0·369 respectively. They had also contributed highly to the major attainment factor, and a correlation of 0·415 between *free meals* and backwardness had been demonstrated. Although these variables undoubtedly derive from home circumstances, after selection at eleven-plus there is a sense in which they may be regarded as school variables in that they reflect the socio-economic conditions of the school intake. They are less indicative of neighbourhood at the secondary level and may reflect the reputation of the school as seen by the parents when confronted with a choice of school. Are there in fact particular schools likely to be chosen by the poorer parents and, if so, what are their characteristics? It was thought that this would be a particularly interesting question in the case of the selective grammar and technical high schools. The provision of free clothing is certainly a more complex variable at the secondary level where it is as much related to the emphasis a school places on the desirability of wearing school uniform as it is to poverty in the home. The schools with the highest incidence of free clothing grants would not necessarily contain the most poverty-stricken pupils, but may have headteachers who place great value on the wearing of uniform by all pupils and therefore press the local authority very hard for the provision of uniform purchasing vouchers.

(vi) AGE OF TEACHERS

The percentage of teachers under thirty and over fifty years of age are two further variables replicated from the primary school survey. Although it had been shown that at primary age the physical aspects of school environment had a much greater importance than either teachers, organization or policy, and that the factor mainly concerned with teachers had contributed only 2% of the educational variance, it was nevertheless felt that the age of the teaching staff might be more important at the secondary level. Certainly our headteachers expressed strong opinions at interview that age and experience of teachers were particularly important determinants of the quality of teaching, and the main indicators of a school's stability. It seemed fairly certain that there would be a different effect of these variables between types of secondary school, but their possible effect on secondary attainment needed to be evaluated.

(vii) PERCENTAGE OF GRADUATES ON TEACHING STAFF

In the primary study this variable had shown the interesting result that graduate teachers had a positive effect with attainment at the lower end of the age range and a negative effect at the upper end. The situation in the secondary schools could not be expected to produce results that could be directly compared with these findings, as a greater proportion of graduate teachers would obviously be found in the selective schools. However, its association with other variables when type of school is held constant was thought to be a profitable area of study.

(viii) TEACHER TURNOVER RATE

A decreasing effect with age on attainment had been found for this variable in the primary study. Although the correlations were low, a steady decline of effect from 0·14 to 0·03 between the ages of seven-plus and ten-plus had been noted. A comparison between this finding and secondary school results was thought to be desirable, as headteachers were in the main adamant that rapid staff turnover was one of their greatest problems. This applied equally to the 'good' schools where staff change was more likely to be associated with professional promotion than dissatisfaction.

(ix) PROPORTION OF MEN TEACHERS

This variable had not appeared in the major attainment factors in the primary school survey. Its negative contribution to the only teacher factor had suggested that attainment at the seven-plus and eight-plus levels was associated with women rather than men teachers. In spite of this very tentative effect it was decided to include this variable again in the secondary school survey because of the frequently expressed opinion, particularly in relation to the secondary modern schools, that the men teachers contributed most to the discipline of the school and adopted a more serious attitude to their professional careers.

(x) SEX OF THE SCHOOL

This variable had shown no significant effects in any of the analyses performed for the primary study. However, it was decided that it might play a greater part in the secondary school system. Any controversy about the effect of segregation by sex is almost entirely centred on the adolescent age group, and the possible effects on attainment in the secondary schools of coeducation could not be ignored.

(xi) AGE OF SCHOOL BUILDING

This variable did not emerge as an important contributor to attainment in the primary school study. It appeared in one of the factors associated with age, and showed its greatest effect at ages seven-plus and eight-plus in the direction opposite to that which would be expected. Warburton (1964) had included this variable in his study of Salford secondary modern schools because of its objectivity, but the results were chaotic and no trend whatsoever was discernible. However, it was not deleted from the present study, as it was hypothesized that—for a sample covering all types of secondary school—as well as being a measure of the physical environment it was also a measure of the weight of tradition, which some of our headteachers valued highly. On the other hand, certain headteachers, whose schools were housed in older buildings, displayed some resentment. They clearly felt that the modern 'show places' had an unfair advantage in attracting staff and equipment.

Information for the above variables—all replications of variables in the primary school survey—was obtained from a questionnaire completed by headteachers, a copy of which will be found in Appendix 2.

The variables listed in the next section are also replicated, but they are the more subjective ones given ratings by our research officers. It was the usual practice to have a lengthy interview with the headteacher, followed by a tour of the school during which classrooms were visited and teachers and pupils engaged in conversation. Notes on interview and observation schedules were made, copies of which are in Appendices 3 and 4. After each visit the variables were rated independently by the two research officers, and the two ratings compared. There was very little divergence between the two sets of ratings and in every case agreement was reached when individual observations and impressions were discussed.

(i) ATTITUDE TO INQUIRY

No correlation for this variable with attainment had been discovered from the results of the primary study. It was felt, however, that it might be a worthwhile discriminator in the secondary schools, as ratings certainly discriminated between headteachers when assessments were made on the amount of cooperative enthusiasm with which we were received. It was felt that any suspicion we encountered may well have been due to the impeding reorganization of schools, as it was necessary to reassure several headteachers that we had nothing to do with 'comprehensivization' and had no interest in assessing the attainment of their pupils for this purpose. On the other hand, there was no doubt that certain schools were overwhelmed with requests for research facilities. We were shown large box files filled to overflowing with outstanding questionnaires and schedules connected with research projects from national, international and local sources, and there is no doubt that such a proliferation of documents can constitute a serious problem for schools, particularly when repeated requests are made for the same information.

(ii) QUALITY OF THE HEADTEACHER

In the primary school survey this variable produced no significant attainment effects. It was retained, as schools at the secondary stage appear to be less homogeneous than primary schools in almost every respect, and it was felt that this variable might produce important results with older children.

(iii) INNOVATION

This variable was hypothesized to be the nearest equivalent to the 'progressiveness' variable of the primary school study, which had rated schools on a formal–free scale ranging from extremely formal and orthodox to most informal, free and progressive. A knowledge of the secondary schools in our sample precluded the adoption of an identical scale for our study, as none of the schools deviated from the orthodox line to any marked degree. It was decided, however, that an assessment could be made on the awareness of new educational ideas, techniques and equipment, and the extent to which they were used. The uses made of television, radio, audio-visual aids, teaching machines, language laboratories, etc., was noted, and participation in Nuffield schemes, Newsom projects, social work projects, work practice schemes, and the number and types of courses which the headteachers themselves regarded as experimental, were assessed.

(iv) EMPHASIS ON EXTERNAL EXAMINATIONS

In the primary study this variable appeared as 'examination technique', where it was a measure of efficiency in preparation for examinations and objective tests. It had appeared in the second most important attainment factor which was clearly important for 'brightness'. In the present study this variable was looked at from a different point of view—as a measure of the importance of external examinations at sixteen and eighteen-plus to the raison d'être of the school. Ratings were based on statements by headteachers and a close look at the system of streaming and course option arrangements. There was little diversity in the selective schools, which were clearly examination orientated, but the effect of the diversity found in the non-selective schools promised to be interesting.

(v) SOCIAL ATMOSPHERE

Disappointingly, this variable showed no significant correlation with attainment in the primary school study. Observation visits to secondary schools, however, made it evident that such a variable very clearly differentiated the social ambience of our secondary school sample and might therefore repay further study.

(vi) HOMEWORK

The correlation between homework and attainment in the primary survey was 0·303, the schools which gave homework at the ten-plus level tending to produce higher scores in attainment tests. This variable also showed a greater effect with age and was one of the outstanding variables in the major attainment factor. Clearly, in the secondary school system, this variable was going to be associated with school type, and the interest would be concentrated on its effects in the non-selective schools where homework was less likely to be rigidly enforced for all pupils.

(vii) OUT-OF-SCHOOL ACTIVITIES

No association of this variable with attainment was reported for the primary school sample. It was retained in the present study because it is generally felt that such activities are appropriately a part of secondary school life, where school clubs and societies are regarded as valuable extensions to the educational content of the school day. They are clearly regarded as important in the Newsom Report, which made strong recommendations for their existence in secondary modern schools.

(viii) FIRST IMPRESSION OF SCHOOL

This very subjective variable had shown no significant effect with attainment in the primary schools. It was retained here because a need was felt to differentiate the effect of the newness of school buildings. There were clearly some new buildings in our sample which received less loving care than some of the older more inconvenient establishments, and where minimal effort was exerted to provide any kind of aesthetic stimulation in the physical environment. The discrepancies were very marked and the effect, if any, of the sometimes outstanding efforts in unpromising buildings was thought to be worthy of assessment.

(ix) APPEARANCE AND SOCIABILITY OF PUPILS

In the primary school survey this was included as a single variable, and had correlated importantly at 0·422 with attainment. Some doubt was expressed, however, as to whether it was a 'home' or a 'school' variable. In the secondary survey we have taken appearance and sociability as two distinct measures, as it was thought that appearance—with its connotations of cleanliness and of care of clothing—is related to home background, whereas the sociability displayed by pupils in the school situation is more likely to reflect the atmosphere of the school.

(x) CORPORAL PUNISHMENT

No important attainment effects for this variable were found in the primary study. It was retained in the present investigation because it was obviously a clear discriminator between secondary schools. It is a very difficult variable on which to make ratings, as a headteacher's stated policy on this subject may bear little relation to the amount of corporal punishment actually being administered in the fastnesses of classrooms. Eventually we used a three-point scale of 'never–sometimes–frequently', and modified headteachers' statements according to the evidence of our own eyes and ears and the voluntary comments of individual pupils.

(xi) QUALITY OF BUILDINGS

Warburton (1964) found a clear association between good school buildings and superior attainment. This had not been an important variable in the Plowden study, except in so far as it loaded significantly in the factor related to age trends. As our sample of secondary schools contained a full range of building qualities, from the very best to the very worst, this variable did discriminate between schools and was worth retaining.

(xii) QUALITY OF SCHOOL EQUIPMENT

This had mattered increasingly with age in the primary study. Several of our secondary schools were extremely well equipped in the way of language labs, teaching machines, calculating machines, aural and visual aids, etc., and other headteachers obviously thought they were being discriminated against in this respect. The provision of science equipment was particularly varied. It is possible that the quality of school equipment also gives a measure of the enthusiasm and energy of the teaching staff, which we have not been able to assess in a more objective way.

(xiii) QUALITY OF LIBRARY

This had not emerged as a particularly important attainment variable in the primary schools but it was thought that, as a well equipped and efficient library is very pertinent to the type of study undertaken in secondary schools, it would show more positive effects at later ages. There was clearly a vast amount of difference in provision both of rooms and books between schools and between types of schools. The uses to which libraries were put also varied tremendously. Some rooms were kept locked with the chairs on the tables until a teacher accompanied a class for a library period, when everybody chose a book and sat down and read it until the bell went. Others were obviously being used for individual study and research purposes. Cataloguing systems ranged from non-existent to extremely professional. Whether there was a special allowance given to a teacher-librarian was a further indication of the seriousness attributed to library facilities.

(xiv) STREAMING

This had been the third most powerful predictor of good attainment in the primary school survey—streamed primary schools had better records of attainment. In the secondary schools, however, it promised to be a very complex variable, as we were dealing with several distinct types of school with different traditional attitudes to this problem. The grammar schools, in the main, did not stream their pupils on entry but waited until the first year had been completed. After that there appeared to be a minimal amount of transfer between streams. The non-selective schools, on the other hand, tended to stream on entry giving great weight to the eleven-plus selection test results, but subsequently there was a greater amount of flexibility, and promotions and demotions between streams were more frequent. We therefore decided to have two measures connected with streaming—*streamed on entry* and *streamed by ability*. A measure of the flexibility of any system of streaming was also calculated by counting the number of promotions and demotions during the first three years.

Thirty-two new variables were added to the above, either at the request of headteachers or because they seemed to us to be particularly pertinent to secondary school organization. Those suggested by headteachers were—(i) *movement between lessons*, (ii) *number of teaching periods per day*, and (iii) *length of teaching day in minutes*. Whether teachers should move to pupils or pupils to teachers' rooms seemed to be of particular concern to the heads of the non-selective schools where it seems to be traditional that pupils move round the school for each lesson and teachers stay put. In the selective schools, however, the teachers usually move to the pupils' form rooms for those lessons where specialist equipment is not needed. There was also a considerable amount of soul-searching as to whether it was 'better' to have many short teaching periods of thirty minutes each, or fewer periods of longer duration. There was a clear suggestion that such considerations as movement and timetable organization had crucial effects on attainment, as they could both be associated with 'wasting valuable teaching time'.

The variables added because they had obvious discriminatory powers in our secondary school sample were—(i) *percentage of pupils leaving at the statutory leaving age*, (ii) *percentage of pupils completing an extra year of schooling*, (iii) *percentage of pupils entering the sixth-form*, (iv) *the size of entry for external examinations at sixteen plus*, (v) *range of external examination subjects offered*, (vi) *percentage of untrained teachers*, (vii) *graduate headteacher*, (viii) *age of headteacher*, and (ix) *authoritarian headteacher*, (x) *the importance attached to the wearing of school uniform*, (xi) *adherence to traditional system of prefects*, and (xii) *house system*, seemed to us to be further measures of orthodoxy, whereas (xiii) the efficiency of *vocational guidance*, (xiv) the amount of *opportunity given to individual pupils to acquire formal status* in the school, (xv) provisions made for the *welfare* of individuals, (xvi) *extent of subject setting*, (xvii) *adequacy of individual pupil records*, (xviii) *the use of a merit mark system* as an incentive to achievement, all had connotations of pupil-centredness. (xix) The number and range of *school journeys* at home and abroad, and (xx) the number and range of *visits during school hours*, were included as general measures of energy and enthusiasm. (xxi) The number of *internal examinations* held in each school year varied from one to three, and this measure was included to reinforce our assessment of the emphasis placed on examinations in the objectives of a school.

In view of the importance attached to parent-school relations in the Plowden Report, we decided to look at this aspect of the secondary schools particularly carefully. Unfortunately we could not use the variable *Parent-Teacher Association* as there was none in any of our schools. We found two parents' associations in grammar schools, but the headteachers were careful to point out that they were run entirely by parents and only parents were active; any suggestion that teachers might become involved would not be welcome. Both had been initiated in the early days of the second world war to fight against the evacuation of pupils to safe areas, and had continued as fund raising bodies ever since. We finally decided to make our measures of parent-teacher interaction as objective as possible by counting the number of formal and informal occasions where it was possible for parents and teachers to meet. A further measure—of the availability of teachers to individual parents—was added, and here an attempt was made to gauge the obstacles in the way of a parent being able to see a particular teacher to discuss his child at any time he thought necessary.

Since this is a follow-up study and our sample of schools could only be assumed to be representative, whereas the primary school sample had been carefully selected, we included *type of school* as a single variable, also *coeducation* and *voluntary school* (*R.C., or C.E.*). Finally, a rating was made on the *quality of specialist rooms*, a clear school discriminator which might have a bearing on attainment. A full list of all the variables used in the school-based study appears in Appendix 5.

When the distributions of scores on these variables were inspected, in many cases they were found to be skewed, and they were therefore normalized and standardized to have a mean of 50 and a standard deviation of 10. This brought them into line, as far as possible, with the distributions of the criteria measures, and would render any intercorrelations capable of a more valid interpretation.

Variables for the study of individuals

Four objective variables used in the analysis of schools were retained for the study of individual pupils. These were—*type of secondary school*, *entered 6th form*, *left school at age 16*, and *left school at age 15*. The remaining variables were acquired from three sources—(i) the Plowden survey, (ii) the pupils, and (iii) the parents of the pupils. From the Plowden survey we obtained data on the twelve test results which had been the criteria variables in that study—tests of intelligence, English and arithmetic given at seven-plus, eight-plus, nine-plus and ten-plus. These scores can be viewed either as predictors of secondary school attainment or additional criteria variables for an investigation of seven-plus to sixteen-plus achievement as a total process. We also included a total score of all the ten-plus selection tests, as this was the single measure on which our pupils had been selected for the type of secondary school attended. *Primary headteacher's rating* was also included in order to compare its association with future attainment with that of primary school test measures, and to assess its relative associations with home environment scores.

Three further variables from the schools analysis of the Plowden survey, which had promised to be very interesting, were dropped after a preliminary correlational analysis, because they revealed only very low and inconsistent associations with secondary school attainment. These were *sex of primary school*, *streamed at primary school* and *progressiveness of primary school*. It was with reluctance that these three variables were dropped as they might have provided us with much needed evidence that aspects of primary school organization have some connection with ultimate attainment. *Progressiveness of primary school* produced consistent results in that all the non-significant correlations operated positively, and there was an association with second year non-academic subjects which was significant at the 5% level. Though this is an extremely attenuated result, there is the suggestion that progressive methods at primary level have the advantage—however marginal—over extreme formality, as a predictor of high attainment in the secondary school.

The remaining environment variables were selected from over three hundred items included in either the parent or pupil interview schedules, copies of which will be found in Appendices 6 and 7. Correlations for each item with each of the criterion variables enabled us to discard those which had little or no association with school attainment, or where they were very obviously measuring the same effect as other items. For example, *absence of a parent* and *change in father's occupational level* produced average correlations over all secondary attainment measures of only 0·027 and 0·054 respectively, and the direction of effect was not consistent over all school subjects at all ages. Where overlapping content was concerned, we dropped *parents' knowledge of best and worst subjects* because it obviously duplicated *parents' knowledge of class position in individual subjects*. The latter was retained in the final analysis because of its generally higher correlations with attainment scores.

The interview with individual pupils produced thirty-three measures of factual circumstances or attitudes to school which were finally discarded because of low associations with attainment level. For instance, *paid job outside school* and *liking for school* produced average attainment correlations of only 0·144 and 0·041 respectively when the variable direction of signs had been ignored. Eleven of the discarded items were attitude measures derived from an adaptation of the College Characteristics Inventory devised by Pace and Stern. This inventory was designed originally to assess the amount of satisfaction college institutions afforded to the basic needs of the students' individual personalities. Each hypothesized 'need' is measured by ten items which require a response of 'true' or 'false' to statements about pressures present in the institutional environment. We included fourteen of these 'need–press' categories originally and then discarded all but three—*affiliation*, *deference* and *order*, as these were the only measures that showed associations with secondary school attainment of any size. The categories of *abasement*, *achievement*, *adaptiveness*, *change*, *conjunctivity*, *counteraction*, *energy*, *nurturance*, *play succourance* and *understanding* produced very low correlations with attainment measures, the highest of which was 0·129 for 'need-achievement'. The full inventory and a copy of the scoring sheet is given in Appendix 8.

A further nine variables were retained from the pupils' own responses at the individual interview—*occupational ambition of child*, *child's preference for extended schooling*, *interest taken by school in leaving decision*, *number of school clubs and societies joined*, *parents ask about school*, *child likes parents and teachers to meet*, and *involvement of child in school activities*. These all correlated significantly with one or more of the attainment measures, as did *cleanliness of child and evidence of care*, and *child's outgoingness at interview*, on which the pupils were rated by the interviewer. The last variable was an assessment of ease of communication in the interview situation.

The remaining variables are measures of the home environment resulting from interviews with the parents of our subsample in their own homes. They are the result of a process of selection made on the basis of a preliminary analysis of the responses to a schedule containing some two hundred questions recorded at a single interview. The criteria of selection or omission of an item from the final matrix included considerations of distribution of rating scores, ambiguity of meaning contained in similar replies, and an awareness that in some cases distinctions on rating scales, though plausible theoretically, were not satisfactory in practice. Undoubtedly some of this item selection could have been facilitated had the planned pilot study proved successful. However, after a remarkable week of attempted interviews with a carefully chosen group of parents from the original primary subsample (whose children were not included in the present analysis as they were not attending schools in the schools study), without the completion of a single interview, pressure of time forced us to abandon the project. It is felt that the elimination of items later rather than earlier has not significantly affected the outcome.

Even though the number of items in the parent questionnaire was considerable, they were not regarded as a complete exploration of the true complexities of home environment, but neither were they the consequence of an entirely random approach. The most important considerations determining the choice of items were the results of the Plowden Survey, which had indicated that the area of parental attitudes to education would provide the most promising exploratory field so far as school attainment is concerned. We were concerned to define more closely the concomitants of 'favourable to education' parental attitudes, shown to be important at the primary stage, and also to obtain evidence as to whether they were equally important to subsequent achievement. All the parental attitude variables from the Plowden Survey were therefore retained, sometimes modified and frequently elaborated with further questions intended to be more searching. A further guide to the inclusion of questions was derived from Bloom (1964), who listed six categories of question found empirically useful in the analysis of home environment and its relation to school attainment. These were—(i) pressure to achievement, (ii) language models, (iii) academic guidance, (iv) stimulation to explore the larger environment, (v) intellectual interests and activities, and (vi) work habits. This analysis was thought to be extremely promising, not so much for its novelty as for the ways in which it set out to define the components of the domestic environment. Thirdly, there were questions devised by the research officers to test such hypotheses as 'family cohesiveness', the relative importance of 'father' and 'mother' variables, and how the pupils' own attitudes to school and their assessment of parental interest rated in importance as educational predictors.

We certainly do not claim to have left no stone unturned in the preliminary analyses but, in view of the wealth of information originally sifted, we feel fairly confident that our selection of home environment variables for the final matrix reflect the most important of those aspects of home likely to be crucial to educational achievement.

Individual interviewing, even when following a structured schedule, is extremely time consuming, especially if the interviewer allows the interviewee time to settle down and expand answers. This approach was always followed as it was felt to be most conducive to an accurate interpretation of the responses made, in that the distortion of initial defensiveness—or even aggression—might be worked out in discussion. The shortest interview was completed in just under thirty minutes and the longest took over three hours.

The final data matrix for the correlational and factor analyses comprised scores on 113 variables. Four related to factual aspects of the pupils' secondary school careers, thirteen related to the pupils' own attitudes and perceptions, sixty-one related to the home environment, and thirty-four were educational measures covering all ages from seven-plus to sixteen-plus. One was the quasi-criterion variable *primary headteacher's rating*. All the distributions were normalized and standardized to have a mean of 50 and a standard deviation of 10 before the intercorrelations were computed. A list of the 113 variables finally included in the individual analysis will be found in Appendix 6.

4 Results—the schools analysis

From the results of our statistical analyses we were concerned to find the answers to the following questions:

(a) Are there any features of secondary school environment which appear, in themselves, to be associated with school attainment?
(b) Does any effect of secondary school environment increase or decrease in relation to attainment as pupils advance in years?
(c) Are there features of secondary school environment that appear to be associated with attainment in particular school subjects?
(d) The age at which a pupil leaves school is another indication of the success of schooling. Are there any features of school environment which appear to be associated with leaving school at the statutory leaving age?
(e) Are the environmental concomitants of internally assessed attainment the same as those for attainment in external examinations?
(f) Can we identify 'improving' and 'deteriorating' schools and isolate the environmental determinants of these conditions?
(g) As the tripartite system assumes that different educational environments are required by different types of pupil, do any environmental attributes relate to attainment in one type of school and not in another?

The discussion of our analyses will be presented, as far as possible, under sub-headings related to these seven areas of investigation. In the discussion of results we must bear in mind that this was a school-based study and thus it was necessary to award a score on each of our variables to each of the fifty-three schools in the sample and to examine how far these scores were associated with **school** attainment scores. To arrive at the school attainment scores we calculated averages from the scores obtained by the Plowden pupils constituting the follow-up sample. It is not possible to assume that the pupils in this sample are strictly representative of a particular school's population, and any reported results are therefore descriptive of the secondary school experience of the Plowden sample only.

Secondary school environment and attainment

Intercorrelations were first of all calculated for the whole matrix of variables to indicate which school attributes had significant associations with secondary school attainment measures. The most striking effect—immediately noticed—was that, when a variable correlated significantly with all the measures of secondary school attainment, it also correlated significantly with the scores obtained in the eleven-plus selection examination, and that the correlations with the latter measures **were often higher.** In order to summarize these correlation data for ease of inspection, we calculated the average correlations of each variable with the eighteen secondary school attainment scores. These average correlations, in order of size, are given in Table 4.1, together with the

Table 4.1 Correlations and average correlations—school environment and attainment

Variable	Average correlation with 18 secondary attainment scores	Correlation with 10+ total score
Intake		
10+ Total score	0·961*	1·000*
10+ Mathematics I	0·954*	0·984*
10+ Mathematics II	0·953*	0·983*
10+ Verbal reasoning	0·950*	0·993*
10+ English	0·950*	0·994*
10+ Composition	0·927*	0·978*
Environment		
34 Type of school	0·905*	0·937*
11 Size of 6th form entry	0·837*	0·862*
17 Graduate teachers	0·827*	0·838*
9 No. of pupils leaving at age 15	−0·824*	−0·856*
13 Size of entry for external exams	0·823*	0·864*
4 Attendance	0·794*	0·811*
5 Free meals	−0·781*	−0·813*
29 School uniform	0·763*	0·805*
31 Homework	0·752*	0·765*
44 Streaming on entry	−0·701*	−0·690*
47 Movement between lessons	0·688*	0·753*
30 Emphasis on external exams	0·661*	0·686*
1 Size of school	0·656*	0·660*
7 Appearance of pupils	0·638*	0·667*
6 Free clothing	−0·620*	−0·639*
38 School journeys	0·531*	0·522*
60 Parents meetings—formal	0·514*	0·514*
37 Out-of-school activities	0·491*	0·498*
12 Migration	−0·477*	−0·488*

Table 4.1—*continued*

Variable	Average correlation with 18 secondary attainment scores	Correlation with 10+total score
22 Graduate headteacher	0·452*	0·449*
18 Untrained teachers	0·431*	0·497*
3 Pupil/teacher ratio	−0·388*	−0·362*
45 Streaming by ability	−0·387*	−0·347*
43 Adequacy of pupil records	0·370*	0·364*
51 Merit mark system	−0·349*	−0·334*
19 Teacher turnover	−0·343*	−0·363*
62 Availability of staff to parents	−0·306*	−0·295*
57 Quality of specialist rooms	0·291*	0·274*
27 Quality of headteacher	0·287*	0·318*
59 Quality of library	0·282*	0·319*
33 No. of internal exams per year	0·252	0·235
39 Visits in school time	−0·232	−0·193
61 Parents' meetings—informal	0·232	0·277*
42 Length of teaching day in minutes	0·227	0·221
14 Subject range in external exams	0·213	0·258
24 Authoritarianism of headteacher	0·210	0·198
46 Extent of subject setting	0·200	0·178
48 Prefect system	0·199	0·212
20 Male teachers	0·195	0·189
36 Absence of corporal punishment	0·175	0·201
58 School equipment	0·169	0·156
10 No. of pupils leaving at age 16	0·165	0·234
21 Sex of school	0·157	0·148
35 Voluntary (RC, or CE)	−0·143	−0·187
54 Age of building	0·142	0·177
53 Extent of transfer between streams	−0·134	−0·181
41 No. of teaching periods per day	−0·136	−0·138
25 Social atmosphere	0·135	0·183
23 Age of headteacher	−0·125	−0·147
32 Vocational guidance	0·113	0·123
40 Coeducation	−0·111	−0·101
49 Opportunities for formal status	0·099	0·166
16 Teachers over age 50	0·092	0·082
15 Teachers under age 30	−0·086	−0·138
50 House system	0·083	0·079
28 Innovation	0·054	0·098
2 Size of class	—	−0·016
26 Attitude to inquiry	—	−0·019
8 Sociability of pupils	—	0·062
52 Welfare	—	0·049
55 First impression of school	—	−0·015
56 Quality of building	—	−0·015

* Correlation significant at the 5% level or over

correlation of each environment variable with the ten-plus total score—the single measure on which selection for secondary school was based.

The blank cells towards the end of the above table occur where the eighteen correlations to be averaged did not operate in the same direction, i.e., they were not all positive or not all negative. The fact that this phenomenon occurs suggests that some environment variables are advantageous to some school subjects but not to others, or differ in effect at different ages. These aspects will be discussed later. A correlation between two measures gives us the extent to which they are in agreement. The precise extent of agreement is measured by the coefficient of correlation which can range in value from −1 (perfect disagreement) to +1 (perfect agreement). A correlation of zero represents complete absence of both agreement and disagreement. For our sample of fifty-three schools, a correlation coefficient is said to be 'significant' if it is as high as 0·270. This figure is significant at the 5% level, meaning that the probability is one in twenty of the relationship occurring by chance. If a coefficient is as high as 0·350, it is significant at the 1% level, and the probability that chance factors are operating is only one in a hundred. An inspection of column 1 in Table 4.1 shows us that, of the 71 predictor variables, 36 were correlated significantly at over 0·270 with the average of all secondary attainment measures, and that the 6 highest correlations were for the 6 ten-plus tests, these forming a coherent band of high correlations, each of which is more important than any of the environment variables that appear below. The highest correlation of all (0·961) is for the ten-plus total score—the measure on which selection for secondary school was based. There seems to be little doubt that the attainment of our Plowden pupils in the secondary school was largely determined by the ability in evidence before transfer at eleven-plus, and that the effect of those factors we have studied in the subsequent school environment is relatively small. The next highest correlation with attainment is *Type of school* (0·905), but this merely reflects the fact that selection for school type was the result of ten-plus test scores.

Column 2 of Table 4.1 impresses upon us that, if a variable is not significantly associated with ten-plus scores, it is unlikely to be significantly associated with subsequent attainment. It is clear from column 1 that eleven-plus selection tests were the best predictors of secondary school attainment and from column 2—because of the generally higher correlations—that they are even better predictors of aspects of secondary school environment. This is tantamount to saying that secondary school environment is more importantly associated with primary school achievement than it is with secondary school achievement. This association can only be rationalized if we look upon eleven-plus selection results as a further measure of secondary school environment called 'quality of intake'. There is every reason to suppose that such a variable would be of prime importance if we take the view that any environment includes the attributes of the individuals inhabiting it. The fact that the brightness or dullness of a school population affects the aims, atmosphere and policies of a school is not surprising.

It was quite obvious that eleven-plus selection had been all-pervading and subtle in its effects and, to test the extent of this pervasiveness, we calculated partial correlations holding ten-plus total score constant for all our environment variables. This procedure helps us to nullify two of the effects of eleven-plus selection—those on subsequent attainment and on subsequent environment. It enables us to discover what effects the environment variables, in themselves, would have had in correlation with secondary school attainment if all the schools had had an intake of equal educational standard. As a result of the partial correlation exercise we found that none of the resulting coefficients was of a size that could be called 'significant' even at the 5% level. The relationships originally found between secondary school environment and secondary school attainment were overwhelmingly dependent on the quality of the school intake, and chance factors could account for any of the residual correlations between environment and attainment. The better the school in terms of the initial abilities of their pupils the better the subsequent attainment scores. This is only to be expected since secondary school attainment is compounded of initial ability at the age of transfer and any subsequent increments or decrements. However, we have also shown that, the better the school intake the higher is the score on most environment variables—in a direction favourable to educational achievement. It looks very much like a case of 'to him that hath it shall be given'.

We would expect intake to be associated with such variables as *size of sixth-form entry*, *graduate teachers*, *number of pupils leaving at age 15* and others of a similar nature that are clearly descriptive of traditional circumstances prevailing in the selective schools. But when we find that the provision of such amenities as *out-of-school activities* and *school journeys* is also largely related to school intake, surprise can be expressed. If such provisions are regarded as either incentives or compensations it would not be unnatural to assume that schools with a lower intellectual intake would have made more use of them and scored highly on such variables, but this is not the case. Even in matters of staffing and physical provision it appears that the rich get rich and the poor get poorer. The better the school in terms of intake the more they had of *graduate teachers*, *graduate headteachers* and *headteacher quality*, and the less they had of *pupils to teachers* and *teachers leaving*. The quality of specialist rooms and libraries is also largely related to the intake level of the pupils. The Manchester Survey for the Plowden Report had clearly shown that the major contributions to success at eleven-plus were derived from the home and neighbourhood circumstances of the sample pupils in their pre-secondary years. This being the case, it is logical to assume that the overwhelmingly important association we found between eleven-plus selection scores and subsequent attainment is also largely the result of the impact of social forces outside school before the age of eleven. It is also logical to assume that the even greater association between secondary school environment and ten-plus total score is also the result of extra-school factors impinging before the age of transfer. Thus, a poor social background at the primary age not only persists in its effects with secondary school attainment, it will furthermore be reinforced by its effects with the school environment encountered later. The all-pervading effect of eleven-plus selection, and therefore of pre-selection social factors, can be demonstrated if we look at their relative associations with aspects of secondary school experience, as presented in Table 4.2. Signs have been ignored in the calculation of average correlations.

Table 4.2 Correlations and average correlations—selection level and secondary attainment

Correlations with 10+ total score		Correlations with average of secondary attainment scores	
Secondary school attainment	0·961*	Type of secondary school	0·905
Type of secondary school	0·937	Secondary home environment	0·708*
Secondary home environment	0·733*	Secondary school environment	0·310*
Secondary school environment	0·323*		
Primary home environment	0·306†		
Primary school environment	0·224†		

* Average correlations † Correlations from Plowden Survey

Eleven-plus selection has been decisive in its effects on secondary school attainment and on the type of secondary school attended, which was its aim; type of school is strongly associated with attainment because of selection. When we isolated those variables strongly indicative of home background—free meals, free clothing, attendance and appearance, and compared their average correlations with those derived from the school variables, we found that selection was strongly associated with home background and this in turn was strongly associated with attainment. Secondary school environment is also significantly associated with eleven-plus selection—more importantly than with attainment. The home variables are more importantly related to both selection and attainment than are the school variables. It is clear that eleven-plus selection has certainly selected for ability, but it has also, in doing so, selected for home background and less importantly, but significantly, for the environment encountered in the secondary school. By adopting the technique of partial correlation and removing the effects of ten-plus total score, we have also removed the effect of social factors impinging before selection, and the resulting negligible partial correlation coefficients suggest that school environment at the secondary stage, in itself, has little relation to attainment.

The answer to our question, 'Are there any features of secondary school environment which appear, **in themselves**, to be associated with school attainment?' is therefore a qualified 'No'. Initial ability is the most important component of secondary school attainment but not quite the whole story. The issue is confused because initial ability is also associated with environment factors—the 'brighter' the intake the 'better' the educational environment. Remove the effects of initial ability with attainment, and initial ability with environment, and school provision, in itself, has little or no impact on secondary school attainment.

Secondary school environment and age trends

We had collected, however, not one measure of average secondary school attainment, but scores in different subjects at different ages. Our investigation of average scores, above, could conceivably have obscured significant environmental effects at particular ages. We had hypothesized that school environment would have an increasing effect over time as children grow into adolescence and become less home-orientated. In order to test this hypothesis we calculated the effect of certain categories of environment variables with the total of first, second and third year attainment scores. The correlations and average correlations are set down in Table 4.3.

Table 4.3 Correlations and average correlations for first three years with secondary school attainment

All Schools $n = 53$	Year 1	Year 2	Year 3
10+ Total score	0·970	0·970	0·966
Type of school	0·915	0·912	0·903
Home environment variables	0·713*	0·714*	0·717*
School environment variables	0·313*	0·313*	0·315*

* Average correlations—signs ignored

The general tendency would appear to be for the effect of *ten-plus total score* and *type of school* (also a selection variable) to decrease with age and for environmental effects, both of home and school to increase. However, none of the differences between correlations from Year 1 and Year 3 is significant, and the changes over time are so small they could have occurred by chance. The environment correlations above, however, are average correlations which may be concealing individual variables where the change over time is significant. In view of the high correlations already reported between *ten-plus total score* and individual environment variables, it was once again necessary to calculate partial correlations holding *ten-plus total score* constant to investigate any intrinsic effect of environment variables with attainment at three different ages. The resulting partial correlation coefficients revealed that five variables did retain a significant association with one or two, but not all the age measures.

Our hypothesis that school environment would have a greater effect with attainment in later years was definitely confirmed in the case of *attendance* (0·07, 0·06, 0·29), *migration* (0·19, —0·033, —0·283), *untrained teachers* (—0·223, —0·242, —0·311), and *opportunities for formal status* (—0·233, —0·275, —0·333), which all increased intrinsically in size until they became significant for attainment in the third year. The variable *migration* was included as a measure of the stability of the pupil population. The negative effect of this variable over all three years, the increase trend, and the fact that it becomes significant in the third year is interesting. Certainly pupil turnover would appear to have greater connection with attainment than teacher turnover, and this variable might well repay further study. It may be a home and neighbourhood variable reflecting the amount of slum-clearance in a school catchment area or a tendency of middle class parents to stay put because of educational considerations. The reasons for population movement cannot be deduced from our data, but it is clear that the low achieving schools are subject to greater changes in this respect.

Attendance and *teacher training* are also significant by the third secondary year, as is *opportunities to acquire formal status*. The last variable was included as a measure of 'incentive' and was assessed by counting the number of offices to which a child could be elected, e.g., prefect, house captain, games captain, form captain, milk monitor, etc. Its negative effect with attainment right across the age categories suggests that 'giving them responsibility' does not appear to have a salutory effect on attainment—rather the reverse, and the adverse effect is significant by the third year. Though negatively associated with attainment, this variable has positive connections with other important aspects of school life—correlating significantly with *sociability of pupils* (0·391), *social atmosphere* (0·389), *innovation* (0·467), *vocational guidance* (0·559), *out-of-school activities* (0·436), *house system* (0·363), *welfare* (0·357) and *number of informal parents' meetings* (0·512). It appears to have a close connection with those aspects of school associated with pleasantness, care and concern and general liveliness. Had we been measuring the effect of our environment variables on social adaptation or even happiness, rather than scholastic attainment, the single variable of *opportunities for formal status* might well have been an important predictor.

When we examine certain other variables that have an increasing effect with attainment over time, though never attaining significance, we are left with the impression that a rather restricted authoritarian orthodoxy becomes increasingly important to examination success. *Teachers over age 50* (0·04, 0·11, 0·18), *male teachers* (0·06, 0·02, 0·19), *homework* (0·08, 0·12, 0·20), *corporal punishment* (0·06, 0·07, 0·18), *sociability of pupils* (—0·12, —0·11, —0·23), *social atmosphere* (—0·15, —0·17, —0·26), *old buildings* (0·10, 0·11, 0·21) and *quality of specialist rooms* (0·10, 0·12, 0·20) all become increasingly important in their effect with attainment. The pattern of our results suggests that 'attainment' is associated with one set of variables and 'socialization' with another, and that there is little overlap. The subjective impression of the research officers was that if a school has high attainment expectations it will be work orientated. If, because of the quality of intake, attainment expectations are low, 'socialization' will take precedence, perhaps as a gesture of despair rather than of positive commitment.

All the variables individually mentioned above, with the exception perhaps of *attendance* are 'school' variables, and a number of them are concerned with teachers and attitudes. In general we can say that, although home environment looked at first sight to be more importantly and increasingly associated with secondary school attainment, this effect was almost wholly due to the social selection which was a concomitant of eleven-plus selection, and that school variables, though statistically significant only at certain ages, tend to increase in effect rather than decrease as the years go by. Our answer to the question—'Does any effect of secondary school environment increase or decrease in relation to attainment as pupils grow in years?' is that there is a slight tendency towards increased effect between the first and third secondary years, though most increases are so small that they could have occurred by chance. The increasing importance of good school attendance, teacher training and a stable school population are the most unequivocal of our findings.

Secondary school environment and subject attainment

Let us now look at the correlations for the five separate subject areas. First we derived an average correlation for each subject from the three correlations for the first, second and third years. Table 4.4 gives these for *ten-plus total score*, type of school, and the home and school variables.

Once again we find that school mean subject scores are more clearly related to quality of intake (*ten-plus total score*) and type of school, than with either home or school variables, and that the latter are the least important. Since eleven-plus selection has been shown to have selected for home background and school environment as well as for the type of secondary school attended, we calculated partial correlations holding *ten-plus total score* constant, to investigate any intrinsic effect of environment variables with specific school subjects. We found that no single variable had a residual association with

Table 4.4 Average correlations—five subject areas

Subject area	10+ Total score	Type of school	Home variables	School variables
English	0·964	0·907	0·708	0·332
Mathematics	0·967	0·903	0·714	0·310
Sciences	0·937	0·890	0·694	0·303
Social sciences	0·966	0·910	0·711	0·319
Non-academic subjects	0·960	0·912	0·709	0·308

attainment in any one subject that could not be accounted for by initial ability. Attainment in any secondary school subject conforms with the level of initial ability, and environment differences do not help us to predict any specific abilities that might be inherent in attainment in different subjects.

The answer to our question—'Are there features of secondary school environment which appear to be associated with attainment in particular school subjects?' is 'No.' Attainment in any of the school subjects measured can be accounted for by the complex influences of initial ability at eleven-plus, and there is no feature in the school environment which, in itself, could be said to favour attainment in one school subject rather than in another.

Secondary school environment and statutory leaving

The foregoing results have been concerned with attainment in the first three years in the secondary school. It will be remembered that, at the close of the third year, secondary education in Manchester maintained schools was reorganized on comprehensive lines. The school experience of many of our Plowden pupils changed after this date, and the data we had collected as evidence of school environment could no longer be assumed to be valid indicators of environmental influence. Sixteen of our fifty-three schools, containing 460 Plowden pupils (30%) were not included in the reorganization plans—three direct grant schools, two Roman Catholic technical high schools, nine RC secondary modern schools, one Church of England secondary modern and one unreorganized RC all-age boys' school. Four maintained schools—one grammar, two comprehensive and one secondary modern were redesignated as high schools but their composition remained virtually unchanged as they were not paired with other schools. This category contained 198 of our Plowden sample (13%). Three maintained secondary modern schools were not included in the reorganization scheme because they were deemed unsuitable by virtue of their size or geographical isolation. They contained 75 (5%) of the sample. In these twenty schools changes in school circumstances were at a minimum, but there was no doubt that their staffing and subsequent intake would be affected by changes taking place in the remainder of the school system. Three of our secondary modern schools had closed completely and their 74 pupils (5%) were transferred to a new custom built comprehensive high school to complete their fourth and any subsequent years of education. The remaining twenty-seven schools were reorganized into comprehensive high schools by amalgamation with other schools geographically as close as possible. Eight of our grammar schools were paired with secondary modern schools, four of our technical high schools were paired with others of the same type, and three with secondary modern schools. Five of the secondary modern schools in our sample were paired with grammar schools, three with technical high schools and four with other secondary modern schools. The amount of change actually discernible to the 737 (48%) of Plowden pupils in these paired schools would depend upon the circumstances and policies adopted in the new institutions, but it was obvious that all these schools were very different places from those in which we had originally collected data on school environment variables.

At the end of the first year after reorganization the schools were approached again for details of sample pupils who had left school during 1968, the year in which they reached the statutory leaving age. We found that 776 of our pupils had done so. The proportions of pupils leaving school at the age of fifteen ranged from 0% to 29% in the original grammar schools, from 3% to 22% in the original technical high schools, and from 32% to 100% in the original secondary modern group. Table 4.5 gives correlations and average

Table 4.5 Correlations and average correlations—leaving school at age fifteen

Variables	Correlations for proportion of pupils leaving at age 15
10+ Verbal reasoning	−0·875
10+ Composition	−0·875
10+ English	−0·871
10+ Mathematics II	−0·859
10+ Total score	−0·856
10+ Mathematics I	−0·846
Type of school	−0·824
Secondary school attainment	−0·824*
Home environment variables	0·650*†
School environment variables	0·304*†

* Average correlations
† Signs ignored

correlations for *proportion of pupils leaving at age 15* with ten-plus selection scores, type of school, and home and school environment variables, for the whole sample of fifty-three schools.

From the above order of correlations we can see that leaving school at the earliest possible moment is more strongly associated with eleven-plus selection and its concomitants of school type and secondary attainment than with factors in the environment, and that school environment has the least effect of all. That the three highest of the selection variables have a strong verbal element is supportive of current educational theories which emphasize that verbal and linguistic ability predetermines the capacity to take advantage of the educational system as it exists.

In order to isolate the environmental characteristics of the schools with a higher proportion of statutory leavers, we calculated partial correlations for *proportion of pupils leaving at age 15* and each of the environmental variables. We have noted that early leaving is strongly associated with eleven-plus selection results, and the partial correlations, with *10+ total score* held constant, tells us what effect the environment variables would have had if all the schools had received an intake equal in terms of ability. Table 4.6 lists those variables which appear to have a direct bearing on early leaving, as the partial correlation coefficients were of a size to be regarded as 'significant'.

Typically, then, the schools with a high proportion of statutory leavers have a negligible entry for external examinations, a small sixth-form entry, few pupils staying at school until the age of sixteen, a small range of subjects studied for external examinations, and they place little emphasis on the

Table 4.6 Partial correlations for proportion of pupils leaving school at age fifteen (*10+ total score* held constant)

Environment variables	Partial correlations significant at the 5% level or over
13 Size of entry for external exams	−0·923
11 Size of sixth-form entry	−0·557
10 No. of pupils leaving at age 16	−0·540
61 Parents' meetings—informal	−0·496
1 Size of school	−0·380
14 Subject range in external exams	−0·377
31 Homework	−0·357
30 Emphasis on external exams	−0·338
29 School uniform	−0·336
2 Size of class	−0·293
60 Parents' meetings—formal	−0·287
6 Free clothing	−0·286
4 Attendance	−0·278
44 Streaming on entry	−0·270

importance of such examinations. They are smaller schools with a weaker insistence on *homework* and *school uniform*, and poorer attendance records, and they tend to organize few occasions, both formal and informal, to which parents are invited. The tendency is for them not to stream their pupils on entry, but this is no doubt due to the fact that streaming is also associated with size of school. The negative and significant association with *free clothing* is interesting. This variable, in the secondary schools, appears to be an indicator of the insistence on school uniform rather than a socio-economic factor, as in the primary schools. Our observers certainly concluded that the schools with the highest incidence of free clothing grants did not necessarily contain the most poverty-stricken pupils. They were more likely to have headteachers who placed great value on the wearing of uniform by all pupils and therefore pressed the local authority very hard for the provision of uniform purchasing vouchers. The relation of statutory leaving to small classes may be a function of the size of school, but it is more probably a reflection of the positive discrimination practised towards schools in the more deprived areas so far as the provision of staff was concerned.

The answer to our question—'Are there any features of school environment that appear to be associated with leaving at the statutory leaving age?' is 'Yes'. Although none of the partial correlations for attainment retained significance when initial ability was nullified, fourteen environment variables were found to be significantly associated with early leaving, irrespective of initial ability. Certain aspects of differential provision between schools, therefore, though not affecting attainment itself, are related to decisions to leave school at the earliest possible moment.

Secondary school environment and external examinations

In spite of the fact that changes in school experience encountered by 50% of our sample in the two years preceding their entry for external examinations could not be assessed, it was felt that some account must be taken of the results of such examinations, as to many people they represent the culmination and raison d'être of secondary education. Our data could provide us with some indication of how early secondary school environment was associated with later success at sixteen-plus. Of those 768 Plowden pupils who continued their education after the statutory leaving age, 731 sat for external examinations at the age of sixteen-plus, either the Certificate of Secondary Education, the O-level of the General Certificate of Education, or a combination of both. Choice of examination appeared to be a matter of school policy, as some schools restricted entry to one examination only, and some schools entered pupils for combinations of subjects in both examinations. Because of this it was necessary to construct a scale of scores that would cover results in both examinations. The examination boards involved could only provide us with the information that a CSE grade 1 pass could be regarded as award equivalent to an O-level pass in the range of grade 1 to grade 6. When the marks of the Plowden pupils were scrutinized it was found that there were 93 pupils with one or more CSE grade 1 passes who had also 'passed' at O-level in one or more subjects. The average O-level pass grade of these 93 pupils was calculated and found to be 4·33. On the basis of this an overlapping points scale was constructed with a CSE grade 1 regarded as equivalent to a GCE O-level grade 4. It must be emphasized that this was a personal decision based on technical needs and such evidence as we had, and that we were not assuming nor implying a statistically or educationally valid overlap. For the purpose of comparison between schools it provided an adequate method of applying a uniform composite score to all the schools in the sample. Table 4.7 gives the correlations for external examinations with ten-plus selection measures, type of school, secondary school average attainment and home and school environment variables.

Table 4.7 Correlations and average correlations—external examinations

Variables	Correlations with 16+ external examinations
10+ Composition	0·790*
10+ Total score	0·783*
10+ English	0·781*
10+ Verbal reasoning	0·780*
10+ Mathematics II	0·767*
10+ Mathematics I	0·766*
Secondary school attainment	0·759*†
Type of school	0·757*
Home environment variables	0·628*†
School environment variables	0·274*†

* Significant at the 5% level or over
† Average correlations signs ignored

Overall the best predictors of success in external examinations at sixteen-plus are the eleven-plus selection measures, followed closely by their concomitants of secondary school attainment and type of school. The least important predictors are the school environment variables, but these are nevertheless significantly associated with sixteen-plus success. However, the correlation coefficients for external examination results with ten-plus test results are overall significantly lower than similar connections between ten-plus measures and internal school examination marks over the first three years of secondary school. Table 4.8 shows the relevant correlations.

We have already stated that there was a slight tendency for the connection between ten-plus scores and subsequent attainment to diminish over time,

Table 4.8 Correlations—10+ selection tests and internal and external examinations

Variables	Average correlations with internal exams Years 1–3	Correlations with 16+ external exams
10+ Total score	0·961	0·783
10+ Mathematics I	0·954	0·767
10+ Mathematics II	0·953	0·766
10+ Verbal reasoning	0·950	0·780
10+ English	0·950	0·781
10+ Composition	0·927	0·790

and the much lower correlations for sixteen-plus results may be reflecting a continuation of this process. Contributing factors to the decline of eleven-plus selection in effect may be the environmental changes encountered by many of our Plowden pupils in the two years after reorganization. There is also the possibility that the 'halo' effect of eleven-plus results on the internal assessment of school examinations has boosted the correlations for attainment in the first three years of secondary school. There is no doubt that the most important single predictor of success at sixteen is *10+ composition*, a logical result when we consider that most external examinations rely heavily on the ability to present information cogently in written form. This particular ten-plus score was the least important selection predictor for attainment in the first three years of secondary school, but by sixteen it has pride of place.

Like internally assessed attainment, however, external examination success is largely predicted by eleven-plus selection tests, though to a lesser extent. Because of this fact, and because environment has also been shown to be connected with eleven-plus selection, we once again calculated partial correlations holding *10+ total score* constant in order to assess the intrinsic effect of our school variables with sixteen-plus attainment. We found that five variables did retain a significant effect, and these are set down in Table 4.9.

Table 4.9 Significant partial correlations for 16+ external examination results (10+ *total score* held constant)

Variables	Significant partial correlations for 16+ external examinations
14 Subject range in external examinations	0·769
35 Voluntary school (RC or CE)	0·373
16 Teachers over age 50	0·335
7 Appearance of pupils	0·308
28 Innovation	−0·276

The overall impression is that voluntary schools with a high proportion of elderly teachers, orthodox teaching methods, entering pupils of clean and neat appearance for a wide range of examination subjects are those with the most successful results at sixteen-plus, when the initial ability of the pupils is discounted. It would not be wise to generalize too far from these rather sparse results when we consider that the collection of data for our environment variables was not coincident in time with the sitting of external examinations. Reorganization had altered many of the schools in terms of the environmental variables studied, and there had been two years in which the impact of these changes could have influenced the aims and motivations of our Plowden sample. The significant partial correlation of 0·373 with *voluntary school* suggests that the schools with a religious foundation achieved better results at sixteen-plus. This may be because these schools had not suffered the upheavals of reorganization, but we can obtain no definite conclusions on this point from our data.

The answer to our question—'Are the environmental concomitants of internally assessed attainment the same as those for attainment in external examinations?' is a qualified 'No'. None of our environment variables were, in themselves, significantly associated with attainment in any specific subject area when measured by internal examinations. Three variables appeared to have a connection with third year attainment—*migration*, *untrained teachers* and *opportunities to acquire formal status*, none of which have any intrinsic bearing on sixteen-plus results. External examination success at sixteen-plus, however, does appear to have associations with the range of examination subjects offered, elderly teachers, pupils of good appearance, and few innovative techniques in the first three years of secondary schooling. The finding must remain tentative, however, because of the relation with the voluntary schools.

Improvement and deterioration in attainment

When we attempted to isolate 'improving' and 'deteriorating' schools we were faced with two main difficulties. Firstly, our Plowden follow-up sample related only to a proportion of a single year's intake in each school and not to the whole age population. We could make no assumptions that our restricted school samples were representative of a particular school's population. Secondly, we had based our attainment measures on internal school examination marks scaled against rank class positions in school subjects. When marks are scaled on this basis—of ranking within a group—it follows that, within a particular group, for every improver there must be a corresponding deteriorator. If a pupil is top of the class in one examination and is placed at the bottom subsequently, it means that he has changed places with another pupil in terms of his scaled score, not that the whole class has deteriorated. They may have done so in absolute terms, but this cannot be discerned from data obtained by scaling rank position against independent criteria. This is the chief difficulty when we apply the concept of 'improvement' and 'deterioration' to schools and not to individuals.

Bearing these qualifications in mind, however, we can obtain an overall impression of how *type of school* was associated, on average, with improvement and deterioration, so far as the Plowden sample was concerned, by examining the mean attainment scores of different types of school. The differences between school types in intake, secondary school attainment, measured ability at age fourteen-plus and external examination results at sixteen-plus are most simply shown by giving the mean scores for each type of school. These are given in Table 4.10, together with the standard deviations to show the spread of scores in each group. As these are normalized standard scores, the mean for the whole sample of 1544 pupils is 50, and the standard deviation is 10.

The gross differences between school types are much as might be expected. All the mean grammar school scores are higher than the mean scores of technical high and secondary modern schools at over 1% significance. Technical high school means are similarly significantly higher than those for the secondary modern schools. It is obvious that selection for secondary school had taken place on the criterion of measured ability at the age of ten-plus, and that the differences in subsequent attainment produced by such selection are maintained throughout the period of secondary schooling. The size of the standard deviations show that the selective schools were more homogeneous in intake than the secondary modern schools, the technical high schools being particularly tight knit in this respect. By the time the Plowden pupils had reached fourteen-plus, however, we see that the reverse is the case. There is now a much wider spread of scores in the selective schools than in the secondary modern schools. The secondary modern schools show little change, but the selective school pupils have become more divergent in ability with the passage of time.

When we examine the mean scores of the school type sub-groups for upward or downward trends over time, we find that, in general, they are contrary to what would be expected. The group of pupils whose scores were above average at ten-plus (grammar and technical high) would be expected, for purely statistical reasons, to make lower scores when retested at fourteen-plus. This effect is known as 'regression to the mean' and is a statistical artefact due to imperfect correlation between two sets of scores. We should have expected the selective groups to show a declining trend between ability on entry, as measured by ten-plus selection tests, and attainment scores at fourteen-plus, and for the secondary modern schools to have shown increase. This is because children who do very well on one test are likely to produce a lower score when next tested. Any inaccuracy in the first assessment is likely

Table 4.10 Mean standard scores of Plowden pupils by *type of school*

	Grammar Mean	Grammar S.D.	Technical High Mean	Technical High S.D.	Secondary Modern Mean	Secondary Modern S.D.
Intake						
10+ Overall score	64·707	4·899	56·372	2·285	44·614	7·022
10+ M.H. Verbal reasoning	63·873	5·247	57·098	3·038	44·666	7·378
10+ M.H. English	62·436	4·973	56·868	3·568	44·969	7·823
10+ Composition	61·108	5·861	56·398	4·927	45·096	8·465
10+ M.H. Mathematics I	62·583	4·601	56·335	3·073	45·035	7·806
10+ M.H. Mathematics II	62·127	4·282	56·737	2·945	45·402	8·757
1st year secondary						
English	63·591	9·378	54·049	6·637	44·644	6·659
Mathematics	63·876	9·177	54·594	6·893	44·860	6·661
Sciences	63·822	9·101	53·992	6·514	44·833	6·619
Social sciences	63·625	9·333	53·805	6·723	44·591	6·401
Non-academic subjects	64·058	9·285	53·816	6·843	45·303	6·695
Total score	65·514	7·758	54·744	5·143	44·640	5·804
2nd year Secondary						
English	63·386	9·044	54·391	7·015	44·531	6·442
Mathematics	63·927	9·912	54·695	6·853	44·683	6·470
Sciences	63·081	8·766	54·331	7·079	44·904	6·810
Social sciences	63·143	8·920	54·241	6·788	44·752	6·553
Non-academic subjects	64·799	9·370	54·323	7·174	46·214	7·560
Total score	65·421	7·591	55·068	5·244	44·688	5·902
3rd year secondary						
English	64·448	10·317	54·515	6·545	45·869	6·337
Mathematics	64·166	9·569	53·891	6·578	44·658	6·483
Sciences	63·591	9·605	53·947	6·618	44·878	6·731
Social sciences	63·286	9·671	54·150	6·906	44·725	6·440
Non-academic subjects	64·757	10·041	54·692	7·152	45·475	6·638
Total score	63·521	5·834	55·658	4·101	45·046	7·716
14+ general ability						
Verbal test	63·958	9·082	53·853	7·579	44·543	6·843
Non-verbal test	59·498	6·278	56·207	6·442	45·143	8·121
Verbal plus non-verbal	62·371	7·445	56·301	5·631	45·227	7·210
16+ external examinations						
Average	68·704	10·771	57·900	9·086	39·132	12·086
n=	259		266		1019	

to have overestimated the real achievement of these pupils. In the same way, children who obtained very low scores on the first test are likely to obtain a higher score on the second occasion, as the chances of obtaining a lower score are much less than the chances of obtaining a higher one. Such observed changes may simply be the result of errors in measurement and need not be reflecting real changes in performance. Because of such regression effects it could be anticipated that the children who obtained high scores on the first occasion of testing would produce lower scores subsequently and vice versa. However, when we compared mean scores at different ages on similar tests we found this was not necessarily the case. Figure 1 compares test performances at different ages between the three school type categories. It plots the school type mean scores at ages ten-plus and fourteen-plus for *verbal intelligence*, at ages ten-plus and sixteen-plus for *external examinations*, at ages twelve-plus, thirteen-plus and fourteen-plus for *sciences, social sciences* and *non-academic subjects*, and at ages ten-plus, twelve-plus, thirteen-plus and fourteen-plus for *English* and *mathematics*.

For those measures for which we have secondary school scores only, i.e. *sciences, social sciences* and *non-academic subjects*, all assessed on the results of internal school examinations, we can see there is little difference in mean scores at twelve and fourteen. The differences between these two sets of means are not significant in any group. Our Plowden pupils, on average, have not improved or deteriorated in these subjects to any marked extent between the first and third years in the secondary school in any type of school. We must remember that, as these internal school marks were scaled on rank order in class, we cannot say that the **schools** have not improved or deteriorated. We can only say that as groups within types of school the Plowden pupils have not changed significantly in either an upward or downward direction over the space of three years in these three subjects.

These considerations do not apply to changes in *verbal intelligence* because the normalized scored derived from the ten-plus Verbal Intelligence Test and the fourteen-plus Verbal General Ability Test are absolute scores not based on ranking. In this area we can see that the only sizeable change over time is a decline of ability in the technical high school group. The difference between the two mean scores for the type of school, taking into account differences in standard deviation and the fact that the means are correlated, is significant at the 1% level. The slight rise in the grammar schools and slight fall in the secondary modern schools are not significant. The technical high school group distinctly converges towards the secondary modern schools in terms of *verbal intelligence*, and the decline is significant. If this had been accompanied by a corresponding fall in the grammar school graph and a rise in the secondary modern, we might have suspected that regression to the mean effects were responsible. The tendencies are the other way, however, and we are forced to conclude that the changes are underestimated and that the decline noted in the technical high schools is a genuine one.

For *English* we find trends in the same direction as for *verbal intelligence*, but more marked. The improvement in *English* attainment in the grammar and secondary modern schools between the ages of ten and fourteen is significant

Figure 1 Mean test scores at different ages by school types

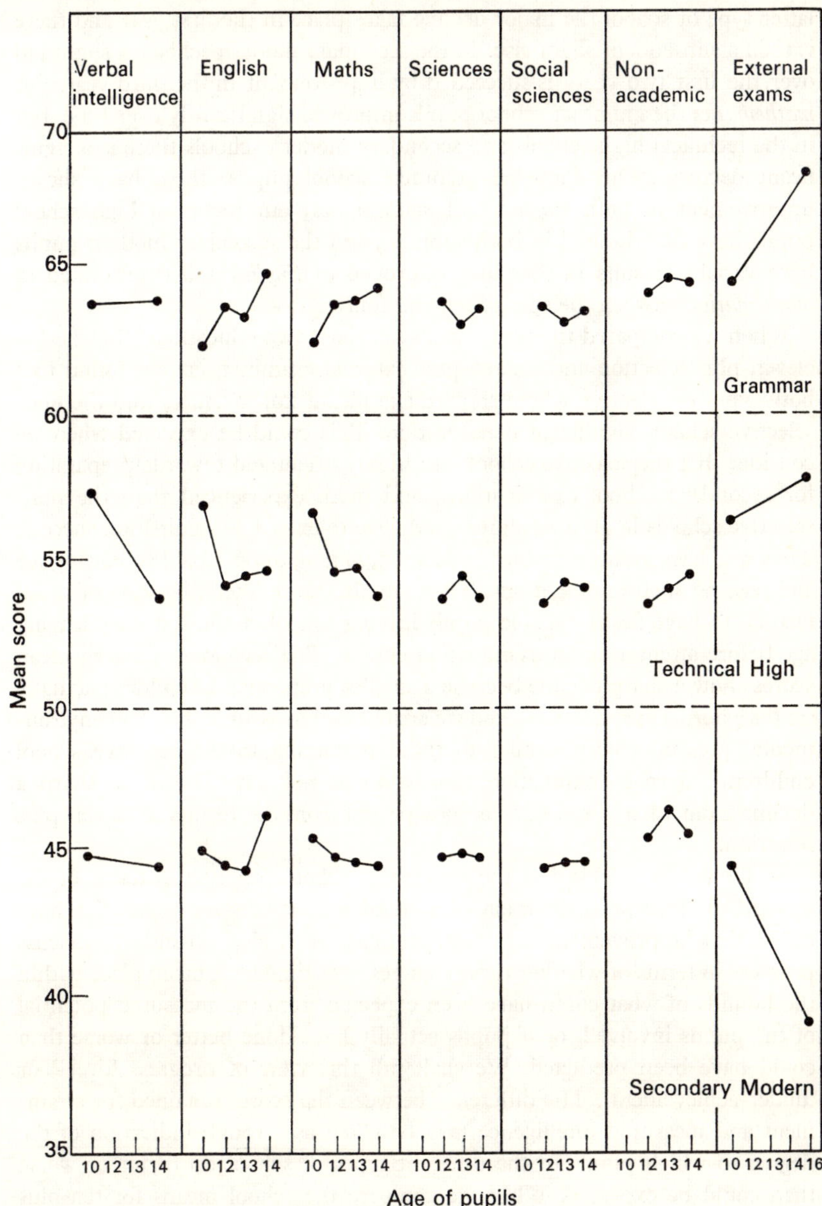

In the figure above, within each column, a trend line summarizes the data in Table 4.10.

at the 1% level, as is the deterioration in the technical high schools. In the latter type of school the major decline takes place in the first year and there is then a subsequent slight rise. In the secondary modern schools a slight fall over the first two years is succeeded by improvement in the third year. For *mathematics* the grammar school pupils improved significantly over time, but in the technical high schools and secondary modern schools there is a significant decrease. Our Plowden grammar school pupils, then, have shown improvement in both *English* and *mathematics*; our technical high school pupils have deteriorated in both subjects, and the secondary modern pupils have variable results in that they improved in *English* and deteriorated in *mathematics* between the ages of ten and fourteen.

When we compared the results between those two educational 'hurdles'—eleven-plus selection and sixteen-plus external examinations, we found that both types of selective school showed significant improvement and the non-selective schools significant deterioration. This could be expected when we consider that the selective schools are highly orientated towards preparation for secondary school examinations, and more experienced than the non-selective schools in all procedures conducive to external examination success. They also have an intake which is deemed, *in toto*, to be capable of sitting for and passing such examinations. They are also more likely, because of social factors, to have fewer capable pupils leaving school at the statutory leaving age before attempting an examination course. The secondary modern mean scores show a sharp decline because a smaller proportion of children actually sat for external examinations, and we are entitled to assume that, had environmental pressures been similar to those pertaining to the selective school children, external examination results would not have shown so sharp a decline from what could have been expected from the results of eleven-plus selection.

So far we have looked at the concept of school progress in terms of the upward or downward direction of a trend over successive years. We have called this 'improvement' or 'deterioration'. It is also possible to discuss progress in terms of whether these changes over time have taken place within the bounds of what could have been expected from the measured potential of the pupils involved, or if pupils actually have done better or worse than could have been predicted. We shall call this view of progress 'over-' or 'under-achievement'. The difference between the scores obtained for attainment and measured intelligence may be taken as a rough indication of the degree to which pupils in the different types of school do better or worse than could be expected. When we compare the school means for ten-plus intelligence and fourteen-plus school subjects we find that in the grammar schools there are no significant differences. On average, therefore, our Plowden grammar school pupils have done no better or worse in school subjects than could have been predicted from their intelligence test scores before entry, even though they have improved significantly in English and mathematics. These pupils have, however, achieved significantly better results in sixteen-plus external examinations than could have been predicted at eleven-plus, if we regard intelligence score as a measure of potential. They have therefore over-achieved in this respect.

All the differences between mean scores for ten-plus intelligence and fourteen-plus school subjects are significant at the 1% level in the technical high school group in the direction of under-achievement, but there is no significant difference between ten-plus intelligence and mean sixteen-plus external examination score. Our technical high school pupils, therefore, have done worse than could be expected in internally assessed school examinations and as well as could be expected in external examinations.

A different pattern is observed for the non-selective group. The secondary modern pupils on average, have significantly over-achieved in English and non-academic subjects, and have done as well as could be expected in mathematics, sciences and social sciences. In external examinations at sixteen-plus there is significant under-achievement.

But we have already noted that there have been some changes over time in measured intelligence. Figure 1 showed a slight rise in the grammar school group, a slight fall in the secondary modern schools, and a significant fall in the technical high schools. In view of these changes in average intelligence level, it is logical to assume that attainment at fourteen-plus will reflect these changes. We therefore inspected the differences between the mean intelligence (Verbal General Ability scores) at fourteen-plus and fourteen-plus school subjects, to assess whether at this stage pupils were over- or under-achieving in terms of their concurrent capacity. In the grammar schools we found no significant differences for school subjects—the Plowden pupils were doing as well on average as could be expected. On the criterion of fourteen-plus mean intelligence, however, the grammar school pupils still over-achieved in sixteen-plus external examinations. An exactly similar result was found in the technical high school group with fourteen-plus intelligence as the measure of potential. In the secondary modern group the same pattern was found as that reported for ten-plus intelligence as criterion. In the grammar and secondary modern schools, therefore, ten-plus and fourteen-plus intelligence scores were similar predictors of attainment, whereas in the technical high school group ten-plus intelligence had overestimated future results in school subjects and underestimated sixteen-plus external examination results.

In general, and on average, we can say that the trend in the grammar schools was towards improvement and over-achievement, in the technical high schools towards deterioration and under-achievement, and in the secondary modern schools towards improvement and over-achievement in certain subjects (English and non-academic) and towards deterioration and under-achievement in sixteen-plus external examinations. These results, however, are for average scores of our Plowden pupils in particular types of school. The average scores suggest that school types are completely homogeneous in terms of intake and attainment. However, this is not strictly the case, and the apparent homogeneity of school types breaks down somewhat when the mean scores of individual schools are examined. Table 4.11 shows that there is an amount of overlap between school types when the ranges of mean scores within each type are inspected.

In intake at eleven-plus (based on the scores of tests taken at ten-plus), there is little overlap of mean scores. Here the three types of school appear as separate distinct groups on all the ten-plus measures with the exception of *composition* where one of the technical high schools attained a higher mean than the lowest of the grammar schools. The difference between these two means is not significant, so the overlap is minimal. This separateness is maintained between the grammar and technical high school groups on all the attainment measures for the first three years with the exception of second year *English*, where one technical high school overlaps into the grammar school band. By the third year, however, this overlap has disappeared. The overlap between the secondary modern schools and technical high schools is more pronounced, but in every case where it occurs the same school is responsible —the one with the highest mean scores on all the ten-plus measures in the secondary modern school group. This school also had the highest mean score on the Verbal General Ability test against which all the school attainment scores were scaled. The overlap, therefore, is only to be expected. In the case of third year *English* and *mathematics*, where the overlap is no longer apparent, the differences between the lowest technical high school mean and the highest secondary modern school mean are not significant. In fact, when we compared the lowest of the mean grammar school scores with the highest of the mean technical high school scores on all measures, no significant differences were found, with the exception of those for third year *sciences* and third year total scores. The difference between sixteen-plus external examination means was also significant. Similarly, when the lowest scoring technical high school was compared with highest scoring secondary modern school, although the means of the latter were higher, the differences were not significant except in the case of performance in external examinations. Variations in attainment within the three types of school were also apparent when the highest and lowest means within each type were compared. The differences were all significant.

There is obviously a wide attainment range within each school type and a degree of overlap between school types, when the average scores of Plowden pupils in individual schools is considered. Mean scores and standard deviations, however, do not throw much light on the extent of the overlap. Such measures are likely to be obscuring overlapping individuals. When we looked

Table 4.11 Range of standard score means of Plowden pupils among individual schools

	Grammar schools	Technical High schools	Secondary Modern schools
Intake			
10+ Total	61·85–75·50	55·04–58·13	40·90–50·85
10+ Verbal reasoning	61·46–71·67	55·61–59·67	40·80–50·65
10+ English	59·12–70·67	55·68–58·83	40·94–51·29
10+ Composition	58·55–67·17	54·63–59·41*	38·90–52·38
10+ Mathematics I	60·23–69·50	54·72–57·55	41·57–50·50
10+ Mathematics II	60·00–69·67	55·63–57·59	40·14–51·74
First year secondary			
English	57·26–74·17	51·82–56·33	40·29–54·41*
Mathematics	57·78–73·00	52·58–56·78	40·00–52·74*
Sciences	57·22–76·17	51·97–56·35	40·88–52·85*
Social sciences	57·61–72·67	52·74–56·76	40·35–53·65*
Non-academic subjects	56·47–78·33	51·90–55·78	41·12–53·71*
Total score	58·30–77·83	53·19–57·35	40·57–54·12*
Second year secondary			
English	57·24–75·00	51·21–57·26*	40·06–53·41*
Mathematics	58·96–76·83	51·89–57·04	40·29–52·85*
Sciences	58·22–73·50	51·61–56·52	40·43–53·68*
Social sciences	57·65–71·50	51·82–56·72	40·29–54·29*
Non-academic subjects	59·78–79·50	51·97–58·63	40·71–55·53*
Total score	61·65–78·33	52·57–58·30	40·29–54·53*
Third year secondary			
English	59·29–77·83	52·82–56·30	41·59–52·50
Mathematics	59·43–74·83	51·71–55·85	39·86–51·50
Sciences	58·39–74·00	51·86–55·65	39·86–53·21*
Social sciences	57·70–73·33	52·46–56·67	39·29–53·53*
Non-academic subjects	60·35–76·67	51·86–58·33	40·47–53·12*
Total score	59·78–72·00	54·21–57·59	37·71–53·50*
14+ general ability			
Verbal test	60·29–76·50	51·21–55·96	40·29–54·76*
Non-verbal test	56·18–63·83	51·64–60·61*	41·41–55·21*
Verbal+non-verbal	58·18–70·83	51·64–60·61*	41·35–55·97*
16+ external exams			
Average	37·78–77·78	42·22–68·89*	23·33–58·89*
n=	12	9	32

* Highest mean score overlaps with lowest mean score in adjacent column(s).

at the 225 pupils who scored over 60% in the fourteen-plus General Ability Test (one standard deviation above the mean), we found that 69% were in grammar schools, 17% in technical high schools and 14% in secondary modern schools. In the middle range of ability, encompassing approximately two-thirds of the sample population, we found 10% were in grammar schools, 23% in technical high schools, and 67% in secondary modern schools. Of those pupils scoring lower than one standard deviation below the mean, none was in a grammar school, one such pupil was in a technical high school and 99·999% in secondary modern school. There is obviously a considerable overlap among individual pupils in the upper and middle ranges of ability which mean scores tend to obscure.

For the reasons stated earlier in the discussion, difficulties arise if we try to compare **individual schools** for improvement or deterioration and over- or under-achievement on any measures where scaled rank order marks are involved. This objection does not arise if we deal with individual school means derived from absolute scores on standardized tests, such as those available for *verbal intelligence* at ten-plus and fourteen-plus. When these two sets of scores were compared for each school individually we found that—out of the fifty-three schools—one grammar school had significantly improved, five technical high schools had significantly deteriorated, two secondary modern schools had significantly improved and three had shown significant deterioration. In the main, therefore, there is little change in *verbal intelligence* during the first three years in the secondary school, and the eleven schools which demonstrated significant changes towards improvement or deterioration provided groups too small for comparison on individual environment variables.

The answer to our question—'Can we identify improving and deteriorating schools and isolate the environmental determinants of these conditions?' must be that we are precluded from doing so in detail by the nature of our data and the constitution of the sample. Our evidence confirms that individual schools can be associated with differential attainment results but, in the absence of standardized test scores, more detailed analyses would not be justified.

School environment and attainment in different types of secondary school

We have previously discussed the results of correlational analyses for the whole sample of fifty-three schools, ignoring the fact that it contained different types of secondary school designed and intended to be different in their organization and aims. From our overall correlations it was clear that many of our environment variables correlated more highly with the single variable *type of school* than they did with measures of attainment, and we could not tell from such correlations whether environment variables were having an equal or similar effect within the different school types. As a tripartite educational system exists to cater for differences in ability and aptitude we could expect differences in school environment to operate in a variable way on the bright and the less bright, the practical and the academic, if the system is a valid one. The Newsom Report specifically advocated radically different kinds of educational provision for the Browns, Joneses and Robinsons within only one type of school (secondary modern) and, in the 'comprehensive' debate, controversy continues to rage as to whether what is good for some is good for all. It seemed to us that, by calculating intercorrelations between attainment and environment variables for each of the three school types separately, we could compare them for differences in effect and find out if any variables operated in the same direction for all types of school and if any operated differentially. Table 4.12 gives the variables which produced significant correlations with average secondary school attainment in at least one type of secondary school.

It will be noted that the variable *type of school* is significantly associated with attainment **within** the grammar and secondary modern groups. This is because the sample of twelve grammar schools represents two school types—three direct grant schools and nine maintained schools—and the thirty-two secondary modern schools include two schools designated as 'comprehensive' before reorganization, but whose mean attainment scores were more akin to those of the secondary moderns than to those of the technical high schools (and there were too few of them to provide a separate category), plus one all-age unreorganized voluntary school. The zero correlation in the technical high school category results from there being only one school type represented in this sub-group. The blank cells occur where the eighteen correlations to be averaged did not operate in the same direction, i.e. they were not all positive or all negative in effect. No direct comparisons can be made between the size of correlation coefficients in the different types of school because of the variable number of schools in each category. Furthermore, correlation coefficients have to be very large to be of significant importance for such small numbers of units of study.

The first conclusion to be drawn from Table 4.12 is that different kinds of initial ability relate to subsequent attainment to differing extents in the three types of school. We have previously shown that ten-plus total score was the best selection predictor of subsequent attainment for the schools as a whole, and the sub-group analysis shows that this is also the case in the secondary modern schools. In the grammar schools, however, ten-plus English takes precedence, and in the technical high schools only the ten-plus mathematics tests are significantly associated with secondary school attainment. This last finding may well be due to the greater homogeneity of the technical high schools in terms of intake and attainment. The differences between the mean

Table 4.12 Average correlation of environment variables with eighteen measures of secondary school attainment

	Grammar $n = 12$	Technical High $n = 9$	Secondary Modern $n = 32$
Intake			
10+ English	0·851*	0·399	0·708*
10+ Total score	0·846*	0·292	0·720*
10+ Verbal reasoning	0·842*	0·293	0·675*
10+ Mathematics II	0·807*	0·860*	0·687*
10+ Mathematics I	0·705*	0·785*	0·707*
10+ Composition	0·693*	0·447	0·618*
Environment			
11 Size of 6th form entry	0·779*	—	0·533*
10 No. of pupils leaving at age 16	−0·733*	0·154	0·373*
6 Free clothing	−0·730*	−0·630*	—
13 Size of entry for external exams	0·704*	0·338	0·497*
5 Free meals	−0·642*	−0·287	−0·447*
34 Type of school	0·594	0·000	0·395*
58 School equipment	0·576*	0·199	0·425*
57 Quality of specialist rooms	0·566*	0·239	0·356*
4 Attendance	0·552*	0·175	0·350*
3 Pupil/teacher ratio	−0·532*	−0·140	0·163
9 No. of pupils leaving at age 15	−0·522	−0·375	−0·509*
17 Graduate teachers	0·440	−0·296	0·389*
1 Size of school	0·419	0·321	0·623*
43 Adequacy of pupil records	0·278	—	0·340*
46 Extent of subject setting	0·260	—	0·438*
14 Subject range in external exams	0·124	−0·450	0·355*
18 Untrained teachers	—	−0·215	−0·549*
37 Out-of-school activities	—	0·218	0·396*

* Significant at 5% level or over

scores of the highest and lowest technical high schools on all measures were significant, but the significances were generally of a lower order than those found between the highest and lowest means in the other school-type groups. An inspection of the ten-plus mean scores for the technical high schools confirmed that selection for this type of school had been based on the total score of all tests, as for other types of school, and not on specific ability in mathematics, which might be thought to have a technical bias. Nevertheless, a very different pattern is shown in the relative importance of significant ten-plus predictors compared with the other types of school. In the technical high schools the only significant intake variables are *mathematics I* and *II* correlating with subsequent attainment at 0·785 and 0·860 respectively. The remaining four ten-plus scores all correlate positively with secondary attainment but do not reach significance. It looks as though mathematical ability is somehow 'utilized' to a greater extent in the technical high schools in the assessment of all school subjects at secondary level, and that—although selection for these schools was based on a range of abilities—those which are associated with mathematics are far more salient to later achievement. The only other significant correlation to be found in the technical high school analysis between any of the individual secondary attainment measures and any of the remaining ten-plus scores is for ten-plus *English* and second year secondary *non-academic subjects* at 0·663, whereas ten-plus *mathematics I and II* correlate positively and significantly with each of the eighteen measures of secondary attainment individually. It may be the case that mathematical ability produces a 'halo' effect which pervades the assessment of all subjects in the technical high schools. Further support for this suggestion that non-verbal problem solving is of greater importance in technical schools is found when the connection between school attainment and the separate forms of the fourteen-plus General Ability Test are compared. These average correlations are given in Table 4·13.

In both the grammar schools and secondary modern schools the best predictor of secondary school attainment is *verbal general ability*, while in the technical high schools the *non-verbal* form takes precedence. If, as we suggest, non-verbal problem solving ability is an advantage in these schools, it is conceivable that verbal ability may to some extent be 'wasted' because it goes without recognition. We are dealing here with mean scores for schools, and it is inevitable that they are concealing individuals who at transfer scored more highly on verbal tests than on mathematical tests. It may be that in the technical high schools such pupils may be doomed to relative failure when they may have done better in a more verbal environment. It is also worth recording that, out of the eight schools previously mentioned as having shown significant deterioration in verbal intelligence scores between ten-plus and fourteen-plus, five of these were technical high schools. There is some evidence that converse conditions apply in the grammar schools where verbal abilities appear as the most important predictors of future success. Table 4.13 showed that in these schools the fourteen-plus verbal test correlated

Table 4.13 Average correlations of 14+ general ability measures with the eighteen criteria of secondary school attainment

	All schools $n = 53$	Grammar $n = 12$	Technical High $n = 9$	Secondary Modern $n = 32$
Verbal test	0·980	0·890	0·651	0·899
Non-verbal test	0·926	0·696	0·842	0·777
Verbal plus non-verbal test	0·964	0·842	0·714	0·867

most importantly with subsequent attainment at 0·890 and Table 4.12 showed that this was closely followed by *ten-plus English* (0·851), *ten-plus total score* (0·846) and *ten-plus verbal reasoning* (0·842). Only then do the correlations with *ten-plus mathematics* scores feature, at 0·807 with *mathematics II* (problem arithmetic) and 0·705 with *mathematics I* (mechanical arithmetic). These last are not so unimportant as verbal ability appeared to be in the technical high schools, as they do correlate significantly and positively with each of the eighteen criteria measures individually, but their position in the hierarchy of significant intake variables seems to support the view that those Plowden pupils with high verbal ability selected for grammar schools did better subsequently than those with relatively high mathematical ability who were so selected. These assumptions are not illogical in that they do not appear to fly in the face of popular notions about the differences between grammar and technical schools. Grammar schools are 'known' to be wordy places, and everybody knows that mathematics is a tool of technology. What is striking is the suggested effect of the grammar versus technical self-image on the attainment of pupils originally selected on the same criteria, though of course at different levels. No such clear assumptions are usually made about the secondary modern schools, and indeed the rank order of highly correlating intake variables reveals no clear advantage of one kind of ability over another in these schools.

It is interesting also to compare the correlations obtained between the two forms of the General Ability Test taken at fourteen in the three types of school. These are given in Table 4.14.

Table 4.14 Correlations—verbal and non-verbal forms of the 14+ general ability test

Grammar ($n = 12$)		Technical High ($n = 9$)		Secondary Modern ($n = 32$)	
r	Significance	r	Significance	r	Significance
0·680	5%	0·158	n.s.	0·832	1%

The correlations between verbal and non-verbal intelligence were significant at the 1% level in the secondary modern schools, at the 5% level in the grammar schools, and they are not significantly associated in the technical high schools. This appears to corroborate the assumptions made above that the abilities of pupils in the selective schools are more polarized towards a particular type of ability, and that this is most marked in the technical high schools. It may be the case that those grammar schools which drew from the eleven-plus pool the children with relatively high verbal ability produced better attainment subsequently than those which received pupils with relatively high mathematics scores, that the opposite is true in the technical high schools, and that in the secondary modern schools all round initial ability produced all round results. It would be straining the evidence too far, in view of the small numbers of schools involved, to say that this is an argument in favour of comprehensive schools in that a particular specialist image may have a backwash effect on all school subjects and that this may lead to the waste of fairly specific talents. However, it could be said that if specialist schools are thought to be desirable, *per se*, they could better fulfil their stated function if their pupils were deliberately selected for specific talents. Certainly it would seem to support the case for subject setting in any type of school.

Having demonstrated that intake variables are associated with subsequent attainment in different types of school in varying ways, we were concerned to find whether attributes in the general school environment also operated differentially. We repeated all our partial correlation analyses for the three school-type sub-groups separately. We found that several variables, which had not retained significance in the sample of schools as a whole when initial ability was discounted, did appear to be intrinsically associated with attainment within a single school type.

In Table 4.15 we give the partial correlations which were of a size to be called 'significant' in the analysis of grammar schools. There are few such interactions for internally assessed attainment, but many more concerned with sixteen-plus external examination results and with statutory leaving. English attainment is, rather surprisingly, associated with *good school equipment*, and mathematics and overall third year attainment with *poor social atmosphere*. A favourable staffing ratio is salient to achievement in the social sciences and non-academic subjects, and to overall attainment in the first and second years. Good specialist rooms and few pupils receiving free clothing also appear to be associated with success in the non-academic area. Just how a favourable attitude to our research in 1967 is associated with attainment in 1965 (first year secondary) is difficult to rationalize. Quite a different set of variables are associated with success at sixteen-plus—good pupil records, homework, a wide range of external examination subjects, extensive subject setting, good first impression, a flourishing house system, larger classes, younger headteacher, good attendance, few men teachers, pupils of neat and clean appearance, absence of corporal punishment and whether it is a girls' school. It was suspected that these correlations were describing conditions applying in the girls' grammar schools, and when we inspected all these variables for their association with *sex of school* we found that the correlations were high and in the right direction. Our partial correlations are reflecting the fact that the mean sixteen-plus score for the girls' schools was significantly higher than that for the boys' schools.

Table 4.15 Significant partial correlations—grammar schools

Variable	English	Maths	Sciences	Social sciences	Non-academic subjects	Year 1	Year 2	Year 3	16+ external exams	No. of pupils leaving at age 15
58 School equipment	0·541									
25 Social atmosphere		−0·528						−0·539		
3 Pupil/teacher ratio				−0·535	−0·676	−0·586	−0·599			
6 Free clothing					−0·628					
57 Quality of specialist rooms					0·615					
26 Attitude to enquiry						0·613				
43 Adequacy of pupil records									0·932	
31 Homework									0·865	
14 Subject range in external exams									0·663	
46 Extent of subject setting									0·609	
55 First impression of school									0·588	
50 House system									0·575	
2 Size of class									0·555	
23 Age of headteacher									−0·555	
4 Attendance									0·533	
20 Male teachers									−0·533	
7 Appearance of pupils									0·531	
36 Absence of corporal punishment									0·530	
21 Sex of school									−0·528	
11 Size of sixth form entry										−0·830
29 School uniform										−0·753
13 Size of entry for external exams										−0·744
17 Graduate teachers										−0·697
52 Welfare										−0·692
32 Vocational guidance										−0·642
16 Teachers over age 50										0·640
49 Opportunities for formal status										−0·640
60 Formal parents' meetings										−0·615
10 No. of pupils leaving at age 16										0·536
62 Availability of staff to parents										−0·530

The characteristics of the grammar schools with a higher proportion of statutory leavers appear to be—smaller sixth-form entry, small emphasis on the wearing of school uniform, a smaller entry for external examinations, fewer graduate teachers, little provision for individual welfare, poor vocational guidance facilities, elderly teachers, few opportunities for formal status, few formal parents' meetings, many pupils leaving at sixteen and many obstacles placed in the way of parent-teacher interaction. The general impression is one of lack of organizational drive, and the weaker insistence on the wearing of school uniform could well represent *laissez-faire* rather than enlightenment. There is also the suggestion of a lack of pupil-centredness. The greater number of significant partial correlations with *statutory leaving* than with internally assessed attainment suggests that although school environment may not have much influence on attainment that cannot be accounted for by initial ability, it does nevertheless have an effect on what may be even more important in the life of individuals—the decision to curtail education at the earliest possible moment. It is also worth noting that the four 'home' variables—*free meals, free clothing, attendance* and *appearance*—do not appear in the statutory leaving list of variables, which suggests that school factors are more influential than home factors when grammar school pupils make the decision to drop out of school at the age of fifteen.

Table 4.16 gives the significant partial correlations for the technical high school analysis. There is only one type of school represented in this category and the sample is very small—only nine schools. Correlation coefficients have to be as high as 0·610 to be significant at the 5% level. *Homework* in the technical high schools is the strongest concomitant of attainment, retaining significant effect with all school subjects and overall attainment, in the first and third years. A small range of external examination subjects also appears to be conducive to high attainment in all school subjects apart from the non-academic, and it has a similar effect at all years of age. Small classes are associated with attainment in mathematics and sciences and with first and second year overall marks. Flexibility of transfer between streams is positively and significantly associated with attainment in English, mathematics and science and with second year overall achievement. A pronounced emphasis on external examinations has its greatest impact in the second year, and large schools are associated with high English attainment. A poor social atmosphere is related to high attainment in science. Where the same variables are concerned with high attainment at sixteen-plus they appear to work in the opposite direction. The schools offering a wide range of external examination subjects, with a good social atmosphere and a not very strong emphasis on homework, appear to do better here. Extensive subject setting and few out-of-school activities are also salient to sixteen-plus attainment.

There are no fewer than twenty-two variables significantly associated with statutory leaving in the technical high schools. Many of these operate in the

Table 4.16 Significant partial correlations—technical high schools

Variable	English	Maths	Sciences	Social sciences	Non-academic subjects	Year 1	Year 2	Year 3	16+ External exams	No. of pupils leaving at age 15
31 Homework	0·860	0·885	0·833	0·815	0·788	0·859		0·831	−0·734	
14 Subject range in external exams	−0·647	−0·633	−0·614	−0·635		−0·634	−0·678	−0·652	0·663	
53 Extent of transfer between streams	0·635	0·621	0·672				0·644			
26 Attitude to enquiry	−0·615		−0·648							0·666
1 Size of school	0·636									−0·799
2 Size of class		−0·672	−0·634			−0·635	−0·705			0·796
25 Social atmosphere			−0·643						0·642	
30 Emphasis on external exams							0·702			
46 Extent of subject setting									0·667	
37 Out-of-school activities									−0·614	
51 Merit mark system										0·969
35 Voluntary school (RC)										−0·928
13 Size of entry for external exams										−0·912
52 Welfare										0·834
7 Appearance of pupils										0·793
27 Quality of headteacher										0·792
50 House system										0·754
18 Untrained teachers										0·729
36 Absence of corporal punishment										0·716
32 Vocational guidance										0·715
49 Opportunities for formal status										0·699
60 Formal parents' meetings										0·694
24 Authoritarianism of headteacher										−0·656
47 Movement between lessons										0·655
59 Quality of library										0·655
17 Graduate teachers										0·644
11 Size of sixth form entry										−0·642
38 School journeys										−0·629
56 Quality of building										0·615

reverse direction when compared with grammar and secondary modern schools. For instance, we see that good *welfare* provision, good *vocational guidance*, many *opportunities to acquire formal status*, a number of *formal parents' meetings* and *graduate teachers* are associated with early leaving in the technical schools, whereas they were related to 'staying on' in the grammar schools. We also find that the provision of a *system of merit marks*, *good pupil appearance*, *headteachers rated high on quality*, a flourishing *house system*, an absence of *corporal punishment*, *non-authoritarian heads*, and good *quality library and buildings*, all rather surprisingly suggest that the 'good' technical high schools have the most statutory leavers. This state of affairs is almost certainly the result of data artefacts arising out of purely historical circumstances, to which the partial correlation of −0·928 for *voluntary school* gives us the clue. There were a significantly higher number of statutory leavers from the maintained technical high schools. At the time of our data collection the school leaving pattern in the voluntary technical high schools closely resembled that of a maintained grammar school. When our survey was beginning the first Roman Catholic voluntary grammar school had just been completed, and prior to this the technical high schools had received pupils who could have been transferred to grammar schools on their eleven-plus performance, had there been places. The correlations for *voluntary school* with the above mentioned environment variables suggest, in the direction of their effect, that such schools did tend to have larger classes, fewer graduate teachers, more corporal punishment, older buildings, etc. The presence of voluntary technical high schools in our sample has somewhat distorted the position, and it would be impossible to generalize from these results. The *statutory leaving* variables in Table 4.16 appear to be describing the general conditions in the maintained schools.

Fewer variables produced significant partial correlations for the secondary modern schools. These are given in Table 4.17. Untrained teachers have a significant negative effect with all internal examinations and with overall attainment at all ages. Mathematics attainment is additionally associated with *migration* (−0·541) and *opportunities for formal status* (−0·366), suggesting that a stable school population and small pupil involvement in the running of the school are salient to good work in mathematics, and both these variables are also significantly associated with overall attainment in the third year. Few *opportunities for formal status* (−0·353) and absence of *streaming by ability* (−0·344) are associated with high attainment in the social sciences. As far as sixteen-plus attainment is concerned, the distinguishing features of the highly achieving secondary modern schools appear to be a *wide subject range* (0·840), *many teachers over age 50* (0·582), a lack of *innovation* (−0·444), and a larger *entry for external examinations* (0·344). As far as statutory leaving is concerned, the partial correlations produce few surprises. In order of magnitude we find that the following variables are significantly associated with

Table 4.17 Significant partial correlations—secondary modern schools

Variable	English	Maths	Sciences	Social sciences	Non-academic	Year 1	Year 2	Year 3	16+ External exams	No. of pupils leaving at age 15
18 Untrained teachers	−0·541	−0·478	−0·437	−0·507	−0·510	−0·556	−0·525	−0·548		
49 Opportunities to acquire formal status		−0·366		−0·353			−0·340	−0·423		
12 Migration		−0·347						−0·408		
45 Streamed by ability				−0·344						
17 Graduate teachers							0·355	0·353		
4 Attendance								0·372		−0·354
21 Sex of school								0·350		
14 Subject range in external exams									0·840	−0·460
16 Teachers over age 50									0·582	
28 Innovation									−0·444	
25 Social atmosphere									−0·385	
13 Size of entry for external exams									0·344	−0·978
10 No. of pupils leaving at age 16										−0·950
30 Emphasis on external exams										−0·450
7 Appearance of pupils										−0·443
11 Size of Form entry										−0·502
40 Coeducation										0·372
42 No. of teaching periods in one day										−0·366
6 Free clothing										−0·350

leaving school at the earliest possible moment. Few *pupils leaving at age 16* (—0·950), small *entry for external examinations* (—0·978), small *sixth-form entry* (—0·502), small *subject range in external examinations* (—0·460), little *emphasis on external examinations* (—0·450), poor *appearance of pupils* (—0·433), *co-educational schools* (0·372), *shorter school day* (—0·366), poor *attendance* (—0·354) and little *free clothing* (—0·350). The last finding is not as paradoxical as it seems because, since the schools with the greatest number of statutory leavers tended to place little emphasis on wearing school uniform, efforts to acquire clothing grants for this purpose were at a minimum.

These three separate school type analyses reveal most clearly that there is no single environment variable that gives partial correlations which could be called significant in all types of school. That certain variables appear to be significant in one type of school only suggests that environment does indeed affect pupils in different sectors of the tripartite system to different degrees. A further indication of the differential impact of environment on school type is to investigate whether the variables operate in the same direction over all three categories, though not necessarily significantly, or if they operate positively or negatively in some but not in all. We found that *size of school*, *quality of specialist rooms*, *homework*, *attendance*, *school equipment* and *size of entry for external examinations* operated positively in all school types when quality of intake had been allowed for. *Streaming by ability*, *number of informal parents' meetings*, *number of pupils leaving at age 15* and *free meals* retained negative associations with attainment in all types of school.

When we investigated whether any environment variables operated in opposite directions in different types of school we found that *pupil/teacher ratio* and *subject range in external examinations* worked negatively in the selective schools and positively in the secondary moderns. In the primary school survey for the Plowden Report *pupil/teacher ratio* did not contribute to the major attainment factor, whereas *size of class* did. The reverse is the case in those secondary schools where *pupil/teacher ratio* correlated significantly with attainment at —0·388, and *size of class* produced almost zero correlations operating in variable directions over the attainment measures. The correlation between these two variables was 0·859 in the primary survey and is 0·485 in our present study. The assumption that large classes are the result of teacher shortage would appear to be truer in the primary school than in the secondary school. However, the lower correlation in the secondary school may well be explained by the fact that such schools necessarily have small sixth-forms and examination groups, practical subjects in Manchester schools are taught in classes limited by convention to twenty pupils, and free periods for the staff are accepted as part of secondary school requirements. *Pupil/teacher ratio* can therefore be seen to be a more realistic measure of the staffing situation of secondary schools than the size of class variable derived from dividing the pupils equally among the number of classes.

Our partial correlations indicate that, in the selective schools, a small number of pupils per teacher was salient to achievement, and that in the secondary modern schools the reverse was the case. However, the secondary modern correlations are very small and, when we consider that the 'low intake' schools tended to have the most favourable staffing ratio because of a policy of positive discrimination, it looks as though—other things being equal—a small number of pupils per teacher is advantageous to secondary school attainment. This is in line with the findings of Warburton (1964), who concluded that in secondary modern schools high attainment is associated with smaller classes. In view of the fact that the primary school survey reported a positive association between high attainment and large classes, there is the suggestion that there may be a genuine primary/secondary difference in this respect, as in the findings of Kemp (1955) and Morris (1966) who also studied primary schools and found associations between large classes and good attainment. *Pupil/teacher ratio*, however, has been shown to have such complex relationships with quality of intake that our findings about the absolute efficacy of small classes in the secondary school must remain as tentative suggestions. This is a very complex variable and we cannot say that we have provided statistical evidence that the present statutory limitations of class size—to forty in the primary school and thirty in the secondary school—make irrefutable sense.

The effect of *subject range in external examinations* is also confused, and the effect of reorganization may well account for the difference in direction of effect in the secondary modern schools. We must also bear in mind that the negative effect demonstrated by the selective schools resulted from the removal of overwhelmingly strong connections between quality of intake and the number of subjects offered at sixteen-plus.

The two variables discussed above at first sight appeared to discriminate between the selective and the secondary modern schools. The variables *number of pupils leaving at age 16* and *school journeys* appear to distinguish the grammar schools from the rest, as far as average attainment is concerned. The technical high schools represent the middle band of ability, and it is interesting to note that in some respects they resemble the grammar schools and in others the secondary modern schools. From our correlations and partial correlations it is clear that in the grammar schools leaving at the age of sixteen constitutes 'early leaving' and is negatively associated with attainment, while in the technical high schools and secondary moderns it represents 'staying on' and is positively associated with attainment. In the grammar and secondary moderns the association is almost wholly a consequence of 'quality of intake' and the residual effect with secondary attainment is negligible. In the technical high schools the high intake schools certainly tended to have fewer pupils leaving at sixteen but, this effect accounted for, the association between leaving at sixteen and high attainment is increased. There is the suggestion that in both the technical high and secondary modern schools the decision to stay at school for an extra year is made on selection and constitutes a positive goal, whereas in the grammar schools leaving at sixteen is 'dropping out'. It should not be overlooked that many technical high school pupils take up trade apprenticeships at the age of sixteen with the full blessing of the system.

As far as *school journeys* are concerned, in the grammar schools the association between quality of intake and the number and range of school journeys is so strong that the residual effect with attainment is actually negative in direction. The opposite is true in the case of the technical high schools. Here the better intake schools are less energetic in this respect. In the secondary moderns we once again find that school journeys have their highest associations with 'quality of intake' but the residual effect is positive.

Three other variables—*visits in school time*, *graduate headteacher*, and *quality of headteacher* give partial correlations which operate positively for grammar schools and link the technical high and secondary moderns together in that they operate negatively. None of the partial correlations approached significance, however. The one variable which distinguished the technical high schools from the rest is *graduate teachers*. In our grammar school sample 83% of the teachers were graduates, as against 49% in the technical high schools and 19% in the secondary modern schools. In the secondary modern schools the partial correlation for this variable was quite high at 0·270—the high attaining schools are distinguished by the number of graduates on the staff. In the grammar schools the residual effect is not so high, and the original high correlation is accounted for by the fact that the grammar schools with the highest intake also had the highest proportion of graduate teachers. The technical high schools are anomalous. Here all the correlations operate in the negative direction, though none is significant.

The answer to our question—'Do any environmental attributes of schools relate to attainment in one type of school and not in another?' is a very tentative 'yes'. Differences in effect, however, are more a matter of degree than of kind. Most variables operate in the same direction over all school types and, where there are differences, the effects with attainment are negligible. The most unequivocal of our findings is that teacher qualifications matter in the secondary modern schools, all attainment relationships with *number of untrained teachers* being significant even with the initial ability of the pupils nullified. There were also significant associations with *graduate teachers* and second and third year school attainment. However, it is almost certain that these two variables did not produce significant results in the selective schools because such schools are more homogeneous in their proportions of graduate and untrained teachers, and the variables have little discriminatory power. It is evident from the distribution of highly qualified teachers that the 'best' schools have the 'best' teachers in terms of these two criteria. Because of homogeneity we have not been able to show that the 'best' schools need the 'best' teachers. However, our results clearly show that the non-selective schools with the better qualified teachers produced the best attainment results.

5 Results—the schools factor analysis

In this correlational study relating our Plowden pupils to their secondary schools, with ninety variables there are 3960 individual correlations to be related to each other. It would be possible to draw from these many millions of comparisons between pairs of coefficients. As we have already demonstrated, the degree of correlation between pairs of variables is not the only information contained in a correlation table, since each pair may also agree in that they both correlate highly with other variables in the matrix. We have shown that attainment variables correlate highly with eleven-plus tests and that both correlate highly with environment variables. We calculated partial correlations holding ten-plus total score constant in an attempt to assess the intrinsic relationship between attainment and environment. It would be possible to calculate such partial correlations holding each variable constant in turn, but this would be less economical of time and effort in ordering the obviously complex interactions than the technique of factor analysis. This procedure replaces the scores on the ninety *variables*, which are partly dependent upon each other, by scores on a smaller number of *factors*, which are completely independent and have far greater powers of implication than any variables examined individually.

The Atlas Computer produced for us principal components analyses, followed by Varimax rotations of the major factors, for the whole sample of schools and for each of the school type sub-groups separately. This technique is not ideal in our particular case as, in each analysis, the number of variables outweighs the number of units of study, i.e. the number of schools. Because of this we can attach no absolute predictive power to the factor loadings, but we are not precluded from examining how the variables are sorted into independent factors and the relative importance of the environment loadings within and between factors. Because of the differing numbers of schools in the three sub-groups we cannot compare the size of the factor loadings on a particular variable between one school type and another, but we can investigate whether any particular environment variable loads importantly in one school type and not in another. Bearing in mind that we must always consider these qualifications when interpreting our factors, we can proceed to analyse the Varimax rotations.

Our main aim in this study of schools has been to isolate and describe the characteristics of those secondary schools in which our Plowden primary school pupils subsequently achieved the best educational results. Thus, when confronted with the Varimax rotations, our first task was to calculate the amount of variance contributed by the measures of secondary school attainment to each of the obtained factors. It would then be possible to concentrate our attention on those factors shown to be concerned with educational achievement. In all cases—for the whole sample of schools and for the school types individually—we found we had relatively simple solutions, with the first factor in each case accounting for a major amount of the educational variance. Factor I for the whole sample of schools accounted for 97% of the educational variance, Factor I for the grammar schools analysis 83%, Factor I for the technical high school analysis 84%, and Factor I for the secondary modern analysis 87%. The remaining factors in each analysis included very low loadings on attainment variables and were therefore of smaller concern to us. As might have been expected from our correlational study, each rotation produced independent factors with high loadings on *external examinations taken at sixteen-plus*, two factors in each of the analyses. The grammar school analysis also produced a factor (III) which had a single high loading on *first year science*, although the loadings on all other attainment variables in this factor were low.

We shall confine our discussion of factor content, in the first instance, to those factors containing 'significant' loadings on one or more of the secondary attainment measures. Of course, no rule of thumb exists that can determine which loadings in our analyses are 'significant'. Our units of study are too few and too variable in number between sub-groups arbitrarily to decide on a loading size which could be termed 'major' in each of our categories. Since our essentially monofactor solutions inevitably correspond closely to the results of the intercorrelational analyses, we have included as 'major' those loadings which would have been significant if they had been correlation coefficients. This is not entirely satisfactory but it does ensure that no important loadings are overlooked. Table 5.1 gives the major loadings for each of the Varimax rotations for the first factors for the overall sample and the sub-groups. It is evident from a first scrutiny of these Factors I, which account for all but a negligible proportion of the secondary educational variance, that the factor analyses do little to add to the findings of the correlational study. They do, however, help us to summarize very complex interactions. They provide further support for our conclusion that eleven-plus selection is the most important contributor to secondary school achievement, and that certain environment variables cannot be thought of as independent of initial ability. The major loadings in each of the analyses are concentrated among the 'quality of intake' variables, and confirm our findings that *ten-plus mathematics* scores are crucially related to achievement in the technical high schools, and that *ten-plus verbal reasoning* and *English* are the best predictors of success in the grammar schools.

In the Factor I for the all-schools rotation, it is clear that there is a close correspondence between eleven-plus selection tests and fourteen-plus attainment scores. If we regard quality of intake as the 'input' of a school and fourteen-plus results as the end-product or 'output', then we can consider our environment variables to be the 'process' to which the 'input' was submitted to produce 'output'. This industrial analogy helps to clarify what is happening in our major attainment factors. 'Input' is the raw material to be processed. No two schools have started with an identical input and no two schools have applied exactly the same process, even in terms of our limited variables. 'Output' is certain to be different between schools, but how much of the difference is due to variations in input and how much to variation in process needs to be established. We are specifically interested to discover which aspects of 'process' are associated with superior output, and it is here that factor analysis is helpful because it isolates for us those aspects of process which go together, by accident, tradition or design, with the quality of the input. It also enables us to see if there are any variables, descriptive of school circumstances, which have no connection with school attainment at all.

The loadings on a single factor are not independent of each other—they measure the amount of influence a variable has on a quality all the variables in that factor hold in common. The quality held in common in our Factors I is clearly one of educational attainment, and the contributing environmental variables are as much concerned with input as with output. It is interesting to compare the proportions of input, process and output variance contained in the first factors in the various sub-groups, and these proportions are given in Table 5.2.

Input in all the analyses corresponds more closely to output than does process. In the case of the all schools analysis, input and output are of almost identical importance in this major attainment factor. The correspondence is less close in the school-type sub-groups. The involvement of input with output is greatest in the grammar schools and least in the technical high schools. The percentage of process variance shows the amount of environmental variance which cannot be isolated from its dependence upon input and, indeed if we inspect the individual loadings in Table 5.1, we can see they bear a close resemblance to the significant correlation coefficients reported in Table 4.1, before we calculated partial correlations to nullify the effects of quality of intake. As we have stated, none of the remaining factors contains sizeable loadings on any of the ten-plus measures. This supports our suggestion that, if a variable is not associated with input, neither is it likely to be associated with output. This can be most clearly seen from our calculation of the percentage contribution to environmental variance in each factor from quality of intake, type of school, and home and school variables. The seven-

Table 5.1 Factors I—test score analysis

A—Major Loadings	All schools	Grammar	Tech. High	Sec. Mod.
1. *School variables*				
(a) *Intake*				
66 10+ Total score	99	93		76
67 10+ Verbal reasoning	98	91		71
68 10+ English	98	91		75
70 10+ Mathematics I	98	82	81	75
71 10+ Mathematics II	98	90	88	75
69 10+ Composition	96	72		64
(b) *Physical*				
34 Type of school	93	63		39
1 Size of school	64			61
12 Migration	−50			
3 Pupil/teacher ratio	−37			
57 Quality of specialist rooms		53		
58 School equipment		53		38
59 Quality of library	28			
(c) *Teachers and teaching*				
17 No. of graduate teachers	84			39
18 No. of untrained teachers	47			−57
22 Graduate headteacher	46			
19 Teacher turnover	−35			
27 Quality of headteacher	28			
(d) *Organization and policy*				
29 School uniform	80			
31 Homework	78			
47 Movement between lessons	74			
44 Streaming on entry	−69			
38 School journeys	52			
37 Out-of-school activities	48			36
51 Merit mark system	−38			
45 Streaming by ability	−37			−38
43 Adequacy of pupil records	36			
46 Extent of subject setting				48
53 Extent of transfer between streams		54		
(e) *Provision for parents*				
60 Parents' meetings—formal	52			
62 Availability of staff to parents	−31			
(f) *School leaving and examinations*				
9 No. of pupils leaving at age 15	−87			−49
13 Size of entry for external exams	87	70		48
11 Size of sixth form entry	86	79		53
30 Emphasis on external exams	70			
10 No. of pupils leaving at age 16		−77		35
2. *Home variables*				
4 Attendance	82	55		34
5 Free meals	−81	−73		−47
6 Free clothing	−64	−76	−66	
7 Appearance of pupils	67			

Note: As is customary, decimal points have been omitted from the loadings above.

Table 5.1 Factors I—test score analysis

B—Percentage variance on secondary educational measures	All schools	Grammar	Tech. High	Sec. Mod.
Total variance	97	83	84	87
Total secondary attainment	98	87	94	91
English	99	87	95	93
Mathematics	99	96	95	92
Sciences	97	68	93	88
Social sciences	99	91	94	93
Non-academic subjects	98	90	89	87
First year attainment	99	96	98	98
Second year attainment	99	96	98	96
Third year attainment	99	97	98	90
14+ Verbal general ability	99	88	46	94
14+ Non-verbal general ability	94	60	45	76
16+ External examinations	68	25	15	12

teen factors in Table 5.3 were the result of the Varimax rotation for the whole sample of fifty-three schools.

With the exception of Factor I, the factors are largely free of input variance and are clearly home/school interaction factors with quality of intake and type of school relatively unimportant. They suggest that certain kinds of home background are associated with certain kinds of school environment, even though the effect of these particular interactions on attainment is minimal. In making the environmental variance calculations for Table 5.3 we have had to make adjustments to take into account the fact that there are different numbers of individual variables in each category. With this adjustment made, we find that our major attainment factor—in its environment variance—derives 38% from intake effects, 34% from type of school, 21% from dependent home effects, and 7% from dependent school effects. The Plowden primary survey showed, in its similar major attainment factor, that ten-plus selection scores were overwhelmingly associated with home and neighbourhood background and that school environment had contributed much less. Our intake and type of school variables, because they are both dependent on ten-plus selection scores (of which they are other aspects),

Table 5.2 Percentage variance in Factors I

	All Schools	Grammar	Tech. High	Sec. Modern
Input variables	98	76	34	56
Process variables	24	13	8	8
Output variables	97	83	84	87

Table 5.3 Percentage contributions to environmental variance and educational test variance in seventeen factors

Factor	% of environmental variance				% secondary attainment variance	% 16+ external examination variance
	Intake	Type of school	Home variables	School variables		
I	38	34	21	7	97	68
II	0	0	41	59	0	0
III	1	2	50	47	0	0
IV	9	7	26	58	1	1
V	3	0	19	78	0	3
VI	2	9	28	61	1	0
VII	2	5	17	76	0	0
VIII	1	18	20	61	0	0
IX	0	2	4	94	0	0
X	1	13	24	62	0	0
XI	1	1	36	62	0	2
XII	4	21	31	44	0	0
XIII	6	0	3	91	0	0
XIV	0	10	37	53	0	2
XV	5	4	25	66	1	21
XVI	1	1	36	62	0	0
XVII	0	14	45	41	0	0

may therefore be regarded primarily as measures of the home and neighbourhood environment of our sample pupils in their pre-secondary years, and may be regarded as 'home' measures in this important sense. If this is accepted, the 21% contribution from home variables reported above is a serious underestimate. Furthermore, because the 7% contribution from school variables is also interrelated with intake and type of school, we can say that home effects pervade any measures shown to be associated with attainment.

Commenting on the major attainment factor found in the primary school study, the Plowden Report stated, 'The adverse forces in the home are, at this stage of education, the overwhelming ones, and the lower loadings (and the fewer loadings) on the school variables suggest that in the present circumstances we are doing little to counteract them by forces within the school.' There is no need to revise this conclusion in the light of our secondary school findings, and indeed we have shown these adverse forces have an ongoing effect, concentrating the effects of adversity to produce differentials in secondary school environment both in terms of provision and organization, as well as in the social background of the pupils. It could be said that eleven-plus selection has operated against amelioration. If we liken secondary school education to running a race, not only has selection decided that pupils will run races of different lengths for different prizes according to their running capacity, which was presumably its aim, but that the fastest and strongest runners are ensured of having the best tracks, the most highly qualified coaches, more individual coaching and the best training equipment. They will almost certainly receive more cheering from the sidelines in terms of social support because they are competing for the most interesting prizes. This analogy, which seems to be pertinent to our findings, does not resemble an attempt at amelioration. The individual loadings among the environment variables in our attainment factors bear a close resemblance to the significant average correlations reported in Table 4.1 before we nullified the effects of eleven-plus selection by calculating partial correlations and as a result reduced them below significance. There is little doubt, therefore, that the major environmental loadings in Factors I are reflections of the quality of intake.

As we have said, the four Varimax rotations produced certain factors which had high loadings on external examination results at sixteen-plus, although the loadings on other attainment measures were low. The most important of these were Factor XV in the whole sample analysis, Factors II and VI in the grammar school analysis, Factors IV and V in the technical high school analysis, and Factors XI and IX in the secondary modern analysis. The 'significant' loadings on these factors are given in Table 5.4. With the exception of Factor IV of the technical high school analysis, all these factors are relatively free of intake variance. Therefore, the high loadings on environment variables describe characteristics in the schools which are associated with high attainment at sixteen-plus where quality of intake is not a significant influence. The factor analyses have shown that, unlike internally assessed examinations, external examination results are associated with aspects of environment not related to eleven-plus selection differentials. 'Environment' here, of course, means those aspects of experience applying in the first three years of secondary school, and not those coincident in time with the sitting of the examinations.

The individual major loadings in Table 5.4 produce few surprises. In the 'all schools' analysis the loading of 0·80 for *range of external examination subjects* is only to be expected, as is the loading of 0·35 for *number leaving at age 16*. The loading of 0·40 for *graduate headteacher* remains interesting. This Factor XV is largely independent of intake and type of school variance, so even when the fact that the high intake schools had the greatest number of graduate headteachers is taken into account, there remains a clear association between having a graduate head in the first three years and success in external examinations at sixteen-plus. The presence of a high loading on *house system* (0·29) must also be noted.

There are two Factors (II and VI) in the grammar school analysis which together account for 53% of the variance for external examination results. Factor II is reminiscent of our correlation findings in that it appears to describe girls' schools, which had a composite mean score of 72·67 for sixteen-plus results against 65·19 for the boys' schools, and has isolated for us the

Table 5.4 Independent external examination factors

	All schools	Grammar		Tech. High		Sec. Mod.	
A—Major loadings	F.XV	F.II	F.VI	F.IV	F.V	F.XI	F.IX
1. *School variables*							
(a) *Intake*							
66 10+ Total score				73			
(b) *Physical*							
1 Size of school				68			
2 Size of class				70			
3 Pupil/teacher ratio		−63					
58 School equipment			79				
59 Quality of library		59			64		
21 Sex of school		−94					
(c) *Teachers and teaching*							
16 Teachers over age 50						53	
20 Male teachers		−94				−35	
22 Graduate headteacher	40						
23 Age of headteacher				76		37	
8 Sociability of pupils		56					
(d) *Organization and policy*							
29 School uniform							68
31 Homework			77				34
35 Voluntary (RC or CE)				62			
36 Absence of corporal punishment		95					
37 Out-of-school activities				−72			
39 School visits		53					
40 Coeducation					84		
41 No. of teaching periods in one day				89			
42 Length of teaching day in minutes				93			
43 Adequacy of pupil records			57				74
46 Extent of subject setting		79			91		
47 Movement between lessons					64		
48 Prefect system						88	
50 House system	29						
(e) *Provision for parents*							
60 Parents' meetings—formal							71
61 Parents' meetings—informal			−66				
62 Availability of staff to parents					90		
(f) *School leaving and exams*							
10 No. leaving at age 16	35						
11 Size of sixth form entry							38
14 Subject range in external exams	80	61		73		55	
2. *Home variables*							
5 Free meals					−89		
7 Appearance of pupils		72					

Note: As is customary, decimal points have been omitted from the loadings above.

Table 5.4 Independent external examination factors

B—Percentage of secondary attainment variance	All schools F.XV	Grammar F.II	F.VI	Tech. High F.IV	F.V	Sec. Mod. F.XI	F.IX
Total variance	1	2	2	4	3	2	1
Total secondary attainment	0	1	1	1	1	1	0
English	0	0	3	1	0	1	0
Mathematics	0	1	1	0	0	0	1
Sciences	0	2	1	0	1	1	1
Social sciences	0	1	1	2	2	0	0
Non-academic subjects	0	3	0	1	1	0	0
First year attainment	0	1	0	0	0	0	0
Second year attainment	0	1	0	0	0	1	0
Third year attainment	0	1	2	0	1	1	0
14+ Verbal general ability	0	2	0	18	21	0	0
14+ Non-verbal general ability	1	2	0	7	1	1	0
16+ External examinations	21	26	27	43	23	24	18

school environment concomitants of 'femaleness'—absence of corporal punishment, few male teachers, good pupil appearance, high sociability, extensive subject setting, more pupils per teacher, wide range of examination subjects, good school equipment and many visits in school time. Grammar school Factor VI, which accounts for 27% of the external examination variance, describes the characteristics of the successful schools where the bias of sex is not apparent. They are good school equipment, homework, few informal parents meetings and good pupil records.

The technical high school analysis produced two factors (IV and V) which together accounted for 66% of the variance on external examinations. Factor IV is not completely free of intake variance as the loading on ten-plus total score is high at 0·73. This loading, and the high loading of 0·77 on *voluntary school*, suggests that this factor is an artefact of the data and is describing those technical high schools which, because of historical circumstances, had an intake which included pupils of grammar school ability. The direction of effect of the loadings on *age of head teacher* (0·76), *size of school* (0·68), *size of class* (0·70), *out-of-school activities* (—0·72), *number of teaching periods* (0·89), *length of teaching day* (0·93) and *subject range in external examinations* (0·73) is in each case in accord with the circumstances found in the intercorrelations with the variable *voluntary school*. Factor V appears to isolate those variables which are not contaminated with either intake or 'voluntary' effects. In order of loading size they are *extent of subject setting* (0·91), *availability of staff to parents* (0·90), *free meals* (—0·89), *coeducation* (0·84), *quality of library* (0·64), and *movement between lessons* (0·64). It will also be noticed that fourteen-plus verbal general ability contributes 18% of the educational test variance on Factor IV and 21% on Factor V. This adds further support to our suggestion that verbal ability had little connection with internally assessed attainment in the technical high schools, but that it came into its own at sixteen-plus with the sitting of external examinations.

The two external examination factors produced by the secondary modern rotations (XI and IX) together account for 42% of the variance on this test. It is difficult to see where the coherence of the major loadings in Factor XI lies. There is a suggestion of elderly orthodoxy in the loadings for *teachers over age 50* (0·53), *age of head teacher* (0·37) and *prefect system* (0·88), but not of maleness, as the loading of 0·35 for *male teachers* is in the negative direction. Factor IX is more helpful in that the high loadings of 0·68 for *school uniform*, 0·34 for *homework*, 0·74 for *adequacy of pupil records*, 0·71 for *formal parents, meetings* and 0·38 for *size of sixth form entry*, suggest circumstances traditionally associated with selective schools. Perhaps this is an 'emulation' factor, giving further support to our suggestion that organization on archetypal grammar school lines is an element in sixteen-plus success in secondary modern schools.

We can say, in general, that external examination results are dependent upon the same intake-environment interactions as internally assessed school attainment but that, within school types—where most of the intake variance is subsumed—two independent factors describe two separate kinds of attributes, both associated with sixteen-plus success.

The characteristics of several of the factors not concerned with educational attainment are of interest. For instance, the 'all-schools' Factor II is clearly a physical amenities factor with no apparent connection with attainment. It links *quality of building* (0·874), *quality of specialist rooms* (0·825), *first impression of school* (0·817), *age of building* (—0·775) and *school equipment* (0·697). It also contains 'significant' loadings on *welfare* (0·437), *out-of-school activities* (0·437), *number of informal parents' meetings* (0·354), *number of formal parents' meetings* (0·348), *quality of library* (0·340), *appearance of pupils* (0·338), *free clothing* (0·322), *flexibility of transfer between streams* (0·285), *emphasis on external examinations* (0·275) and *innovation* (0·344). Although good physical provision may not have much effect on school attainment in itself, it is clearly associated with other 'good' qualities in the school environment.

Factor III is clearly a 'sex' factor with its heaviest loadings in *sex of school* (0·916), *male teachers* (0·885) and *corporal punishment* (0·705). These are the highest loadings on these variables in any factor and it would be safe to say that corporal punishment can be accounted for by the maleness of a school rather than by any other school characteristics we have measured. Significant loadings in this factor are also contributed by *appearance of pupils* (—0·404) *number of exams per year* (—0·374), *pupil/teacher ratio* (0·341), and *extent of subject setting* (—0·283). Maleness must therefore be assumed to be having some effects on these aspects of school environment and, with the exception of *pupil/teacher ratio*, not altogether 'good' ones.

Factor X has isolated those variables which could be called measures of progressiveness. It contains the heaviest loadings on *sociability of pupils* (0·817), *social atmosphere* (0·725) and *innovation* (0·569). It also contains significant loadings on *migration* (0·468), *quality of headteacher* (0·424), *opportunities for formal status* (0·328), *welfare* (0·328), *leaving at age 16* (—0·318) and *appearance of pupils* (0·270). It is encouraging to note that the loading on *size of sixth form entry* is in the positive direction so, although we cannot say the pleasanter aspects of school environment have had any significant effect on attainment in themselves, the suggestion remains that a progressive atmosphere does encourage staying on at school and, of course, vice versa. The major loading on *quality of headteacher* (—0·432) appears in Factor XI along with the major loading on *adequacy of pupil records* (—0·718), and significant loadings on *number of formal parents' meetings* (—0·482), *teacher turnover* (—0·328) and *number of internal examinations per year* (—0·281). This factor is associated with 2% of the external examination variance, in the same direction, and it suggests that the administrative ability of the headteacher is a salient feature in its connections with records, parents meetings and examinations. It is not without interest that *teacher turnover* and *quality of headteacher* have high loadings in the same factor, and that the loadings operate in the same direction.

The remaining factors are fairly specific to single environment variables and produce little evidence to illuminate the nature of the non-attainment characteristics of schools.

6 Results—the study of individuals

Our study of 114 individual pupils attending forty-one of the fifty-three schools in the school-based study, involved 113 variables. In addition to secondary school attainment measures for *English*, *mathematics*, the *sciences*, the *social sciences* and *non-academic subjects* in the first three years, we also included *external examinations* at sixteen-plus and all the primary school standardized tests taken between the ages of seven-plus and ten-plus. In all there were thirty-four educational measures which also included the scores on the *verbal* and *non-verbal general ability* tests administered by us at fourteen-plus, a total score for the *ten-plus selection tests* and total scores for the *three years of secondary attainment*.

Environment predictors numbered seventy-nine in all. In the main these were derived from a parent interview schedule relating parental attitudes to education, the physical conditions in the home, indicators of socio-economic level, reading and literacy, and the parents' own educational experiences. Three variables found to have a relationship to attainment and concerning the child's attitude to his or her school were also included, and several others connected with ambition for the future and involvement in school activities. Our statistical analyses were concerned with finding the answers to the questions which follow.

(a) Which of our variables are associated with school attainment, and what is their relative importance as predictors of achievement?
(b) Do any such variables become more important or less important at secondary school age?
(c) Are there any features in the home background which appear to be associated with attainment in particular school subjects?
(d) Are there any features in the home background which appear to be associated with the age at which a child leaves school?
(e) Are there any features in the home background particularly associated with success in external examinations taken at sixteen-plus?
(f) Can we identify 'improvers' and 'deteriorators' and isolate the environmental determinants of these conditions?

(a) Environment and school attainment

First we calculated the average correlations with attainment at all ages and stages from seven-plus to sixteen-plus, for all the environment measures. We found that forty-two environmental predictors were significantly associated with attainment at every age. The average of all the secondary attainment correlations was 0·386, marginally higher than the average of all the primary correlations at 0·371, which suggests that environment has a greater influence at the secondary school stage. However, when the differences between primary and secondary correlations for each individual variable were tested for significance, we found that no single variable had a significantly greater effect at one stage than another. The impact of this group of variables is all-pervading and, as a cluster, it describes aspects of the environment importantly associated with all educational results. These forty-two variables with their attendant average age correlations are set down in Table 6.1. An inspection of this list of variables clearly shows that there is a good deal of overlapping content and few, even at face value, would be expected to be completely independent of all others. Rather, they represent a complex of environmental attitudes and conditions favourable to educational achievement at all ages. Immediately striking is the number of such variables concerned with parents' ambitions for their children in terms of education and careers, their awareness of school work and progress, the reading habits of the family, and the educational experience of the parents. No less striking is the absence from this list of the socio-economic measures—*father's occupation*, *material needs*, *rateable value*, *housing standard*, etc. This is in direct agreement with the results of the Plowden primary survey which stated—'Although there is some slight association with social class, what matters is the degree of literacy within the home, and the attitudes of parents towards books and towards school. These correlations emphasize the existence of many good homes in the working class and many bad homes in the middle class.'

There is no doubt that the variables which correlate highly with educational attainment—in that they also correlate strongly with each other—constitute a syndrome describing the most crucial features of the 'education-orientated' home. We attempted to measure, rather crudely, the cohesiveness of these environment variables by calculating the average correlation of each variable with all other environment variables. We were not surprised to find that of fifty-five variables which had average correlations of 0·180 or over with all the educational tests, forty-four correlated at least at an equal level of significance with all other aspects of the environment. The eleven which did not can be assumed to be relatively independent of the 'home-education' complex. They include *order*, *number of clubs and societies joined*, *deference*, *child's outgoingness at interview*, *affiliation* and *parents ask about school*, all of which were scored on the child's own responses, in the absence of their parents.

Table 6.1 Average correlations—individual analysis

Variable	All tests	Primary 7+	8+	9+	10+	All	Secondary Year 1	Year 2	Year 3	16+	All
12 Type of secondary school	0·703	0·630	0·633	0·656	0·767	0·668	0·799	0·803	0·777	0·699	0·723
19 Preferred age of leaving—parents	0·589	0·554	0·538	0·612	0·655	0·582	0·641	0·630	0·616	0·816	0·589
21 Earliness of leaving decision	0·581	0·568	0·566	0·623	0·664	0·597	0·616	0·611	0·575	0·789	0·565
26 Interest taken by school in leaving decision	0·567	0·506	0·532	0·581	0·640	0·562	0·604	0·648	0·585	0·667	0·567
79 Primary headteacher's rating	0·563	0·548	0·617	0·607	0·645	0·595	0·606	0·584	0·580	0·457	0·537
13 Entered sixth form	0·556	0·468	0·509	0·519	0·584	0·515	0·619	0·648	0·640	0·689	0·587
50 Amount of homework	0·551	0·555	0·506	0·559	0·591	0·539	0·596	0·637	0·593	0·546	0·556
14 Left school at age 15	−0·537	−0·501	−0·487	−0·547	−0·599	−0·527	−0·570	−0·578	−0·556	−0·842	−0·539
59 School performance important to child's future	0·521	0·467	0·488	0·523	0·582	0·513	0·583	0·558	0·560	0·603	0·524
32 Duration of child's library membership	0·518	0·513	0·507	0·541	0·576	0·524	0·593	0·544	0·521	0·597	0·509
23 Type of further education desired	0·487	0·431	0·490	0·530	0·550	0·497	0·533	0·528	0·488	0·595	0·478
16 Occupational ambition of child	0·476	0·457	0·429	0·463	0·521	0·460	0·512	0·539	0·528	0·617	0·488
36 Nature of child's reading matter	0·472	0·457	0·457	0·500	0·502	0·467	0·535	0·532	0·481	0·548	0·474
24 Career qualifications desired	0·455	0·388	0·412	0·484	0·491	0·440	0·513	0·502	0·475	0·600	0·462
51 Parents' knowledge of homework content	0·440	0·431	0·380	0·473	0·487	0·432	0·460	0·520	0·463	0·497	0·444
33 Parents influenced child to join library	0·439	0·391	0·405	0·438	0·481	0·423	0·521	0·488	0·428	0·572	0·444
20 Child's preference for extended schooling	0·417	0·343	0·350	0·433	0·442	0·383	0·474	0·488	0·434	0·577	0·432
46 Family involvement during long school holidays	0·394	0·430	0·334	0·404	0·422	0·387	0·443	0·437	0·420	0·466	0·401
47 Parents 11+ selection	0·380	0·366	0·364	0·388	0·397	0·368	0·396	0·418	0·436	0·485	0·387
22 Influence of education on long term plans	0·363	0·373	0·361	0·379	0·383	0·366	0·378	0·385	0·397	0·403	0·357

34 Child likes reading at home	0·361	0·318	0·346	0·383	0·397	0·356	0·407	0·403	0·369	0·413	0·361
17 Cleanliness of child and evidence of care	0·356	0·333	0·349	0·334	0·384	0·344	0·377	0·411	0·381	0·413	0·360
58 Parents' visit to secondary school before entry	0·342	0·344	0·331	0·331	0·407	0·351	0·364	0·374	0·342	0·375	0·331
61 Parents' knowledge of class subject positions	0·340	0·330	0·325	0·388	0·422	0·364	0·356	0·373	0·310	0·358	0·321
27 Parents' library membership	0·331	0·250	0·281	0·333	0·381	0·318	0·407	0·367	0·331	0·446	0·343
35 Nature of publications bought for child	0·325	0·346	0·281	0·350	0·341	0·316	0·344	0·338	0·376	0·421	0·326
38 Provision for child to store own books	0·313	0·275	0·250	0·310	0·329	0·285	0·351	0·397	0·343	0·395	0·334
28 Amount of mother's reading	0·304	0·260	0·269	0·317	0·289	0·273	0·378	0·357	0·340	0·356	0·330
67 Child likes parents and teachers to meet	0·292	0·268	0·268	0·314	0·279	0·268	0·315	0·367	0·318	0·310	0·305
54 Parents' formal education level	0·278	0·256	0·197	0·266	0·288	0·249	0·314	0·336	0·305	0·393	0·298
64 Amount of parental discussion on school reports	0·277	0·309	0·257	0·313	0·295	0·280	0·311	0·299	0·259	0·367	0·268
78 Order	−0·274	−0·229	−0·221	−0·320	−0·316	−0·269	−0·326	−0·344	−0·220	−0·371	−0·276
49 Parents' further education involvement	0·267	0·248	0·219	0·263	0·279	0·249	0·292	0·273	0·331	0·389	0·279
42 Nature of child's hobbies and interests	0·264	0·219	0·219	0·221	0·247	0·222	0·329	0·346	0·295	0·288	0·294
63 Amount of family discussion on school progress	0·256	0·326	0·215	0·308	0·283	0·268	0·270	0·258	0·239	0·354	0·239
37 Nature of books bought for child	0·247	0·237	0·264	0·236	0·265	0·245	0·290	0·241	0·265	0·309	0·246
77 Deference	−0·229	−0·214	−0·221	−0·311	−0·236	−0·232	−0·274	−0·256	−0·212	−0·334	−0·231
71 Attendance	0·227	0·217	0·183	0·198	0·215	0·195	0·231	0·280	0·284	0·308	0·245
40 Nature of radio listening	0·224	0·221	0·191	0·221	0·251	0·219	0·260	0·260	0·234	0·199	0·228
72 Child has own room	0·212	0·198	0·183	0·282	0·247	0·219	0·227	0·228	0·224	0·282	0·212
29 Nature of mother's reading matter	0·218	0·175	0·185	0·228	0·187	0·184	0·261	0·272	0·249	0·340	0·244
55 Secondary school chosen on educational grounds	0·184	0·188	0·176	0·188	0·185	0·179	0·209	0·188	0·216	0·211	0·191

These results suggest that, though home background is overwhelmingly important, educational attainment is also associated with aspects of the child's own attitudes and opinions which are not necessarily highly involved with factors in the home background. There is some comfort in this finding, which suggests that efforts made by schools to modify pupils' attitudes to education need not be abandoned as useless because parental attitudes are so strong in their effect. Further support for this view is given by *no attendance problems* and *educational value of peer group influence*, both of which are significantly associated with overall attainment, but with few other environment variables. We cannot, therefore, assume that conditioning to parents' attitudes and habits is total. The personal characteristics of the child remain viable as predictors of attainment.

This being said, we must examine the relative importance of the stronger of the environmental influences. In Table 6.1 the highest correlations of all are given by *type of secondary school*, the variable most highly correlated with both primary and secondary attainment. It takes precedence over all others at all ages except sixteen-plus, when external examination results are more importantly associated with variables concerned with parental ambition for the child—*preferred age of leaving* and *earliness of leaving decision*. So far as individuals are concerned, *type of secondary school* is a quasi-criterion variable, in itself a measure of attainment (because of eleven-plus selection), and as much associated with primary as with secondary school achievement.

The next highest correlation is given by *preferred age of leaving* (0·589), a sure indicator of parental attitude towards education. This variable also gave the highest correlation with attainment in the primary survey. The very high correlation of 0·816 with *external examinations at sixteen-plus* is boosted by the zero score awarded to those pupils who did, in fact, leave school at the age of fifteen in accordance with their parents' wishes. The temporal quality of this variable is manifested by the next highest correlation (0·581) for *earliness of leaving decision* with which it correlates at 0·766. There is no doubt that the parents of high achieving children formulated their high educational ambitions very early in the child's school career if not before. The latter variable is an indicator of the time span of parents' thoughts about education. We cannot assume from our data that its relationship with attainment necessarily indicates that it is the child's acceptance of his parents' goals which have provided him with scholastic motivation over a long period of time. Both these 'goal' variables have stronger associations with measures of intelligence than with other measures of attainment. *Preferred age of leaving* and *earliness of leaving decision* correlate strongly with the *picture intelligence test* taken at the early age of seven-plus at 0·601 and 0·607 respectively, and it is at least as likely that parents of ultimately high-achieving children recognized potential at an early age. 'Goal-setting' and 'recognition of potential' are both plausible hypotheses for the connection between these two variables and attainment. An equally plausible hypothesis would be the one put forward by Wiseman in the Plowden Survey: that there is a strong connection between the intelligence of children and that of their parents, and that intelligent parents display attitudes and habits that foster the abilities of their children. Unfortunately we have no measure which could be accurately described as 'parents' intelligence', in order to test this hypothesis. The best measure we have is *parents' 11+ selection*, a three-point rating on whether neither, one or both parents achieved the possibility of taking up selective education in their post-primary years. This variable correlates significantly with all the pupils' educational measures—and at a higher level with intelligence tests—than with other educational measures. Its average correlations are 0·374 for English tests, 0·356 for mathematics tests and 0·407 for intelligence tests. When we consider that both *parents' 11+ selection* and all the pupils' intelligence test scores correlated significantly, not only with each other, but also with sixty out of our seventy-nine environment variables, we are forced to the conclusion that parental ability or child's intelligence—or a compound of both which might be termed 'background ability'—could possibly account for most of the significant environment-attainment correlations. In order to see if there were any environmental effects which could not be so accounted for, we calculated partial correlations holding *parents' 11+ selection* and *child's 7+ intelligence* constant in turn, for all the environment variables. Out of the fifty-five significant correlations with overall attainment, thirty-eight fell below significance as a result, indicating that the characteristics described by these variables could not usefully be separated from 'background ability' in all its ramifications.

The partial correlations clearly divided our significant attainment variables into three categories—(i) those that were related to attainment more than to background ability because they retained significance when either *parents' 11+ selection* or *7+ intelligence* was partialled out, (ii) those that were related to both aspects of background ability to such an extent that the residual effect with attainment was not significant, and (iii) those that were not highly related to *parents' 11+ selection* but which derived most of their effect with attainment from their association with the initial intelligence level of the child. These three types of interaction are separated into Sections 1, 2 and 3 of Table 6.2. They relate only to the variables given in Table 6.1 which were significantly associated with attainment at all ages and stages. We cannot assume any causal relationships from correlations, but our results appear to suggest that the variables in Section 1 are the 'purest' of the environmental attainment predictors, and those in Section 3 are intelligence predictors. Section 2 contains those variables that relate background ability and school attainment to such an extent that the interaction cannot be realistically separated.

The sixteen variables in Section 1 of Table 6.2 can be thought of as the

Table 6.2 Average and partial correlations—overall attainment

Variable	Average *r* with all attainment measures	Partial *r* with Parents' 11+ Selection constant	Partial *r* with 7+ Intelligence constant
Section 1			
19 Preferred age of leaving	0·589*	0·508*	0·275*
21 Earliness of leaving decision	0·581*	0·479*	0·254*
26 Interest taken by school in leaving decision	0·567*	0·482*	0·231*
13 Entered sixth form	0·556*	0·484*	0·306*
50 Amount of child's homework	0·551*	0·474*	0·200*
14 Left school at age 15	−0·537*	−0·444*	−0·254*
59 School performance important to child's future	0·521*	0·453*	0·259*
32 Duration of child's library membership	0·518*	0·525*	0·232*
23 Type of further education desired	0·487*	0·402*	0·227*
16 Occupational ambition of child	0·476*	0·384*	0·181*
36 Nature of child's reading matter	0·472*	0·364*	0·219*
24 Career qualifications desired	0·455*	0·378*	0·224*
33 Parents influenced child to join library	0·439*	0·332*	0·188*
20 Child's preference for extended schooling	0·417*	0·330*	0·179*
34 Child likes reading at home	0·361*	0·270*	0·205*
27 Parents' library membership	0·331*	0·178*	0·205*
Section 2			
54 Parents' formal education level	0·278*	0·124	0·089
64 Amount of discussion of school reports	0·277*	0·140	0·042
49 Parents' further education involvement	0·267*	0·141	0·084
63 Amount of discussion of school progress	0·256*	0·160	0·022
29 Nature of mother's reading matter	0·218*	0·066	0·051
72 Child has own room	0·212*	0·114	0·068
55 School chosen on educational grounds	0·184*	0·103	0·048
Section 3			
79 Primary headteacher's rating	0·563*	0·517*	0·170
51 Parents' knowledge of homework content	0·440*	0·327*	0·119
46 Family involvement during long holidays	0·394*	0·307*	0·111
47 Parents' 11+ Selection	0·380*	—	0·116
22 Influence of education on long-term plans	0·363*	0·289*	0·076
17 Cleanliness and evidence of care	0·356*	0·295*	0·144
58 Parents' visit to secondary school	0·342*	0·238*	0·124
61 Parents' knowledge of subject positions	0·340*	0·235*	0·087
35 Nature of publications bought for child	0·325*	0·276*	0·108
38 Provision for child to store own books	0·313*	0·192*	0·167
28 Amount of mother's reading	0·304*	0·179*	0·129
67 Child likes parents and teachers to meet	0·292*	0·207*	0·110
78 Order	−0·274*	−0·257*	−0·139
42 Nature of child's hobbies and interests	0·264*	0·203*	0·159
37 Nature of books bought for child	0·247*	0·187*	0·080
77 Deference	−0·229*	−0·232*	−0·103
71 Attendance	0·227*	0·176*	0·059
40 Nature of radio listening	0·224*	0·179*	0·083

*Significant at 5% level or over

strongest environmental predictors of attainment, in that their relation to background ability is not the whole story. They include four 'ambition' variables—*preferred age of leaving*, *earliness of leaving decision*, *type of further education desired* and *career qualifications desired*. Parental ambition for the child is therefore, **in itself**, related to attainment. *Interest taken by school in leaving decision* is also significantly related to high attainment irrespective of the two aspects of background ability. This is probably a school variable but, as it was scored on information received from the child, it also contains overtones of the pupils' awareness of the amount of interest displayed by his school in regard to plans for the future. Its strongest environmental correlations are for *preferred age of leaving* (0·709), *left school at age 15* (—0·703) and *earliness of leaving decision* (0·697). Its highest attainment correlation is with *sixteen-plus external examination results* (0·667). It appears that close consultation with both parents and pupils on the subject of education after the statutory leaving age is very much associated with aspects of parental ambition and that maximum effort appears to be expended on those pupils with fairly obvious educational prospects. Those pupils intending to leave school as soon as possible do not get the same attention. These findings support the subjective impressions of the research officers when they discussed methods of pupil guidance with headteachers. They were left with little doubt that thought and discussion about the future prospects of individual children took place largely in the context of likely external examination results.

It is not surprising that *entered sixth form* should be significantly associated with attainment at all ages, and that the highest correlations (Table 6.1) should be with *sixteen-plus external examinations*. Its correlations with environment variables, and their implications, will be discussed later when a more detailed analysis of this sub-group will be presented. At this stage it is sufficient to say that partialling out the effects of 'background ability' does not reduce its relationship to attainment to below significance.

As in the primary school survey, *amount of child's homework* correlated very highly with attainment at all ages, and overall at 0·551. This is also probably a school variable as it correlates at 0·559 with *type of secondary school* but, because it was assessed by parents, it could also be an indicator of parental awareness and interest, and a partial indicator of the extent to which parents accept the demands of the school. We have evidence for this in that it correlates significantly with fifty-nine of the seventy-nine environment variables, including all those concerned with parental ambition, child ambition, literacy, family cohesiveness and all other homework variables. It has high associations with *7+ intelligence* (0·606) and *parents' 11+ selection* (0·385) but, with the effects of these partialled out, it is still significantly associated with attainment.

Left school at age 15 discriminates only very slightly between primary and secondary school attainment, and is significantly and negatively related to attainment at all ages from seven-plus to sixteen-plus. Statutory leaving could obviously have been largely predicted at the age of entry to junior school. As a single variable it is most complex in its interactions, correlating significantly with sixty-three of the environment variables. The implications of this will be discussed later when the fifteen-year-old leavers are investigated as a sub-group. It is also concerned with attainment, as partialling out the effects of background ability does not produce attainment correlations which are non-significant.

School performance important to child's future appears to be a very important indicator, not only of school attainment at all ages, but also of the life-style of the home, as it correlates significantly with fifty-seven of the environment variables. Not surprisingly it has its highest association with *leaving school at age fifteen* (—0·645), followed by *earliness of leaving decision* (0·635), *preferred age of leaving* (0·623) and *type of further education desired* (0·605). These are all more important than the correlations with attainment at any age. If this group of variables represents an 'ambition' complex, the single one of relevance of school performance to the future seems to be a useful one for its descriptive qualities alone. It is logical that, if parents think school performance has little relevance to adult aspirations, then their children will leave school at the earliest possible moment. There would be little positive planning about this event, an early leaving age would be preferred, and further education ambitions would be at a minimum. There is no doubt that this variable is associated with 'background ability' as it correlated with *7+ intelligence* at 0·504 and with *parents' 11+ selection* at 0·334 but, when these effects are nullified, it is still significantly associated with overall attainment. One wonders how parents value school performance when they are unconvinced of its relevance to the child's adult life. Our findings certainly point out that in these circumstances children are unlikely to do well at school.

Table 6.1 gave ten variables descriptive of reading habits in the home, which are significantly associated with attainment at all ages, and Table 6.2 shows that five of these are not overwhelmingly related to aspects of 'background ability'. They are *duration of child's library membership*, *parents influenced child to join library*, *child likes reading at home*, *nature of child's reading matter* and *parents' library membership*. It is interesting that these five most important 'reading-attainment' variables are concerned with library membership and liking for reading, as these are surely aspects of literacy which are open to influence by schools and teachers, either by guidance and assistance to parents or direct approaches to the children.

In preceding paragraphs it has been pointed out that the most important environmental predictors of attainment are those connected with parental ambition for the child. In Table 6.2 we can see that *occupational ambition of child* and *child's preference for extended schooling* are also, in themselves, associated with overall attainment, though to a lesser degree than several of the parent ambition variables. As they have their highest correlations with the parent ambition variables, there is no doubt that a high degree of consensus exists within families about plans for the future.

Section 2 of Table 6.2 separates those variables which initially appeared to have a high relationship with overall attainment, but were related to 'background ability' to such an extent that partialling out the effect of *7+ intelligence* or *parents' 11+ selection* reduced the association to a value below significance. The single partial correlation given by *parents' 11+ selection* supports the view put forward by Wiseman (1967) that intelligent parents tend to have intelligent children, in that when *7+ intelligence* is nullified, the correlation between parental ability and the child's attainment (0·380) is reduced to below a level of significance (0·116). Two further variables concerned with the educational experience of the parents appear in Section 2. They are *parents' formal education level* and *parents' further education involvement*, and are clearly related to attainment because of their involvement with 'background ability'. The Plowden survey was forced to a rather pessimistic view of the low average correlation of 0·154 between parents' education (measured by *age parents completed education*) and their child's attainment, and inferred that education alone cannot be the instrument of radical change with succeeding generations. Our measure of *parents' 11+ selection* does, however, take into account those parents who, though selected at eleven-plus and presumably of high ability, did not, for economic or social reasons, attend selective secondary schools. Our higher attainment correlations for this variable suggest that parents' ability level, rather than length of schooling, is the most important factor involved. The possibility exists that, if all parents of high ability had actually undertaken extended schooling in appropriate institutions, the two aspects of ability and length of education could have been compounded to produce higher child-attainment correlations. In other words, as long as economic and social wastage exists, we are unlikely to see clearly what the full impact of parents' education on the attainment level of progeny could be.

Amount of discussion of school reports, amount of discussion of school progress, nature of mother's reading matter, child has own room and *school chosen on educational grounds* also owe their association with school attainment to the fact that they are strongly associated both with parental ability level and the child's measured intelligence.

Section 3 of Table 6.2 gives those variables which have significant associations with overall attainment and derive most of their effect from the initial intelligence level of the child but are not strongly related to the ability level of the parents. *Primary headteacher's rating* is the first of these. This is a quasi-criterion variable and one would expect the high average correlations of 0·595 and 0·537 with primary and secondary attainment respectively, reported in Table 6.1. The correlations for secondary school attainment are not as high as those for any of the individual primary school test scores, and we can conclude that it has been a less reliable predictor of potential than actual test results. Primary English tests (0·671), primary mathematics tests (0·675) and primary intelligence tests (0·736) are all stronger predictors. The social variables which correlate highly with *primary headteacher's rating* closely correspond, both in size and rank order, to those which correlate highly with attainment at all ages, with certain exceptions. For instance, *family discussion on school progress*, *discussion of school reports*, *nature of books purchased for child*, *provision for child to store own books*, *parents' formal education level*, and *nature of radio listening*, although correlating significantly with both primary and secondary school attainment, have low correlations with *headteacher's rating*. Conversely, *family health*, *cleanliness of home* and *material needs adequate* all have significant correlations with the primary headteacher's assessment, but much lower associations with actual attainment. There is the suggestion that, if social factors do influence headteacher's subjective ratings, the more overt aspects—likely to affect a child's appearance—are taken into account, rather than the more educationally important qualities of the home background about which headteachers may have little information. It has often been suggested that headteachers' ratings could provide valid replacements for standardized test scores, but from our findings it would now seem that, if this procedure were to be followed, then it would be necessary for headteachers to familiarize themselves with the more educationally predictive aspects of the child's home environment before reaching conclusions, and not to place too much reliance on appearances.

Parents' knowledge of homework content is largely related to the child's intelligence level, thus producing associations with attainment. This is probably because the low ability pupils were not likely to have any homework and so their parents could not be aware of it. Four of the reading variables are also strongly related to the initial intelligence of the child—*nature of publications bought for child*, *nature of books bought for child*, *provision for child to store own books* and *amount of mother's reading*. The first three of these are logical in their effect. The brighter children would probably choose 'better quality' reading matter, less ephemeral than comics and magazines, and they would need somewhere to keep it. It is more difficult to understand how *amount of mother's reading* is largely dependent on the intelligence of the child for its associations with attainment, but it does suggest that the mothers of bright children are seen to read frequently.

Three of these 'brightness' dependent variables are concerned with activities. The brighter children have more serious and long standing hobbies and interests; their parents take them away for holidays during the long vacations, and they listen to the radio for things other than pop-music. The parents of bright children have allowed educational considerations to influence their long term plans; they probably both visited the secondary school before their child's entry; they were aware of their child's position in class in individual subjects, and the children themselves were assessed as being clean and well cared for. The brighter the child, the more welcome were encounters between parents and teachers.

In Section 3 there are also two variables, largely related to the child's intelligence level, which measured the pupils' reactions to aspects of the school environment. These have been named *order* and *deference*, and in that order they correlate significantly and negatively with attainment at all ages. Their average correlations with overall attainment are −0·274 and −0·229 respectively. These variables were measured by a response of 'true' or 'false' to questionnaire statements, ten for each variable, concerning the amount of pressure it was felt the secondary school exerted towards conformity to: (i) *order*—the organization of the immediate physical environment in terms of preoccupation with neatness, arrangement and meticulous detail; and (ii) *deference*—voluntary submission to the opinions and preferences of others perceived as superior. It will be remembered that out of fourteen 'need–press' categories only three were found to have significant correlation with attainment at any age, those two already mentioned and *affiliation*—the formation of many close, warm and friendly relationships with others.

Typical questionnaire items educing significant negative responses with attainment are, for *order*: (i) 'Many teachers make pupils do work over again to make it neater', (ii) 'Classrooms are always kept very clean and tidy', (iii) 'Staff and pupils pay great attention to the rules for moving about the school', and (iv) 'At this school the motto seems to be, "a place for everything and everything in its place"'; for *deference*: (i) 'Pupils hardly ever express opinions different from those of the teachers', (ii) 'Pupils never make fun of the teachers when talking amongst themselves', and (iii) 'Teachers go out of their way to make sure that pupils address them with respect'; and, for *affiliation*: (i) 'Pupils often go out to support the school teams', (ii) 'There are lots of projects in which groups of pupils can work together in and out of school', and (iii) 'There is a lot of school spirit'. *Order* and *deference* correlate negatively and significantly with attainment at any age, and with each other at 0·313. Not unexpectedly, when a school is seen to exert strong pressure towards meticulous neatness, a pressure towards deferential attitudes to superiors is also felt. When the effect of 7+ *Intelligence* was nullified in partial correlation, the effect with attainment fell below significance in each case. There is no doubt that the initially bright children failed to see their schools as very orderly or demanding of deference. We cannot assume that these negative perceptions represent accurate assessments of actual school environments in view of the small number of pupils in each school but, as these variables also correlate negatively with *type of school*, we may suggest that the pupils lower in the hierarchy of school types feel the impact of such environmental factors most strongly. It may be the case that the more prestigious schools are work-orientated, and their pupils are less conscious of pressures to conform to the pressures of order and submission. School rules and regulations about orderliness, neatness and deference to superiors may well be more obtrusive in the non-selective schools where such pressures are likely to be regarded as 'social education' and as much a feature of schooling as academic achievement. We must not, of course, rule out that a critical attitude towards environment may be associated with intelligence, and that the very able children may have developed such high standards of what they consider to be orderly and respectful, that few school institutions could live up to their expectations.

Attendance, which correlates significantly with attainment at all ages, is also shown to be strongly related to the child's initial intelligence level. Correlations do not indicate whether intelligent children attend school more regularly or whether attendance at school has affected intelligence. However, the existence of the relationship is demonstrated, and, as long as the latter possibility exists, schools are more than justified in their efforts to maximize attendance.

The answer to our question, 'Which of our variables are associated with school attainment, and what is their relative importance as predictors of achievement?' is that forty-two variables were found to be significantly related to attainment at every age from seven-plus to sixteen-plus, but that most of the associations could be accounted for by the intelligence already displayed shortly after entrance to the junior school. The variables which, in themselves, demonstrated significant effects with attainment were largely concerned with educational and career ambitions and with aspects of reading in the home.

(b) **Environment and age trends**

The variables which did not appear in Table 6.1 were those which did not show significant correlations with all the age and stage measures. These are set down in Table 6.3, and the significant average correlations are in bold type. It will be noted that, in general, where a variable is significant at one age it is likely to be significant at all others, and that where no significance exists there is likely to be none at most ages. There are very few variables which can be said to be specifically concerned with attainment at a particular age or stage. But, as already stated, the overall tendency is for the environment variables to correlate more strongly with attainment in the secondary school. This is borne out by the fact that fifty-four of the variables had average correlations which increased in size when averages for all primary tests were compared with averages for all secondary school tests, and twenty-five decreased in effect. The differences, however, were small and none approached significance. The highest increase (0·073 to 0·166) was given by *father from small family*, which was significantly associated with three out of four secondary age measures, but with none of the primary age tests. As this variable is significantly related with all others connected with father's literacy and education, it seems clear that the attributes of fathers are valuable predictors of children's attainment in post-primary years.

Two variables concerned with the child's own activities—*nature of child's hobbies and interests* and *number of clubs and societies joined* increase in weight from significance at the 5% level to significance at the 1% level at the secondary stage. *Family weekend activities* also become significant at the secondary level. The same remarks apply to *nature of mother's reading* and *amount of father's reading*, and the increased effects of both *nature of father's reading* and *amount of mother's reading* are of about the same order of size. *Attendance* and *no attendance problems* also increase in significance from 5% at the primary stage to 1% at the secondary level, and the increased effect of *no history of truancy* (the other attendance variable) is of the same order.

Two aspects of the physical environment of the home—*material needs adequate* and *cleanliness and evidence of care* are significant at the secondary stage though not at primary level. The negative association of *child helps at home* becomes significant in the secondary school also. This variable correlates at 0·228 with *sex of child*—positively with being a girl. Helping at home is therefore very much bound up with sex, and it would appear that adolescent girls give help of a domestic nature to the detriment of their school work. (Women's Liberation please note.)

The variables which show the major decreases in effect after primary school are those containing a temporal element—*earliness of career plans* (0·231 to 0·182) and *earliness of leaving decision* (0·597 to 0·565). *Parents influenced choice of books* (0·254 to 0·185) declines from a 1% to a 5% level of significance after transfer, and *parents check homework* (0·232 to 0·181) and *parents' knowledge of class subject positions* (0·364 to 0·321) decline about the same amount. These variables seem to be redolent of parental pressure rather than interest and awareness.

The answer to our question—'Do any variables become more important or less important at secondary school age?' is 'Yes'. Parental literacy and the ability to provide and encourage activities become more valuable as the child grows up. Good physical provision in the home in terms of cleanliness and material welfare and all aspects of school attendance also become more important. Helping at home becomes increasingly detrimental. Certain variables redolent of parental pressure decline in effect as the child grows in years.

(c) **Environment and subject attainment**

In order to find whether any aspects of environment had a differential effect with the five subject areas that contributed to average correlations, we calcu-

Table 6.3 Average correlations—individual analysis

Variable	All tests	Primary 7+	8+	9+	10+	All	Secondary Year 1	Year 2	Year 3	16+	All
43 Number of school clubs and societies joined	**0·260**	**0·191**	0·155	**0·237**	**0·300**	**0·222**	**0·289**	**0·332**	**0·320**	**0·324**	**0·287**
56 Father involved in choice of school	**0·229**	**0·195**	0·161	**0·260**	**0·261**	**0·217**	**0·249**	**0·246**	**0·251**	**0·277**	**0·231**
18 Child's outgoingness at interview	**0·229**	**0·210**	**0·214**	**0·271**	**0·278**	**0·242**	**0·284**	**0·240**	**0·222**	0·129	**0·223**
76 Affiliation	**−0·225**	**−0·219**	**−0·311**	**−0·278**	**−0·268**	**−0·264**	**−0·244**	**−0·210**	**−0·186**	−0·170	**−0·193**
30 Amount of father's reading	**0·213**	**0·187**	0·170	**0·184**	**0·216**	**0·188**	**0·275**	**0·233**	**0·223**	**0·375**	**0·235**
31 Nature of father's reading matter	**0·213**	**0·220**	0·157	0·164	**0·200**	**0·181**	**0·267**	**0·228**	**0·231**	**0·414**	**0·233**
39 Parents influenced choice of books	**0·207**	**0·229**	**0·276**	**0·252**	**0·273**	**0·254**	**0·235**	**0·194**	0·170	**0·225**	**0·185**
25 Earliness of career plans	**0·203**	**0·182**	**0·228**	**0·264**	**0·250**	**0·231**	**0·220**	**0·199**	0·157	**0·299**	**0·182**
53 Parents check homework	**0·202**	**0·280**	0·173	**0·223**	**0·265**	**0·232**	**0·191**	**0·179**	**0·215**	**0·220**	**0·181**
75 Educational value of peer group influence	**0·199**	**0·220**	**0·187**	0·170	**0·188**	**0·182**	**0·254**	**0·187**	**0·206**	**0·257**	**0·201**
66 Parents ask about school	**0·185**	**0·192**	**0·182**	**0·215**	**0·203**	**0·199**	**0·183**	**0·252**	**0·163**	**0·196**	**0·195**
48 Parents regret aspects of own education	**0·181**	**0·189**	0·165	**0·230**	0·172	**0·176**	**0·213**	**0·188**	**0·186**	**0·275**	**0·182**
70 No attendance problems	**0·176**	0·162	0·150	0·144	0·167	0·150	**0·208**	**0·214**	**0·215**	0·166	**0·192**
74 Both parents control child	0·173	**0·186**	0·127	**0·175**	**0·194**	0·164	**0·199**	**0·188**	**0·180**	0·171	0·172
3 Rateable value	0·172	**0·192**	**0·191**	**0·176**	0·172	**0·176**	**0·194**	0·167	**0·192**	**0·224**	0·171
4 Material needs adequate	0·170	0·161	0·112	0·150	**0·180**	0·148	**0·201**	**0·222**	**0·191**	0·156	**0·183**
73 Child helps at home	−0·169	−0·114	−0·169	**−0·179**	−0·152	−0·149	−0·154	**−0·207**	**−0·225**	**−0·216**	**−0·181**
45 Nature of family weekend activities	0·165	0·165	0·095	0·127	0·169	0·138	**0·190**	**0·219**	**0·172**	**0·321**	**0·184**

52 Parents' approval of homework	0·155	**0·221**	0·163	0·110	0·151	0·153	0·165	0·170	**0·176**	**0·207**	0·161
57 Parents want to assist in the teaching process	0·154	0·118	0·148	0·168	0·125	0·133	**0·190**	**0·176**	**0·180**	**0·274**	0·173
60 Parents' assessment of child's effort at school	0·150	0·169	0·126	**0·175**	0·106	0·131	0·148	**0·225**	0·157	**0·213**	0·164
44 Involvement of child in parents' activities	0·145	0·109	0·127	0·124	**0·211**	0·150	0·158	0·142	0·133	**0·186**	0·137
41 Selectivity of child's TV viewing	0·141	0·116	0·123	**0·181**	0·152	0·136	0·150	0·166	0·136	**0·194**	0·140
2 Father's occupation	0·140	0·131	0·123	0·088	0·157	0·129	**0·179**	0·172	0·123	0·164	0·144
15 Left school at age 16	0·139	0·170	0·122	**0·179**	**0·183**	0·160	0·126	0·111	0·095	**0·360**	0·118
68 Involvement of child in school activities	0·134	0·114	0·127	0·139	0·114	0·117	0·146	**0·187**	0·148	0·051	0·141
9 Father from small family	0·128	0·067	0·070	0·097	0·079	0·073	**0·177**	0·169	**0·190**	**0·196**	0·166
10 Mother from small family	0·126	0·107	0·107	0·166	0·138	0·124	0·125	0·141	0·146	**0·220**	0·133
62 Child talks about school	0·126	0·164	0·051	0·077	0·143	0·110	0·162	0·145	0·135	**0·212**	0·137
69 No history of truancy	0·123	0·079	0·117	0·071	0·107	0·095	0·133	0·170	**0·179**	0·129	0·146
6 Housing standard	0·121	0·052	0·147	0·096	0·128	0·114	0·130	**0·181**	0·088	**0·220**	0·127
5 Cleanliness of home	0·114	0·024	0·044	0·064	0·131	0·075	0·131	**0·189**	0·132	**0·213**	0·141
65 Nature of parental help with school work	—	0·077	—	0·144	0·170	—	—	0·163	0·133	**0·261**	—
7 Smallness of family	0·093	0·112	0·065	0·144	0·136	0·111	0·088	0·091	0·064	0·122	0·077
11 Mother not working	—	—	0·090	0·081	0·068	—	—	0·112	0·084	0·097	—
8 Family health	—	0·079	0·054	0·087	0·096	0·077	0·059	0·075	0·055	0·065	—
1 Sex of child	—	0·064	0·059	—	—	—	—	—	—	0·005	0·052

Significant at 5% level or over in bold type
— correlations to be averaged do not operate in the same direction over all measures

lated the average correlation for the three year scores in each individual subject, and then nullified the effect of initial ability by producing partial correlations holding *10+ total score* constant. As a result we found that only nineteen of the seventy-nine environment variables produced partial correlation coefficients of a size to be called significant with one or more of the individual subjects. These are set down in Table 6.4.

Table 6.4 Partial correlations significant for one or more subject areas

Variable	English	Maths	Sciences	Social sciences	Non-academic
Entered sixth form	0·225	0·253	0·261	0·273	
Child likes reading at home	0·193				
Child likes parents and teachers to met	0·184				
Attendance		0·188			
Interest taken by school in leaving decision			0·183		
Nature of mother's reading matter				0·193	
School performance important to child's future				0·187	
Family involvement during long school holidays				0·179	
Nature of child's reading matter	0·209			0·182	
Amount of child's homework	0·175				0·236
Preferred age of leaving		0·188	0·223		
Occupational ambition of child			0·250		0·183
Child's preference for extended schooling			0·186		0·187
Father from small family			0·175		0·208
Nature of child's hobbies and interests			0·204	0·209	
Amount of mother's reading			0·194	0·213	
Influence of education on long-term plans		0·212			
Child's outgoingness at interview	0·209				
Deference					−0·183

It will be seen that the highest number of significant partial correlations, eight in all, is given for the sciences, followed by the social sciences (seven), English (six), non-academic subjects (five) and last of all mathematics (four). The first three subject areas show the highest environmental involvement, and 'tool' subjects of English and mathematics the least. This finding is supported by the rank order of the average of the nineteen partial correlations for each subject. English and mathematics are most dependent upon initial ability for their relation to features in the home background.

The single variable which has expectedly high associations with attainment in all school subjects is *entered sixth form*, significantly so with all subjects except non-academic. The remaining variables are less general in effect. The fact that is immediately striking about these variables is that they overwhelmingly refer to 'literacy' and 'ambition'. In order to derive a more precise assessment of the nature of their impact we averaged the partial correlations in these two areas of environment for each subject area. The four literacy variables—*child likes reading at home, nature of mother's reading matter, nature of child's reading matter* and *amount of mother's reading*, when averaged revealed that their strongest effect was with social sciences (0·186) then English (0·185), followed by sciences (0·123), non-academic subjects (0·097) and mathematics (0·078) last of all. The five 'ambition' variables—*preferred age of leaving, occupational ambition of child, child's preference for extended schooling, school performance important to child's future* and *influence of education on long-term plans* produced quite a different picture. The order is now sciences (0·185), mathematics (0·154), non-academic subjects (0·136), social sciences (0·111) and last of all English (0·078). Mathematics was associated with literacy least of all, and English with ambition least of all. It is interesting that the important literacy variables are concerned with the reading habits of mother and child. All the partial correlations are higher than those for the two concerned with father's reading, neither of which approached significance with any specific subject area.

As far as English is concerned, two of the significant variables are specifically concerned with the child's reading habits. These are logical associations emphasizing the importance of reading as a component of success in English at school. *Nature of child's reading matter* is also significantly associated with attainment in the social sciences. Two further variables significantly associated with English only are *child likes parents and teachers to meet* and *child's outgoingness at interview*. These both have connotations of ease in social situations, which suggests that it is verbal fluency which connects English attainment and social confidence. *Amount of child's homework* also has a significant relation to English attainment, and we note a similar but rather surprising effect with non-academic subjects.

Apart from *entered sixth form*, there are three variables significantly associated with mathematics—*influence of education on long-term plans, pre-*

ferred age of leaving and *attendance.* These are clearly aspects of parental ambition coupled with a serious attitude to education as a long term process. The first and last of these variables are exclusive to mathematics as far as significance is concerned, but *preferred age of leaving* has an even higher relation to science attainment.

Attainment in the sciences has its strongest association with the cluster of ambition variables, three of which individually reach significance—*occupational ambition of child, preferred age of leaving* and *child's preference for extended schooling.* These are not exclusive to science by virtue of significant interaction, the first and last duplicating this effect with non-academic subjects, and *preferred age of leaving* with mathematics. The only literacy variable significantly related to science is *amount of mother's reading,* which is even more strongly associated with achievement in the social sciences. Of the 'family size' variables only *father from small family* appears in Table 6.4. This is positively related to high attainment in all school subjects, significantly so with sciences and non-academic subjects. While English and the social sciences appear to share common ground so far as mother's reading habits are concerned, it is a father variable which relates the sciences to non-academic subjects in that *father from small family* is significantly related to both. It is at least plausible that the practical elements of subjects are related to the father's early life experiences, and the verbal elements are dependent on the mother's influence. There is tentative supporting evidence for this hypothesis in the direction of effect of the non-significant partial correlations given for *mother from small family* and *parents check homework.* The first of these has negative partial correlations with mathematics (—0·016) and non-academic subjects (—0·026) and positive results with English (0·107), social sciences (0·096) and sciences (0·009). *Parents check homework* (an activity likely to be undertaken by the father) has the reverse effect in that it correlates positively with non-academic subjects (0·035) and mathematics (0·005), and negatively with English (—0·110), social sciences (—0·103) and sciences (—0·042). Science and non-academic subjects are also similar in direction of effect when we examine the partial correlations for *child's outgoingness at interview* and *deference*—they are all negative, tentatively suggesting that inarticulateness (or perhaps introversion) and perception of low deference demands have a similar relationship to attainment in both subjects. *Nature of child's hobbies and interests* is also significantly and positively related to *science* attainment, a condition it shares with the *social sciences.*

The social sciences, as we have already stated, have the highest association with the literacy variables in Table 6.4, three out of four achieving significance —*amount of mother's reading, nature of mother's reading, matter* and *nature of child's reading matter. School performance important to child's future* and *family involvement during long holidays* both achieve significance with the social sciences only, though they are positively associated with all subject attainment. *Nature of child's hobbies and interests* has its highest association with the social sciences.

High attainment in the non-academic subjects has, surprisingly, its highest significant connection with *amount of child's homework* (0·236), followed by *father from small family* (0·208), *child's preference for extended schooling* (0·187) and *occupational ambition of child* (0·183). After mathematics, this subject area has the lowest connections with the literacy variables and the 'ambition' involved is obviously concerned with the child's own aspirations rather than those of the parents. Interpretation of these tendencies is difficult because of the vague nature of this attainment measure. It will be remembered that contributing scores included art, music, handicrafts, etc., which cannot be presumed to have anything in common as far as abilities are concerned. However, it is almost certain that most of these subjects would be taught in a less formal way than the other subjects studied, and it is interesting that *deference* has a significant negative partial correlation with non-academic scores. High non-academic attainment is related to a school atmosphere perceived by the child to be low in its demands for a deferential attitude to those in authority.

The answer to our question—'Are there any features in the home background which appear to be associated with attainment in particular school subjects?' is a tentative 'Yes'. While literacy and ambition are fairly general in effect with all subjects, the overall impression is again that the verbal and literary aspects of attainment are concerned with mother's reading habits and practical aspects with father's early family experience. This is not to say that the child's own attitudes, aspirations and perceptions are not important. Six of the variables with significant partial correlations with one subject or another were assessed on the child's own personal responses. Outgoingness at interview and reaction to deference demands are the two which most clearly distinguish one school subject from another, the comparatively large correlations with the former and English attainment, and the latter with non-academic attainment being particularly noticeable. There is some evidence that personality traits, largely unmeasured in this study, are intervening variables with school subject attainment as criteria.

(d) **Environment and school leaving**

The foregoing results have been concerned with the environmental correlates of attainment up to the end of the third year in secondary schools. Because of the organization of comprehensive education in Manchester, which took place at the beginning of the fourth year, 47% of our individual subsample (54 pupils) now found themselves to be comprehensive high school pupils without actually having been transferred to a new institution. Ten pupils (9%) began life afresh as far as school was concerned, as their secondary modern schools were closed and they transferred to a new purpose-built comprehensive high school. The remaining 44% (50 pupils) suffered little change, as their schools were untouched organizationally by the new regime, since they were either direct grant schools, schools which had been called 'comprehensive' for some years before reorganization, or secondary moderns left unchanged because of their inadequate size or geographical isolation. The Roman Catholic schools of all types had also not been reorganized.

By the end of the fourth year, 58 pupils (51% of the subsample) had left school at the statutory leaving age. After a further year, 38 pupils (33%) left at the age of sixteen, and the remaining 18 pupils (16%) entered the sixth-form after taking external examinations at the age of sixteen-plus. Of the 56 pupils who stayed at school after the statutory leaving age, 54 sat for one form of external examination or another. In the schools study we drew attention to the fact that the organizational changes in schools could have affected both attainment at the age of sixteen-plus and school leaving decisions. We must also bear in mind that such changes may also have modified both parent and child attitudes to school in the intervening period between reorganization and the final decision about when the child should leave school.

In view of the fact that *10+ total score* had higher correlations with *left at age 15*, *left at age 16* and *entered sixth form* than any of the subsequently acquired secondary attainment measures, it seemed obvious that leaving decisions were very much associated with long standing circumstances and attitudes, just as attainment had proved to be. From a perusal of the appropriate correlations, it appeared that the environmental concomitants of school leaving were well established before transfer at eleven-plus and, for this reason, we once again calculated partial correlations holding *10+ total score* constant. Initial ability and the environment features associated with it are so much related to leaving decisions that, without nullifying their effects by partial correlation, it would be difficult to isolate the background circumstances and attitudes which were, in themselves, related to the 'leaving' aspect of educational experience.

The large number of partial correlations of a size to be called significant was immediately apparent. Similar calculations for the average of three years' secondary attainment gave only two variables—*amount of child's homework* and *entered sixth form* of an equally high order. This is an important finding. Secondary attainment has little association with home background features that could not be accounted for by initial ability at the time of entry. On the other hand, the major decision about when to leave school, which is likely to affect the whole of adult life, is shown to be highly involved with many aspects of environment, even when the ability and social effects of selection are nullified. This is particularly the case for statutory leaving which has significant partial correlations with forty-two of the environment variables. *Left at 16* by comparison, gives seventeen significant coefficients, and *entered sixth form* gives twenty-five. From the direction of signs it would seem that the general tendency is for leaving at the age of fifteen to be clearly distinguished from staying on at school voluntarily for one or more years. Forty-seven variables operated negatively for *left at age 15* and positively for the two staying-on categories, and three variables operated positively for early leaving and negatively for staying on.

Perhaps the most useful method of examining the very complex results from the three analyses is to attempt to formulate tentative descriptive profiles of the three leaving categories on the evidence of their significant partial correlations with particular environment variables, and to examine individual cases for support or refutation of our interpretations. Table 6.5 gives the partial correlations significant for statutory leaving.

There is no doubt that, as a group, the statutory leavers are characterized most importantly by a decided lack of ambition on the part of both parents and children. Eight of the 'ambition' variables partially correlate negatively and significantly with statutory leaving, and their average (—0·472) is higher than any of the remaining individually significant variables. The nature of this lack of aspiration can be discerned from the relative size of the eight significant partial correlations. *Earliness of leaving decision* (—0·771) and *preferred age of leaving* (—0·641) give the highest associations, which suggests that parents' ambitions for their children to leave school at the earliest possible moment have been largely satisfied, although a conscious decision was left until the last minute. It would probably be truer to say that a decision was never made at all, and the stance adopted was more like acquiescence to what was considered inevitable. In some cases, of course, it actually was almost inevitable, as the schools attended by their children made no provision for courses after the end of the fourth year.

The next highest partial correlation is *child's preference for extended schooling* (—0·520), a clear indication that the wishes of the children have also largely been fulfilled. Their wishes, nevertheless, appear to carry less weight than those of their parents. When the original data were examined this was seen to be the case. The parents of fifty-four of our fifty-eight statutory leavers expressed a preference for their children to leave school at the earliest possible moment, so 93% were satisfied in this respect. The remaining four had very limited ambitions in that they thought any time up to the age of sixteen was preferable and, in three of these cases (all girls), it is clear that the wishes of the child prevailed at the last moment. One of these girls stated that she had always hated school and had refused to take up a grammar school place at eleven-plus, preferring to go to a technical high school to be with her primary school friends. She knew the advantages of staying on at school and had reluctantly agreed to do so up to the time of the interview. In her own words, she found lessons and teachers so old fashioned and boring that she dreaded every lesson. 'They punish you here by trying to bore you to death.'

Table 6.5 Significant partial correlations—leaving at age 15

Variable	Partial correlation
21 Earliness of leaving decision	−0·771
19 Preferred age of leaving	−0·641
20 Child's preference for extended schooling	−0·520
59 School performance important to child's future	−0·455
32 Duration of child's library membership	−0·427
26 Interest taken by school in leaving decision	−0·420
33 Parents influenced child to join library	−0·419
24 Career qualifications desired	−0·405
16 Occupational ambition of child	−0·373
23 Nature of further education desired	−0·368
57 Parents willing to assist in teaching process	−0·344
17 Cleanliness of child and evidence of care	−0·321
51 Parents' knowledge of homework content	−0·293
38 Provision for child to store own books	−0·280
27 Parents' library membership	−0·277
36 Nature of child's reading matter	−0·274
30 Amount of father's reading	−0·270
47 Parents' 11+ selection	−0·265
48 Parents regret aspects of own education	−0·265
29 Nature of mother's reading matter	−0·257
65 Nature of parental help with school work	−0·255
45 Family weekend activities	−0·252
31 Nature of father's reading matter	−0·248
72 Child has own room	−0·247
71 Attendance	−0·241
25 Earliness of career plans	−0·240
6 Housing standard	−0·239
64 Amount of discussion of school reports	−0·234
50 Amount of child's homework	−0·232
58 Parents' visit to secondary school before entry	−0·230
35 Nature of publications bought for child	−0·223
78 Order	0·217
77 Deference	0·213
28 Amount of mother's reading	−0·212
41 Selectivity of child's TV viewing	−0·205
54 Parents' formal education level	−0·200
34 Child likes reading at home	−0·188
9 Father from small family	−0·186
52 Parents' approval of homework	−0·182
60 Parents' assessment of child's effort	−0·175
62 Child talks about school	−0·175
5 Cleanliness of home	−0·175

Note: 10+ total score held constant

was a typical remark, and her mother had become so exasperated by her 'moans' about school, she had been forbidden to mention the subject again. Her parents' limited ambitions for extended education were, in the event, thwarted as she left at the age of fifteen.

A not dissimilar, though less belligerent, girl—again from a technical high school—told the interviewer that she had already decided in her own mind to leave at fifteen, although the school and her parents were still expecting her to complete a further year. She had done badly in school examinations and had consequently lost interest in school work. She was not prepared to work any harder to pull up, and was more interested in her part-time hairdressing job, which she regarded as a blessed escape from study. She said that, as she was a 'spoiled only child', she could easily get her way, and that her parents would not put up much of a fight when she finally announced her intentions. If they did, they clearly lost. Another girl, who had obtained a selective place in a secondary modern school, knew she should stay on as she wanted a 'job in chemistry', and was aware that her brother and sister who had left school at fifteen had not made anything of themselves. She felt, however, that she had to maintain a neutral attitude at home and fall in with her parents' wishes, as they were going through a difficult period financially. The remaining last minute decision to leave at fifteen was made by the mother of a girl at one of the 'old-established' comprehensive schools. This girl had also obtained a selective place at eleven-plus, was happy at school and set to stay for longer than her parents had foreseen. She had aspirations for a job that was 'better than typing but not as high as teaching'. Her mother, however, found her a 'good job in computers' and removed her from school. Thus, with few exceptions, the wishes of the parents prevailed, though there was a high degree of agreement between parents and children. Of the fifty-four parents who wanted statutory leaving, thirty-nine had children who agreed with them, eight had children who wanted to stay on in spite of their parents' wishes, and seven had children who had no preference, said they would leave it to their parents to decide.

Apart from parent and child leaving preferences, we also found that the statutory leavers were characterized by negative effects with *school performance important to child's future* (—0·455), *career qualifications desired* (—0·405), *child's occupational ambition* (—0·373), *nature of further education desired* (—0·368), and *earliness of career plans* (—0·240), all indicative of low career aspirations, and a lack of foresight and long term planning. It would also seem to be a characteristic of early leavers that they attend schools which do not interest themselves in the leaving decisions of their pupils to any great extent. *Interest taken by school in leaving decision* has a partial correlation of —0·420 with *left at age 15*. We cannot say from our findings that a greater interest would reduce the number of statutory leavers, but we can at least assume that it would be worth trying.

Next to these 'ambition' variables, family reading habits are most crucially involved in statutory leaving. Apart from *nature of books purchased for child* and *parents influenced choice of books*, all the literacy variables are significantly and negatively associated with *left at age 15*. The most important of these are concerned with library membership of parents and the age at which the child joined the library. The two cleanliness variables—of child and of home are also significantly and negatively associated with early leaving. The homework correlations—*amount of child's homework* (—0·232) and *parents' knowledge of homework content* (—0·292) are probably very much a function of the school attended, in this context, as parents cannot know the content of non-existent homework. However, we do know from the negative correlation of —0·182, that the parents of the statutory leavers significantly disapprove of homework.

There is little doubt that there is close correspondence between the length of parents' education and that of their children. *Parents' 11+ selection* (—0·265) and *parents' formal education level* (—0·200) are significantly associated with statutory leaving, indicating that parents who did not pass the eleven-plus examination, and consequently had a limited secondary school career, tend to have children who leave early. Neither parent of forty-three of our fifty-eight statutory leavers had 'passed'; thirteen had one parent who had been selected and, in two cases, both father and mother had been selected. These last two cases are particularly interesting in that the decision for the child to leave school at fifteen had been made on the advice of the head-teacher. One of these was a girl who had ambitious parents who would have liked her to stay on, but the headteacher had advised against it and recommended night school or day release. She wanted to leave as soon as possible and her mother told her she could do so providing she obtained good marks in the last school examination. 'I have got to stay on if I get a bad report' she said—a somewhat paradoxical situation. As she did in fact leave school at fifteen, one can only assume that she must have done rather well in her final year at school. The second girl clearly wanted to stay at school but was frustrated by lack of opportunity, as only the express stream had been offered the option of extended schooling. She said she had tried hard to get into this clearly privileged stream because her older sister had been in it, but if you had not been selected by the first year 'you stood no chance because of the French'.

A very interesting result from the parents' education variables—in that it is negative in effect—is the significant partial correlation for *parents regret aspects of own education* (—0·265). Although the parents of the statutory leavers had in the main not derived the maximum benefit themselves from the educational system, they are the only group significantly satisfied with the education they had themselves received. The physical aspects of the home measured by *housing standard* (—0·239) and *child has own room* (—0·247) have their only significant effects with early leaving. Parental interest in the child's work and activities is also conspicuously lacking in this group, as evidenced by the significant negative correlations for *parents want to assist in the teaching process* (—0·344), *parents visit to secondary school before entry* (—0·230), *nature of help with school work* (—0·255), *family weekend activities* (—0·252) *amount of discussion of school reports* (—0·234), *child talks about school* (—0·175), *selectivity of child's TV viewing* (—0·205), and *attendance* (—0·241). Rather surprisingly, in view of their apparent lack of interest and awareness, the parents of the statutory leavers are the only group significantly dissatisfied with their child's effort at school.

The only variables to be significant and positive in effect are *order* (0·217) and *deference* (0·213) and there is no doubt that high demands for meticulous neatness and deference to superiors is associated with leaving at the statutory age. The *father from small family* result (—0·186) suggests that the fathers of statutory leavers were significantly likely to have had many brothers and sisters.

To summarize, the home background of statutory leavers, discounting initial ability, is characterized by lack of ambition, low literacy level, dirtiness, poor housing conditions, overcrowding, limited parental ability and education, lack of parental interest in school work and an unwillingness to help with it, low involvement in the child's activities, a disapproval of homework, satisfaction with their own education together with a rather poor view of their child's own efforts. This complex has nothing to do with social class or poverty as the low correlations for *father's occupation* (0·001) and *material needs adequate* (—0·083) testify. It is more importantly associated with *smallness of family* (0·151) and significantly with *size of father's family* (0·186). The frequency with which *father from small family* produces significant results is interesting in that a man's early experience of family life seems to be a crucial predictor of the lifestyle of the marital home. It is possible that particular paternal attitudes underly many of the statutory leaving associations which might be expressed as—'What was good enough for me is good enough for mine.'

From the seventeen variables significantly partially correlated with *left at age 16*, no fewer than six are concerned with aspects of ambition—*earliness of leaving decision* (0·576), *child's preference for extended schooling* (0·403), *school performance important to child's future* (0·338), *interest taken by school in leaving decision* (0·340), *preferred age of leaving* (0·241) and *earliness of career plans* (0·177). The impression given by these conditions is that parents' long-held plans for an extended but limited school career have largely been fulfilled. None of the parents of the thirty-eight sixteen-year-old leavers would have preferred their child to leave at the statutory leaving age, although five of their children resented being made to stay on. One of these dissenters was a grammar school boy who was well aware of the advantages of staying at school until sixteen in accordance with his parents' wishes, but felt that he

Table 6.6 Significant partial correlations—leaving at age 16

Variable	Partial correlation
21 Earliness of leaving decision	0·576
20 Child's preference for extended schooling	0·403
26 Interest taken by school in leaving decision	0·340
59 School performance important to child's future	0·338
17 Cleanliness of child and evidence of care	0·301
32 Duration of child's library membership	0·294
57 Parents willing to assist in the teaching process	0·280
33 Parents influenced child to join library	0·270
19 Preferred leaving age	0·241
48 Parents regret aspects of own education	0·239
24 Career qualifications desired	0·231
58 Parents' visit to secondary school before entry	0·231
51 Parents' knowledge of homework content	0·213
11 Mother not working	−0·205
7 Smallness of family	0·186
41 Selectivity of child's TV viewing	0·178
25 Earliness of career plans	0·177

Note: 10+ total score held constant

would get nowhere if he 'stayed to be a hundred'. He thought he had done well in his unstreamed first year as all his marks had been over 60%. He nevertheless was placed at the bottom of the class because all the other boys were 'outstandingly clever' and, as a consequence, he was placed in the lowest second year stream, away from his friends and with a new set of 'dumb lads who messed about all day'. He was disappointed with himself, but nevertheless thought that anyone staying in the sixth form must be mad. As his parents' ambitions for him centred on sixteen-plus leaving, he had only to tolerate one extra year. Another boy, with a selective place at an RC secondary modern school, wanted, like some of his friends, to leave at fifteen to earn money as an electrician, and thus have their freedom to spend. He had not mentioned his doubts either at school or at home, and was going to keep quiet as long as possible. In the event his parents won, and he stayed on to obtain four CSE passes, three at Grade 4 and one at Grade 5. A boy with a selective place at one of the secondary modern schools not involved in reorganization reacted strongly against teachers who were 'always on your back'. 'I am in a class of non-volunteers, and even if they asked me to play soccer for the school I would refuse, even though I play it at home every night.' However, his parents' wishes clearly prevailed, and he ultimately achieved seven CSE passes in Grades 2 to 5. All three boys were selected at eleven-plus, as were four resentful girls who obviously deferred to their parents' wishes in the end. The girls were less specific in their adverse reactions to school, but regarded school subjects as boring and 'no use when you leave'. Between them they collected seventeen CSE passes from Grades 1 to 5.

The thirty-eight families of sixteen-plus leavers also contained thirteen parents who would have preferred their children to stay at school for a sixth-form course. They included one grammar school boy with clear ambitions to go into banking or the Civil Service. His three O-level passes at Grades 3, 5 and 6, however, may have been considered insufficient for a promising sixth-form career. Two technical high school boys with definite sixth-form ambitions achieved only four O-level passes between them, none higher than Grade 4, and this had no doubt been a limiting factor so far as the length of their school careers was concerned. One boy with a selected place in an RC secondary modern school had clearly considered most options. His father had had to forgo a grammar school education for himself, but wanted his son to avail himself of all opportunities. The boy said he had opted for the easiest examination course in order to be near the top of the class and, although he did not feel fully stretched, the resulting good school marks would impress his future employers who would not know any better. He thought his parents' high academic aspirations for him were slightly unrealistic, and in the event he was proved right as he obtained five CSE passes, none higher than Grade 2. The only boy who had clearly benefited from comprehensivization at the time of interview had transferred from a disbanded secondary modern school to a purpose-built high school. He had not obtained a selective place at eleven-plus, but the teachers in his new school were encouraging him to stay for a sixth-form course. However, he did not achieve any O-level passes, passing six CSE subjects in a range from Grade 1 to Grade 4. The remaining boy in this group of sixteen-year old leavers with high aspiring parents had shown so little promise in the primary school that he had not been entered for the eleven-plus selection tests. He wanted to be a draughtsman and his parents wanted him to have a 'proper trade', no matter how long it took him. He finally collected four CSE passes but, as none of these was higher than Grade 4, it was considered unrealistic to transfer him to a grammar school for sixth-form study. None of the boys in this group made any adverse comments about school, except for one who thought the uniform trousers were 'too dull', and a very fat boy who complained about the small portions given at school dinners.

There were seven girls whose parents had unfulfilled sixth-form ambitions for them. The one grammar school girl obtained four O-level passes but, as she wanted to work in a 'dogs' beauty parlour', it was no doubt decided that a sixth-form course was irrelevant. The one technical high school girl with university aspirations did not obtain any O-levels, but gained six CSE passes, only one at Grade 1. An aspiring primary school teacher from a comprehensive school obtained similar CSE grades, but no O-levels. Two selected secondary modern girls wanted to stay in the sixth-form but did not obtain any O-levels, and two girls, who had not been selected at eleven-plus, acquired three O-levels between them—none with a higher grade than 3. One of these girls was clearly very disturbed, and thought her father compared her unfavourably with her clever brother, who attended a direct grant grammar school. It seems apparent that, in most of the cases where the parents' sixth-form ambitions for their child were not satisfied, it was the child's performance in sixteen-plus external examinations that had caused a change of plan.

Only two of the literacy variables are significant in their partial correlation with *left at age 16—duration of child's library membership* (0·294) and *parents influenced child to join library* (0·270). These also have overtones of parental dominance. Parental interest in education is represented by *parents willing to assist in teaching process* (0·280), *parents' visit to secondary school before entry* (0·231), *cleanliness of child* (0·301), *parents regret aspects of own education* (0·239), *parents' knowledge of homework content* (0·213), *mother working* (0·205), *smallness of family* (0·186) and *selectivity of child's TV viewing* (0·178). These are all positive and significant in relation to staying at school for an extra year. These variables are very different in correlational size and direction of effect from those reported for leaving at age fifteen. The general impression is of parents with high aspirations for their children, taking an active and possibly dominating interest in their schooling. They have smaller families, the children are clean and well cared for, and the mother goes out to work—no doubt to augment the family income. *Father's occupation* is negative in effect (—0·122), which leads us to the conclusion that, in isolating the group with the limited ambition of one year's extra schooling, we have also isolated working class families with higher social aspirations. As the parents of this group were significantly dissatisfied with aspects of their own education, an underlying attitude might be expressed as 'What had to be good enough for me is not good enough for mine'. It is interesting that the two partial correlations for *smallness of father's family* and *smallness of mother's family*, unlike those for the statutory leaving group, operate in a positive direction at 0·126 and 0·120.

Table 6.7 clarifies the differential effect of the family size variables when

Table 6.7 Partial correlations—school leaving, family size and father's occupation

Variable	Left at age 15	Left at age 16
Father from small family	—0·186*	0·126
Mother from small family	—0·161	0·120
Smallness of marital family	—0·151	0·186*
Father's occupation	0·001	—0·122

* Significant at 5% level or over

the acquiescent parents of the statutory leavers are compared with the more socially aspiring parents of the sixteen-year-old leavers.

Family size appears to have an ongoing effect in succeeding generations. For the statutory leavers, the father's early family experience dominates and, for the group with higher ambitions, the experiences of both father and mother are approximately equal in effect.

It has been noted previously that twenty-five of the environment variables have significant partial correlations with entry to the sixth-form. These are given in Table 6.8.

Table 6.8 Significant partial correlations—entry to sixth-form

Variable	Partial correlation
19 Preferred leaving age	0·489
12 Type of secondary school	0·365
16 Occupational ambition of child	0·307
3 Rateable value	0·288
23 Nature of further education desired	0·285
30 Amount of father's reading	0·285
52 Parents' approval of homework	0·277
67 Child likes parents and teachers to meet	0·264
31 Nature of father's reading matter	0·259
65 Nature of parental help with school work	0·243
11 Mother not working	0·238
27 Parents' library membership	0·237
49 Parents' further education involvement	0·223
36 Nature of child's reading matter	0·214
29 Nature of mother's reading matter	0·211
38 Provision for child to store own books	0·197
45 Family weekend activities	0·195
22 Influence of education on long term plans	0·195
34 Child likes reading at home	0·189
24 Career qualifications desired	0·187
2 Father's occupation	0·187
44 Involvement of child in parents' activities	0·185
63 Amount of discussion on school progress	0·180
47 Parents' 11+ selection	0·179
28 Amount of mother's reading	0·175

Note: 10+ total score held constant

Only five of these variables are concerned with ambition—*preferred age of leaving* (0·489), *occupational ambition of child* (0·307), *nature of further education desired* (0·285), *influence of education on long term plans* (0·195) and *career qualifications desired* (0·187), whereas no fewer than eight are concerned with reading habits in the home. These are—*amount of father's reading*

(0·285), *nature of father's reading matter* (0·259), *parents' library membership* (0·237), *nature of child's reading matter* (0·214), *nature of mother's reading matter* (0·211), *provision for child to store own books* (0·197), *child likes reading at home* (0·189) and *amount of mother's reading* (0·175). It is clear that, whereas leaving school at sixteen is largely the result of parental ambition, staying for a sixth-form course has more to do with family literacy, and the 'father' variables have the greatest positive effect. The educational experience of the parents has an obvious ongoing effect, the correlations for both *parents' further education involvement* (0·223) and *parents' 11+ selection* (0·179) being significant and positive. The parents of sixth-formers also significantly approve of *homework* (0·277), and give detailed and specific *help with school work* (0·243). They make educational expeditions at weekends (0·195) and their children are involved with them in family activities (0·185). There is a significant amount of family discussion on the subject of school progress (0·180) and the child is happy about his parents talking to his teachers (0·264). Even at first sight these variables appear to be describing middle class activities and attributes and, when we consider that the only significant associations for *father's occupation* (0·187), *rateable value* (0·288) and *mother not working* (0·238) are with sixth-form entry, we cannot but conclude that the ability to extract the maximum advantage from the secondary school system is very much bound up with social status and its concomitants. When we reflect that the partial correlation for *entered sixth form* with average secondary school attainment was 0·249, it seems clear that sixth-form entry has as much connection with certain social class variables as it has with attainment.

Our hypothesis that social class is involved in very specific ways with school leaving age is substantiated when we examine the percentages of broad social class groups leaving at each age. Table 6.9 gives these figures.

On the evidence of partial correlations we postulated that statutory leaving was related only marginally to social class. The above figures show that this

Table 6.9 School leaving age—social class percentages

Occupational group	Left at age 15	Left at age 16	Entered sixth form
Professional and managerial	12	38	50
Skilled manual and non-manual clerical	51	31	18
Semi-skilled manual and non-manual operative	59	33	8
Unskilled manual and unemployed	57	43	0
Percentage of sample	51	33	16

is indeed the case as far as the skilled, semi-skilled and unskilled grades are concerned, as there is little difference between these groups. The class bias in this distribution clearly differentiates the professional and managerial grades from the rest. Our contention that sixteen-plus leaving is related to the aspiring working class is wholly borne out by Table 6.9. The highest percentage of sixteen-plus leavers comes from the unskilled grade and, as none of their children entered the sixth form, it does appear that one year's extra schooling represents the peak of ambition for a particular group of ambitious lower working class parents. The social class bias for entry to sixth form is obvious. There is no need, on the basis of the original data, to modify our interpretation of the correlations. Leaving at the statutory age or staying at school for one extra year is associated with differences within social class groups in terms of environment, whereas differences between social classes are related to sixth-form entry.

The answer to our question—'Are there any features in the home background which appear to be associated with the age at which a child leaves school?' is a definite 'Yes'. Sixth-form entry is as much connected with social class as it is with attainment; sixteen-year-old leaving is largely a working class phenomenon connected with conscientiousness and aspirations towards upward mobility, and statutory leaving has some less significant connections with social class level but is conspicuously characterized by lack of ambition, low literacy level and attitudes of acquiescence.

(e) **Environment and sixteen-plus external examination results**

Selection for sixth-form entry usually takes into account the results of external examinations taken at sixteen-plus, and we must therefore look at the environmental correlates of success in O-level and CSE to see if this conclusion is justified, and also to see if internal and external assessment of attainment have the same environmental concomitants. Table 6.10 gives the forty-seven significant partial correlations obtained for external examination results, with the effect of initial ability at eleven-plus nullified.

There are very many more significant partial correlations here than were obtained in any of our analyses of internally assessed attainment over the first three years of secondary schooling. The very high correlation of −0·739 with *left at age 15* is to be expected, as all the statutory leavers left school before taking external examinations. We find that all the ambition and parental interest variables which were significantly associated with sixth-form entry appear in Table 6.10. It will be noted, however, that *father's occupation* (0·076), *rateable value* (0·147), *mother not working* (0·069), *child likes parents and teachers to meet* (0·164), *parents approval of homework* (0·144) and *child's involvement in parents' activities* (0·051) do not appear as they are not significantly associated with sixteen-plus results. These 'middle class' variables,

Table 6.10 Significant partial correlations—16+ external examinations

Variable	Partial correlation with 10+ *total score* held constant
14 Left school at age 15	−0·739
19 Preferred age of leaving	0·658
21 Earliness of leaving decision	0·602
13 Entered sixth form	0·478
20 Child's preference for extended schooling	0·415
16 Occupational ambition of child	0·409
24 Career qualifications desired	0·408
31 Nature of father's reading matter	0·396
26 Interest taken by school in leaving decision	0·390
33 Parents influenced child to join library	0·373
23 Type of further education desired	0·345
12 Type of secondary school	0·335
15 Left school at age 16	0·334
59 School work important to child's future	0·328
32 Duration of child's library membership	0·325
30 Amount of father's reading	0·323
47 Parents' 11+ selection	0·314
36 Nature of child's reading matter	0·313
29 Nature of mother's reading matter	0·300
45 Nature of family weekend activities	0·291
49 Parents' further education involvement	0·282
54 Level of parents' formal education	0·280
35 Nature of publications bought for child	0·270
27 Parents' library membership	0·268
57 Parents willing to assist in teaching process	0·266
46 Family involvement during long school holidays	0·259
51 Parents' knowledge of homework content	0·243
77 Deference	−0·243
38 Provision for child to store own books	0·241
64 Amount of discussion on school reports	0·234
63 Amount of discussion on school progress	0·226
71 Attendance	0·226
28 Amount of mother's reading	0·223
48 Parents regret aspects of own education	0·221
50 Amount of child's homework	0·219
78 Order	−0·219
17 Cleanliness of child	0·214
34 Child likes reading at home	0·202
65 Nature of parental help with school work	0·202
9 Father from small family	0·200
22 Influence of education on long term plans	0·200
60 Parents' assessment of child's effort at school	0·197
6 Housing standard	0·185
25 Earliness of career plans	0·178
75 Educational value of peer group influence	0·178
37 Nature of books bought for child	0·177
10 Mother from small family	0·175

which have a lot to do with sixth-form entry, have little or nothing to do with external examination results, *father's occupation* and *mother not working* being little removed from zero. It appears to be fairly conclusive that, as far as our Plowden pupils were concerned, entry to sixth form was not wholly dependent on ability, but that high scores on certain social class variables were a contributing factor. The upper reaches of secondary education do not represent perfect meritocratic selection.

Most of the remaining variables which give significant partial correlations for sixteen-plus external examinations are those which also correlated significantly with leaving school at the age of sixteen, and, on the whole, Table 6.10 contains those variables concerned with staying on at school after the statutory leaving age for any length of time. However, there are a few variables which, though not significantly related to school leaving at any age, are nevertheless concerned with high achievement in external examinations, even when initial ability is discounted. These are—*parents' level of formal education* (0·280), *nature of publications bought for child* (0·270), *educational value of peer group influence* (0·178), *nature of books bought for child* (0·177) and *mother from small family* (0·175). This last result is interesting. It looks as though both mother's and father's early family experience have a significant effect with secondary school achievement as measured by sixteen-plus external examinations, but only that of the father is measurably relevant to decisions about leaving school.

The answer to our question—'Are there any features in the home background particularly associated with success in external examinations taken at sixteen-plus?' is 'Yes'. While in the main they are the same features as those related to school leaving, there is evidence that the standard of reading matter in the home, the parents' own experience of extended education, the mother's childhood experience, and the pupil's circle of friendships are additionally concerned in external examination success.

(f) **Environment and 'improvement' or 'deterioration'**

One of the specific initial briefs for this inquiry was to identify individuals who had improved or deteriorated in terms of school attainment during secondary school years, and to investigate features in the environment which appeared to bear some relationship to such changes in performance. The best predictor of probable performance in the secondary school was given by *10+ total score*—the criterion of secondary school selection. By comparing individual scores on this measure with total attainment score at the end of the third secondary year, it was possible to separate groups of children who had improved, remained constant or deteriorated in their expected level of performance, and then compare the scores on environment variables obtained by the three groups. In order to do this, both ranges of scores were divided into twelve class intervals, each representing five points of normalized score. An individual was deemed to have improved or deteriorated if he had moved towards the mean by one or more class intervals. But, before attempting any comparisons between such groups in environmental terms, it was necessary to minimize any possible effects of regression to the mean implied in the regression coefficient of 0·816 for the two sets of scores. This was done in two ways. First, those pupils in the top and bottom class intervals on the ten-plus tests were deemed to be 'constant' if they had improved or deteriorated by no more than one class interval. In practice, it was found that none of the pupils in either of the two top class intervals had deteriorated at all in these terms. In the bottom class interval, however, four pupils had improved by only one class interval, and these were classified as 'constant', as their apparent improvement might well have been due to the statistical artefact of imperfect correlation. This adjustment left us with 32 improvers, 39 deteriorators and 43 pupils who had shifted only minimally after transfer. Then a further control of regression was attempted by performing separate analyses for two different levels of transfer score—(i) a high-score group achieving a total ten-plus score at least equal to the lowest transfer score obtained by any child granted a selective place (presumably an eleven-plus pass mark), and (ii) a low-score group containing children whose total transfer score was below this mark. Chi-squared analyses were then calculated to test the possibility of there being differences in the numbers of improvers and deteriorators in either of the two eleven-plus selection groups, in terms of high or low scores on the environment variables.

A preliminary chi-squared analysis contrasting the selected group from the non-selected group in terms of improvement or deterioration between transfer and fourteen-plus attainment showed no significant differences. The frequencies involved are given in Table 6.11.

The chi-squared analyses produced few significant associations between improvement or deterioration and environment variables, and no single environment variable was significantly related to change in performance in

Table 6.11 Significance of selection level differences in improving, constant and deteriorating groups

	Improved	Constant	Deteriorated	TOTAL
High at transfer	5	13	14	32
Low at transfer	27	30	25	82
TOTALS	32	43	39	114

Chi-squared = 3·74 with 2 degrees of freedom
A value of 5·99 is required to reach significance at the 0·05 level

both the 'high at transfer' and 'low at transfer' groups. It would appear that rising or falling attainment is not associated with the same environment measures for children of high and low initial ability. Table 6.12 shows the values of chi-squared for those variables significantly associated with improvement or deterioration in the high level group.

Table 6.12 Variables giving significant level of chi-squared—high at transfer group

Variable	Degrees of freedom	Chi-squared	Significance
Type of secondary school	6	24·722	0·001
Number of school clubs and societies joined	2	11·883	0·01
Entered sixth form	2	10·264	0·01
Preferred age of leaving	2	10·253	0·01
Family involvement during long school holidays	2	7·650	0·05
Nature of publications purchased for child	2	7·489	0·05
Child has own room	2	7·392	0·05

When discussing the above results it is evident that the small numbers of pupils involved precludes us from generalizing from our sample to a wider population. For our high level transfer group, however, it appears—from the distribution of frequencies associated with Table 6.12—that improvement is related to position in the hierarchy of school types, to joining more than one school club or society, to entering the sixth form, to parental preference for education beyond the statutory leaving age, to long holidays being taken as a family group, to the purchase of publications other than comics, and to housing space and/or privacy implied by the *child has own room* measure. The first three of these conditions may well be 'school' variables related to orientation towards academic achievement in grammar schools, but parental ambition is also involved. The last four could equally well be expressions of parental interest, middle-class mores, or reflections of adequate material needs.

The variables giving significant levels of chi-squared for the 'low at transfer' group are given in Table 6.13.

Inspection of the frequency distributions over the improving, constant and deteriorating groups suggests that, for this group of pupils, parental attitudes and interest are the salient concomitants of improvement. Progress at school is related to family discussion of the child's performance at school, which is regarded as important to the child's future. There is little interest in listening

Table 6.13 Variables giving significant level of chi-squared—low at transfer group

Variable	Degrees of freedom	Chi-squared	Significance
Amount of parental discussion of school reports	2	11·283	0·001
Nature of radio listening	2	7·668	0·05
Amount of family discussion of school progress	2	7·430	0·05
Father from small family	2	6·813	0·05
Family health	2	6·742	0·05
School performance important to child's future	2	6·374	0·05

to pop-music on the radio in the homes of the improvers and serious illness in the family has not been experienced. Once again we have the curious appearance of *father from small family* as an educational asset.

The most striking difference between the separate analyses for the two initial ability groups is that the 'high level' group appears to be advantageously affected by factors related to school, parental ambition and aspects of the home background not unrelated to material advantage, whereas the 'low level' group improves where there is high parental interest in school work and a serious attitude to the process of education. The results are admittedly rather meagre and, in view of the small numbers of pupils involved, must remain tentative. The high frequencies for constancy in attainment between transfer and the end of the third secondary year were only to be expected from the correlational analysis, which showed high relationship between all eleven-plus selection test scores and all secondary attainment scores. It is also realized that our method of analysis is based on a rather narrow view of the nature of school progress, as third year marks cannot realistically be regarded as the culminating criteria of a school career. Over- and under-fulfilment of promise may also be discussed in the context of school leaving and results obtained in external examinations taken at sixteen-plus. Table 6.14 gives a breakdown of the number of children leaving school at different ages in relation to the type of school attended during the first three years after transfer.

As we have previously reported, 57% of these 114 pupils spent their later secondary years in newly organized comprehensive high schools with sixth-form facilities but, in spite of these new opportunities, the pattern of leaving expected in a tripartite system had not yet substantially changed. The majority of grammar school pupils entered the sixth form, the majority of technical high school pupils left school at sixteen, and the majority of pupils

Table 6.14 Age at leaving school and type of school attended

	Grammar		Technical high		Non-selective		TOTAL	
	n	%	*n*	%	*n*	%	*n*	%
Left school at age 15	0	0	2	13	56	67	58	51
Left school at age 16	4	27	8	50	26	31	38	33
Entered sixth form	11	73	6	37	1	2	18	16
TOTALS	15	100	16	100	83	100	114	100

originally in the non-selective schools left at the statutory leaving age. The four grammar school selectees who left school at sixteen have not taken full advantage of educational facilities considering their measured potential, the two technical high school pupils who left at fifteen clearly 'dropped out', and the twenty-seven non-selective pupils staying at school beyond the statutory leaving age have taken above the minimum advantage of educational opportunities.

The two statutory leavers from the technical high schools are the two rather rebellious girls previously described. They did not attend the same school. The four sixteen-plus leavers attending schools which were originally maintained grammar schools and later became comprehensive high schools included two boys and two girls. The very dissatisfied boy described on pages 105–6 was one of this group. The other boy had had a chequered secondary school career, transferring to a different comprehensive high school in his fifth year because of differences of opinion between his father and the original headmaster on haircuts and school uniform. He preferred his new school to the old one and thought he was doing better work, hoping eventually to obtain good enough O-levels to justify his entry to a sixth-form course. In the event, however, he was entered for only two O-level subjects, obtaining a Grade 8 in one and being unclassified in the other. The girl whose ambition was to work in a dogs' beauty parlour was also one of this group, and the remaining girl—although obtaining five O-level passes above Grade 6 and expressing a preference for a sixth-form course—clearly had a difficult home situation, and received little educational support from her widowed mother. Her mother had never envisaged schooling for her daughter after the age of sixteen, and thought that, as the girl had so many boyfriends, marriage was the obvious objective. The girl herself said that her school work and future career were never discussed at home, not because they talked about other things but 'because we never talk at all'.

Table 6.15 gives the numbers of pupils attending the non-selective schools during their first three secondary years, subdivided into three groups—(i) those who obtained a selective place at eleven-plus, (ii) those who did not, and (iii) those who were considered at primary school as incapable of sitting for any of the eleven-plus selection tests. The four selected pupils who left at the statutory leaving age may also be considered to have fallen below expectations. They are all girls, two of whom have already been described. A further girl, originally in a 'comprehensive' school, said she had never got over being demoted from the 'A' stream to the 'B' stream in her second year. She had then decided she would never do very well and would just do as her friends did. She encountered no opposition from her parents, who left her to determine her own future. She felt that little interest was taken in her at home, as her mother had just given birth to a tenth child. The last member of this group was also a girl—very attractive and talkative—who had originally intended to become a nurse, but who had latterly felt that she could not tolerate anything involving further study. She really wanted to break into the world of 'pop', and had a formed singer-guitar group with her girl friend. The dark secret that she had written to the *Musical Express* to try to get engagements had to be kept from her parents. She hated school for being too restrictive, loathed having to wear uniform, and being treated like a child. 'Even the easy teachers here put a block on discussion if they think it will go too far.'

Table 6.15 Non-selective schools—school leaving and 11+ selection

	Selected at 11+		Not selected at 11+		Not entered for 11+		TOTAL	
	n	%	*n*	%	*n*	%	*n*	%
Left school at age 15	4	29	48	76	4	67	56	69
Left school at age 16	10	71	14	22	2	33	26	30
Entered sixth form	0	0	1	2	0	0	1	1
TOTALS	14	100	63	100	6	100	83	100

Of the twenty-six pupils from non-selective schools who stayed at school for an extra year, fourteen had not been allocated a selected place at eleven-plus, and two pupils had not even been entered for the selection tests. These children are success stories in so far as they received schooling comparable in length to that undertaken by twenty-four of their selected contemporaries in all types of school. In this group there were two boys and twelve girls. The questionnaire responses of the twelve girls were remarkably similar. They were all favourably disposed towards school and realized that qualifications were necessary for the jobs to which they were aspiring—two nurses, one nursery nurse and nine shorthand-typists. Their parents were all pleased they were staying on at school, and the interviewer noted that they were all quiet and conformist. Two of the decisions to stay at school were of recent origin, one due to the new opportunities afforded by the comprehensive system and one because she had been encouraged by promotion to a higher stream. A typical remark was, 'Schools are O.K. for people who behave themselves.' One of the boys in this group had been encouraged by the teachers in his new comprehensive school to try for CSE subjects, although he would not have thought himself capable, and his parents were pleased with the new opportunities offered. The other boy had found his niche in art and had received so much encouragement from his teachers that his enthusiasm had spilled over into interest in other subjects. He wanted to obtain sufficient qualifications to be accepted at evening classes at a college of art and design and train to become a commercial artist. The one non-selected girl who stayed for a sixth-form course wanted to be a primary school teacher. She was partially deaf and was full of gratitude and praise for the help she had received from school. Her parents were delighted with her progress and the girl was very happy that she had been able to please them.

If we look at Table 6.16 we may compare the size of external examination entry in each type of secondary school, the average number of papers taken per entrant, and the average grade acquired by those entrants achieving marks which could be classified.

47% (54 pupils) out of the total subsample of 114 pupils entered for one or more papers in one or more of the sixteen-plus external examinations.

Table 6.16 Size of entry for external examinations, average number of papers taken and average grade achieved per entrant

	Grammar		Technical high		Non-selective		TOTAL	
	n	%	*n*	%	*n*	%	*n*	%
O-level GCE								
Size of entry	15	100	14	100	10	12	39	34
Average number of papers taken	7	—	4	—	2	—	5	—
Average grade achieved	5	—	6	—	2	—	5	—
CSE Examination								
Size of entry	5	33	10	63	22	27	37	33
Average number of papers taken	3	—	5	—	6	-	5	—
Average grade achieved	3	—	3	—	3	—	3	—
O-level and/or CSE	15	100	14	100	25	30	54	47

As would be expected, the most popular examination in the selective schools is GCE O-level and, in the non-selective schools, it is the CSE. The average number of papers taken per entrant declines from seven in the grammar schools to two in the non-selective schools, but there is little to choose between the average grades obtained when school types are compared. If we compare the combined scores on both sixteen-plus examinations of the various sub-groups, we see there is a degree of overlap which can account for the small differences in mean scores between school types. It will be remembered that, for purposes of comparison, we constructed a points scale to cover a combination of O-level and CSE results, with a Grade 4 O-level pass regarded as equivalent to a Grade 1 CSE pass. For the subsample of 114 pupils, this produced a range of points from 4 to 58. The top six scores, ranging from 40 to 58, were all obtained by pupils transferred to grammar schools at eleven-plus, and the bottom five scores, ranging from 4 to 9, were obtained by children transferring to non-selective schools. It is in the range of scores between 11 and 38, obtained by 40 pupils (74% of the examination entrants), that overlap between the various eleven-plus selection groups occurs. In this range there are nine grammar school pupils, fourteen technical high school pupils, six pupils who obtained selected places in the non-selective schools, and eleven pupils who attended non-selective schools in non-selected places. If we crudely dichotomize the overlapping group—necessary because of the small numbers involved at each point of score—the distribution given in Table 6.17 results.

Table 6.17 Range of external examination scores and 11+ selection group

11+ Selection Group	Range 40–58 *n*	Range 25–39 *n*	Range 11–24 *n*	Range 4–10 *n*	No. of exam. entrants
Grammar	6	5	4	0	15
Technical high	0	7	7	0	14
Selected place at non-selective school	0	1	5	2	8
Not selected at 11+	0	3	8	4	15
Not entered for 11+ tests	0	0	0	2	2
TOTALS	6	16	24	8	54

The extent of overlap can be clearly seen. Seven technical high school pupils achieved better scores than four of the grammar school pupils. In all, four pupils in the non-selective schools had higher scores than four grammar school pupils, and three of these did not obtain a selective place at eleven-plus. These three pupils did better at sixteen-plus than sixteen pupils who, at eleven, were assessed as being potentially capable of a secondary examination course. In overall educational terms they are clear improvers. The partially-deaf girl and the aspiring commercial artist—both from the same school—are in this group, together with the boy who was described as being encouraged by his teachers in his new comprehensive school. The feature they have in common is that they all mentioned the help and encouragement they, as individuals, had received from their teachers, and their parents' delight with their progress.

Although very small numbers are involved in the lowest range of scores, where no selective pupils appear, there is nevertheless food for thought in that two pupils who were not entered for the eleven-plus tests did as well as two pupils who had received selected places. One of these was a partially-sighted girl with some artistic talent, and the other was a boy displaying a certain precocity of manner, a pronounced interest in clothes, and a dread of having to work in a factory where people are not 'nice'. General statements cannot be substantiated when the sources of evidence are subsamples that can be counted on the fingers of one hand, but we are struck by the fact that, when we look at our four clearest improvers in overall terms, we find they have certain attributes in common. Two had obvious physical handicaps, and two had obvious artistic ability. All four were enthusiastic about school because of the help and encouragement they had received from teachers, and the word 'grateful' appeared in comments recorded on their interview schedules. Did these receive extra attention because they stood apart from the crowd as 'something special', or because their appreciation was gratifyingly obvious? There is certainly nothing in this admittedly meagre evidence to refute the view that care, concern and practical help on a very personal and individual level are salient to progress and high attainment.

The answer to our question 'Can we identify "improvers" and "deteriorators" and isolate the environmental determinants of these conditions?' is 'Yes'. Selective school pupils who improve over time appear to be affected by certain aspects of school, by parental ambition, and aspects of home not unrelated to material circumstances, whereas the improvers in the non-selective band are most affected by parental interest and a serious attitude in the home towards the process of education. Though few in number, our clearest improvers in overall terms appear to have distinguishing features—either handicaps, talents, or both, which attract attention and encouragement to the benefit of their scholastic attainment.

7 Results—the individual factor analysis

The principal components analysis, followed by a Varimax rotation of twenty-seven factors, which was computed from the data gathered for 114 individuals, adds very little to our findings from the study of correlations. It does, however, help us to get a clearer picture of the pattern of relationships between our variables and, in effect, summarizes our conclusions in the most economical way. When the variance contributed by the primary and secondary educational tests to the twenty-seven factors was calculated, it was found that 82% of this variance lay in the first factor. Most of the remaining educational test variance was distributed over a further seven factors with fairly heavy loadings on single areas of attainment. The remaining nineteen factors are specifically 'environmental', having very low loadings on all the educational tests. Table 7.1 gives the major loadings on Factor I. Its content bears a close resemblance to the previously reported correlation data, and the heaviest loadings are for the two quasi-criterion variables—*type of secondary school* and *primary headteacher's rating*.

High attainment at any age from seven to sixteen is associated with sixth-form entry and low attainment with leaving at the statutory age. Leaving school at the age of sixteen has a loading of only 0·09 in this factor, and we can assume a different composite of variables, not highly associated with overall attainment, has affected decisions to stay at school for one extra year. The parents of high achieving children are clearly ambitious. They want their children to have extended school careers and have high aspirations for both further education and career qualifications. They formed these ambitions early in the child's life, and are prepared to consider education as a factor when making long term family plans. The children themselves also prefer extended schooling, and aspire to occupations high in the Registrar General's classification. Parents' ambitions, in general, carry more weight than those of the child. The schools of high achieving children take a greater interest in the leaving decisions of their pupils and give regular amounts of homework. The interest and educational awareness of the parents of high achievers is characterized by their opinion that school performance is important to the child's future, they know the content of homework and are aware of the child's position in class in individual subjects. They frequently discuss the child's reports and general progress between themselves. They are likely to have visited the secondary school of their choice before the child entered, and both father and mother will have been involved in the choice of school. Family literacy is obviously associated with high attainment. Both parents and children are members of a library, and the child joined as a result of parental influence at an early age. The child likes reading at home and reads a variety of 'superior' books. Good books and publications are bought for the child and he has somewhere of his own to store them. The crucial feature of parental reading habits is the amount of time the mother gives to reading. That high achieving parents have high achieving children is borne out by the appearance of the three parent-education variables in this attainment factor. They are are however, on the whole, less important than ambition, literacy and awareness. The families of high achievers take long holidays together, are discriminating in their radio listening, and are satisfied with the educational effect of their children's friends.

The high achieving child is of clean and neat appearance, his attendance at school is good and at home he is likely to have a room to himself. He joins school clubs and societies, has serious and long-enduring hobbies, and does not help with household chores. He is not withdrawn in interviews and is happy about encounters between his parents and teachers. He does not feel his school to be obsessed with neatness and orderliness, nor does he feel required to be highly deferential to those in authority. At the same time he does not feel that school is a place where warm personal relationships are established.

The variables mentioned above are the concomitants of good overall scholastic attainment. They are the strongest environmental predictors of school performance and all have a common element. It is equally important in this context to see which variables are not highly involved in this educational factor. Sex, father's occupation, rateable value of house, material needs, cleanliness of home, housing standard, family size, family health, size of parents' childhood families, non-working mothers, leaving school at sixteen, nature of mother's and father's reading matter, amount of father's reading, parents' influence on book choice, television viewing habits, involvement of the child in parents' activities, weekend activities, parents' dissatisfaction with their own education, approval of homework, checking of homework, choosing a secondary school on educational grounds, being willing to assist in the teaching process, whether the child or parents talk about school, specific help with school work, being involved in school activities, truancy and attendance problems are unimportantly involved overall with attainment. The low loadings on these variables support the findings of the correlational analyses in that physical, material and social class factors, and those connected with direct participation in school work, are unimportant compared with ambition, literacy, interest and awareness.

Table 7.1 Factor I—test score analysis

A—Major loadings

Variable	Loading
12 Type of secondary school	817
79 Primary headteacher's rating	667
13 Entered sixth form	620
19 Preferred age of leaving	601
26 Interest taken by school in leaving decision	594
50 Amount of child's homework	594
21 Earliness of leaving decision	582
14 Left school at age 15	−537
59 School performance important to child's future	527
32 Duration of child's library membership	506
16 Occupational ambition of child	471
23 Type of further education desired	468
36 Nature of child's reading matter	466
24 Career qualifications desired	433
51 Parents' knowledge of homework content	425
33 Parents influenced child to join library	408
20 Child's preference for extended schooling	387
46 Family involvement during long school holidays	382
34 Child likes reading at home	372
22 Influence of education on long-term plans	370
47 Parents' 11+ selection	352
17 Cleanliness of child and evidence of care	345
58 Parents' visit to secondary school before entry	341
35 Nature of publications bought for child	310
61 Parents' knowledge of class position in individual subjects	307
27 Parents' library membership	300
78 Order	−300
67 Child likes parents and teachers to meet	295
43 Number of school clubs and societies joined	282
38 Provision for child to store own books	259
28 Amount of mother's reading	256
42 Nature of child's hobbies and interests	255
76 Affiliation	−255
18 Child's outgoingness at interview	254
64 Amounts of parental discussion of school reports	231
54 Parents' formal education level	229
37 Nature of books bought for child	229
77 Deference	−228
73 Child helps at home	−218
49 Parents' further education involvement	215
63 Amount of family discussion on school progress	212
56 Father involved in choice of school	208
40 Nature of radio listening	201
75 Educational value of peer group influence	201
71 Attendance	189
72 Child has own room	176

Note: As is customary, decimal points have been omitted from the loadings above

Table 7.1 Factor 1—test score analysis

B—Percentage variance on educational measures	Primary	Secondary	Overall
Intelligence	86	81	84
English	77	86	81
Mathematics	79	87	82
Sciences	—	85	—
Social sciences	—	82	—
Non-academic subjects	—	74	—
16+ external examinations	—	60	—
Total educational	81	83	82

As the percentage variance on sixteen-plus examination results in Factor I (60%) is much lower than that for other attainment measures, it was only to be expected that other factors would be concerned with O-level and CSE results. There are three factors which had loadings on this particular attainment measure of over 0·185—Factor XXIII (loading 0·311), Factor III (loading 0·303) and Factor XIII (loading 0·185). As these three factors derive their major variance from environmental variables, we can conclude that external examinations are involved with three independent aspects of environment in addition to the more important complex of variables associated with high attainment at any age. Table 7.2 gives the major loadings on these three factors which have 'significant' loadings on sixteen-plus achievement.

These three factors remind us of the separate analyses of correlations for the three leaving ages. Factor XXIII, which accounts for 11% of the external examination variance, is predominantly concerned with the literacy of the father, and in general the factor substantiates our suggestion that paternal attributes come into their own at sixteen-plus. The 'father' reading variables have their highest loadings here. Most of the variables also appear in Factor I, but additionally we have *parents regret aspects of own education*, *parents' approval of homework*, *nature of family weekend activities*, *secondary school chosen on educational grounds* and *involvement of child in parents' activities*. The nature of these, and that of the other major loadings, reminds us of the complex of correlations associated with sixth-form entry, for which the loading is 0·408. *Type of secondary school* is also involved, and *interest taken by school in leaving decision*. The aspiration attitudes characterized by a preference for maximum length of schooling, early formation of this preference and all the parent-education variables are shown to be concerned with sixteen-plus results and sixth-form entry. Literacy is manifested in *parents influenced child to join library* and *library membership of parents* in addition to the two 'father' reading variables, but neither of the 'mother' reading variables is

Table 7.2 Factors with high loadings on 16+ external examinations

Variable	XXIII	III	XIII
30 Amount of father's reading	712		
31 Nature of father's reading matter	708		193
44 Involvement of child in parents' activities	421		
13 Entered sixth form	408	−259	194
52 Parents' approval of homework	399		312
27 Parents' library membership	399		
45 Nature of family weekend activities	372		290
47 Parents' 11+ selection	358		
54 Parents' formal education level	337		224
19 Preferred age of leaving	280	317	388
33 Parents influenced child to join library	238	255	
46 Family involvement during long school holidays	231		305
49 Parents' further education involvement	220		352
14 Left school at age 15	−215	−653	−210
12 Type of secondary school	214		
55 Secondary school chosen on educational grounds	192		235
26 Interest taken by school in leaving decision	189	391	
21 Earliness of leaving decision	188	495	230
67 Child likes parents and teachers to meet	186		
48 Parents regret aspects of own education	182	177	
68 Involvement of child in school activities	−176	−241	
56 Father involved in choice of school	176		
20 Child's preference for extended schooling		386	186
59 School performance important to child's future		310	312
57 Parents want to assist in the teaching process		207	277
24 Career qualifications desired		190	676
15 Left school at age 16		893	
17 Cleanliness of child and evidence of care		337	
58 Parents' visit to secondary school before entry		303	
32 Duration of child's library membership		302	
41 Selectivity of child's TV viewing		195	
35 Nature of publications bought for child		182	
2 Father's occupation		−173	
23 Type of further education desired			709
37 Nature of books bought for child			409
16 Occupational ambition of child			345
22 Influence of education on long-term plans			323
61 Parents' knowledge of class subject positions			281
38 Provision for child to store own books			277
6 Housing standard			258
29 Nature of mother's reading matter			244
36 Nature of child's reading matter			239
25 Earliness of career plans			785
53 Parents check homework			197
69 No history of truancy			196
65 Nature of parental help with school work			194
63 Amount of family discussion on school progress			183
34 Child likes reading at home			178
Major educational loadings:			
16+ external examinations	311	303	185
14+ non-verbal general ability			195

Note: As is customary decimal points have been omitted from the loadings above importantly involved. The two variables concerned with family activities—*involvement of family in long school holidays*, and *involvement of child in parents' activities* are also concerned, and operate the opposite way to *involvement of child in school activities*. The children are happy about parent-teacher encounters, and father has been concerned in the choice of secondary school. The loading for *father's occupation* is 0·132 in this factor. The general impression is one of a home-orientated family dominated by the attributes of the father.

Factor III has isolated the features of the environment concerned with high attainment in external examinations coupled with leaving school at the age of sixteen, as *left at age 16* has its highest loading (0·893) in this factor, and both *entered sixth form* and *left at age 15* operate in the opposite direction. The major environment loadings support our interpretation of the partial correlations for the sixteen-year-old leavers, in that parent and child ambitions, cleanliness of child, long duration of parent-influenced library membership, schools taking an interest in the leaving decision and parental visit to secondary school before entry are associated with the parents' willingness to assist in the teaching process, the purchase of good publications, selective television viewing and, once again, a low child involvement in school activities. The only parental education variable involved is *parents regret aspects of own education*. The quite heavy and negative loading for *father's occupation* (−0·173), confirms our suggestion that sixteen-plus school leaving reflects the upward aspirations of the ambitious, clean and conscientious working class. The negative loading for *mother not working* (−0·113), although too low to appear in Table 7.2, is also in line with the correlation analysis.

Factor XIII accounts for a further 4% of the external examination variance, and differentiates the sixth-form entrants from the statutory leavers. It also accounts for 5% of the fourteen-plus non-verbal general ability test variance. The heaviest loadings are for the three ambition variables—*earliness of career plans*, *nature of further education desired* and *career qualifications desired*. Each of these has its highest loading in this factor, as does *nature of books bought for child*. Additional variables which do not have major loadings in Factor I are *parents' approval of homework*, *nature of family weekend activities*, *secondary school chosen on educational grounds*, *nature of father's reading matter*, *nature of mother's reading matter*, *parents check homework*, *no history of truancy* and *nature of parental help with school work*. This appears to be a 'career ambition' factor, associated with the content of parents' reading and direct instrumental help with school work. As it is involved with non-verbal general ability, we have the impression that there is an element of family 'practicality' here which is related to a small extent to sixteen-plus results.

In general, we conclude that high achievement in external examinations is involved with the same environmental conditions as any other kind of attainment, but that three distinct and independent types of home background—

(i) the home-orientated, father-dominated middle class family atmosphere, (ii) the upward-aspiring, clean and conscientious working class home with clear but limited ambition, and (iii) the family with high career ambitions backed up with active and practical assistance—also produce a positive effect.

The Varimax rotation produced four further factors which had high loadings on single specific aspects of secondary school attainment. Factor VI accounted for 5% of the second year non-academic variance and had its major loadings in *parents check homework* (0·669), *nature of parental help with school work* (0·616) and *parents' knowledge of homework content* (0·604). These are the highest loadings for these variables and they suggest that practical help from the parents is conducive to success in non-academic subjects. Factor XI is also concerned with non-academic attainment, accounting for 11% of the third year variance in this subject area. It has its highest in *father from small family* (0·790). Social science attainment is mininally associated with Factors XIX and XII—3 and 4% respectively. Factor XIX contains the highest loading on *parents willing to assist in the teaching process* (0·683), and Factor XII the highest loading on *outgoingness of child at interview* (0·741). The educational variance for English, mathematics and the sciences is almost wholly accounted for by Factor I, the general educational variables, and we can say that, of all the school subjects investigated, only social sciences and non-academic subjects differ from the rest in that they appear to be additionally concerned with certain environment features not highly involved with overall attainment.

There are seven environment variables which do not load to a major degree on any of the 'educational' factors already mentioned. They are *sex of child*, *material needs adequate*, *cleanliness of home*, *mother not working*, *parents' assessment of child's effort*, *parents ask about school*, and *no attendance problems*. Factor VIII is clearly the 'sex' factor and its loadings confirm our correlation findings that being a girl is associated with a liking for reading, no history of truancy, cleanliness, helping at home and talking about school, and being a boy with the opposite circumstances. Factor IX clearly links dirt and poverty, *cleanliness of home* (—0·818), *material needs adequate* (—0·727) and *cleanliness of child* (—0·387) having their highest loadings here. They are supported by *child talks about school* (—0·304), *child likes parents and teachers to meet* (—0·249), *parents' approval of homework* (0·210), *housing standard* (—0·207), *family health* (—0·189), *attendance* (—0·189), *nature of publications bought for child* (—0·198), *nature of books bought for child* (—0·175) and *child's involvement in parents' activities* (—0·187).

While the connections between dirt, poverty, attendance and health are expected, this factor is interesting because it demonstrates that certain other parent and child attributes are not unconnected with poverty. The children from poor homes do not talk about school to their parents, and they are unhappy about parent-teacher encounters. These facts should be borne in mind when parent-school relations in educational priority areas are under consideration. It is obvious that the needy children cannot be relied upon to provide the communication channel between home and school. Several children admitted to our interviewer that they never delivered messages to their parents from the school about school activities, because they did not want them to attend. Thus, the efforts of the school were being sabotaged by those who were supposed to benefit. Direct approaches to parents are obviously necessary, and these must be of a nature that will not threaten the child's self-esteem and cause apprehension. Though the parents described by this factor have low involvement in activities with their children and do not purchase (or are unable to purchase) books and publications of a worthwhile nature for their children, there is the suggestion that they are not hostile to the aims of education in that they appear to approve of homework.

Factor XIV has its strongest loading (0·843) with *mother not working*. Controversy still ranges on many fronts about whether mothers should or should not go out to work. We have seen from our study of correlations that working mothers are associated with staying at school to the age of sixteen, and non-working mothers with sixth-form entry, and there was a social class bias in the expected directions for these two aspects of school leaving. In general, however, the variable has little association with level of school attainment. Factor XIV shows that, in our sample, working mothers were related to good *family health* (0·476) and *small families* (0·193). They contribute to the adequacy of material needs (0·280), and purchase good quality reading matter for their children (0·407). There is, however, an association with *no history of truancy* (—0·193) which cannot be overlooked.

The role of social class, as measured by *father's occupation*, should be considered specifically, as we have previously theorized that, although it may not be particularly associated with level of attainment, it is nevertheless associated with whether a child will extract full advantage from the educational system in terms of length of schooling. This variable has high loadings in six factors. The highest of these is in Factor XV which also has loadings of 0·194 and 0·186 on *9+ English* attainment and *10+ English* attainment, supporting the view that social class and verbal ability are related in their association to school achievement. Its next highest loading is in Factor XVI (0·264). This is obviously a 'posh home' factor, as its highest loading is for *rateable value* (0·831). It also contains a reasonably high loading on *7+ arithmetic* (0·188). Factor XVIII is clearly the attendance factor, having high loadings on all variables concerned with school attendance. It also has a loading of 0·236 on *father's occupation*, which indicates that social class and going willingly to school are not unconnected. We have already stated that father's occupation is involved with the non-academic subject Factor VI which is the 'instrumental help' factor. It is also concerned in Factor XXI which is dominated by *educational value of peer group influence* (0·765), and in Factor III, the school leaving factor. To summarize, social class has associations with housing, attendance, practical help to the child, satisfaction with child's friends and school leaving, though its connection with attainment is not explicit. There is also the suggestion of a relationship with early arithmetic and English attainment which apparently does not persist into the secondary school.

The factor analysis has, very usefully, provided us with further statistical support for our interpretations of the correlation analyses. It has neatly summarized the major relevant interactions and allows us to feel confident that we have drawn valid conclusions from the data we collected from the pupils and parents in our individual subsample.

8 Conclusions—the analysis of schools

This report was concerned with the statistics related to fifty-three secondary schools and their environment, and to a lesser extent to the home environment of their pupils. We attempted to discover how, and to what extent, aspects of environment were associated with the scholastic achievement at the secondary stage of a group of children whose primary school record had already been studied for the Plowden Report. The unit of analysis was the school and not the individual pupil. We had to bear this in mind when surveying our results, and also that we had made certain assumptions that the attainment of the Plowden sample in each school was representative of the attainment level of that school.

We analysed the intercorrelations of ninety separate variables, nineteen of them attainment scores at four different ages, six attainment scores in the last year of primary education, three general ability measures at the age of fourteen, and sixty-two measures of environment. Our analysis was first made by means of average and partial correlation and then, more comprehensively, by factor analysis. We replicated each stage of the analysis for all fifty-three schools with separate analyses for sub-groups approximating to the three types of school in the traditional tripartite system, in order to find whether environmental factors had operated in the same way in three different types of school.

The most important of our findings was that achievement in the secondary school was overwhelmingly dependent upon what had happened to the pupils before entry, and there was no sense in which transfer at eleven-plus could be regarded as a 'fresh start'. We have demonstrated that the pre-secondary experience of our pupils had exerted influences on secondary school attainment of a complex and all-pervading nature—some obvious and expected and some rather surprising. The most obvious and expected effect was that secondary school attainment measures had their strongest associations with scores obtained on eleven-plus selection tests. The secondary pupils entering with high scores have finished with high scores, and vice versa. As primary school ability is subsumed in secondary school ability, it was inevitable that the level of ability at any secondary school stage would have an important relation to level at entry. Eleven-plus scores provide the base-line from which subsequent progress is measured. The abilities acquired before entry to secondary school were therefore the crucial determinants of the level of secondary school achievement. One of the ostensible aims of eleven-plus selection is to ensure that pupils begin their secondary education at a level appropriate to the skills and abilities they have already acquired and, in so far as eleven-plus scores have emerged as the best predictors of subsequent attainment, it has been successful in this.

Secondly, we have also demonstrated that selection scores were not straightforward predictors of ability simply providing an essential base on which to build further educational achievement. The Plowden Survey, in respect of these same pupils, showed that abilities acquired during the primary school years (and measured by eleven-plus scores), were largely the fruits of influences from home and neighbourhood background. Because of this, it was not surprising that we initially found our home environment measures of *attendance*, *appearance*, *free meals* and *free clothing* were strongly related to secondary school achievement. This was the inevitable result of eleven-plus scores and social factors being interrelated. Eleven-plus selection differentiated one secondary school from another in terms of the initial ability level of their pupils—which was its aim—but, as a secondary and unavoidable effect, it also differentiated one school from another in terms of the social background of their pupils. This was made quite clear by the fact that our home environment measures correlated more strongly with eleven-plus scores than with secondary attainment scores. That selection by ability also results in social selection may even be an attractive feature of eleven-plus allocation procedures to some of those who look upon the higher achievement of the selective schools as a vindication of selection. However, the results of our partial correlation calculations appear to show that social background in itself had little effect on that part of attainment accruing in the secondary school. The effect of our home variables on secondary attainment could be almost wholly accounted for by the association between initial ability and home background. We therefore came to the conclusion that the effects of an advantageous or disadvantageous home background were largely complete by the age of transfer and that the social selection aspect of eleven-plus examinations is not an essential component of prediction, even though it is an inevitable consequence.

Having demonstrated the important association between initial ability and home background, it was nevertheless obvious that some aspects of 'home' were stronger in effect on that part of attainment accruing after entry to secondary school than others, and it was suggested that, as in the primary school survey, parental attitudes were more importantly associated with attainment than poverty or affluence. Our clearest indicator of the economic level of a school's intake was the variable *free meals*. Of our four home variables this appeared to have the least important association with attainment, as it produced partial correlations little different from zero in any of our analyses, and also varied in the direction of its effect. *Free clothing*, which was a less clear indicator of economic level because of its association with school uniform, also produced low partial correlations which were variable in effect, except in the technical high schools where all the negative correlations approached significance. *Attendance* and *appearance*, which are more concerned with parental attitudes and care, were more consistent in effect. All the partial correlations for attainment and *attendance* were positive, and significantly so for third year attainment in the whole sample of schools and in the secondary modern schools, and with sixteen-plus results in the grammar schools. *Appearance of pupils* also produced significant partial correlations in the whole sample and grammar school analyses for sixteen-plus external examinations. There was also evidence that these two 'attitude' variables were related to statutory leaving, in that both *attendance* and *appearance* were negatively and significantly associated with leaving school at age fifteen in the secondary modern schools, and in the whole sample as far as attendance only was concerned. On the evidence of these four variables alone, it would seem that parental attitudes rather than socio-economic factors are salient to attainment and to extracting maximum advantage from the secondary school system, and we suggest that all efforts to produce cooperative attitudes in parents are tasks well worth undertaking in the secondary schools as well as in the primary schools.

The third effect of eleven-plus selection which we have demonstrated is that school environment variables are also crucially interrelated with initial ability. There is little room for complacency about this finding, even if it can be said that the connections between eleven-plus scores, secondary attainment and home background are self-evident inevitabilities. If it is admitted that selection is a method of ensuring that the most promising pupils receive an advantageous share of existing facilities, then the eleven-plus tests have undoubtedly done their job in this respect also. However, it is rarely stated baldly, that eleven-plus selection is designed to isolate the 'more deserving' from the 'less deserving' as far as provision of facilities is concerned, but this is how the system has appeared to operate for our Plowden pupils. If selection for provision is a desired effect of eleven-plus procedures then it has been successful, but if the concepts of compensation, amelioration or remediation are anywhere inherent in the existence of the tripartite system, then in practice the system has operated against such concepts.

The pupils of lower initial ability, from disadvantaged homes, have also had poorer school facilities in most of those areas originally shown to be associated with achievement. This effect was most grossly seen when types of school were compared but, even within school types, we have found that 'provision' hierarchies emerged related to the initial ability of the school intake. It is not suggested that such differential provision is the result of deliberate intent on the part of the appropriate authorities. This may have been the case, but it is more likely that a conglomeration of adverse factors stemming from low initial ability and poor home background have a defeating effect on the provision of ameliorating facilities. Our school results have shown how selection operates in the direction of self-fulfilment. That high initial ability produces high final achievement is obvious, but this may blind the unwary observer to the fact that all aspects of environmental provision conspire to make this inevitable. We can say that the level of scholastic ability of our Plowden pupils in the secondary school has overwhelmingly been the result of abilities acquired in the primary school, plus such differences in secondary school environment as were characteristically associated with different levels of ability.

In addition to showing that few of our school environment partial correlations reached significance when the effect of initial ability was removed, we also demonstrated that no single school variable operated in a consistent direction over all school subjects, at all ages, in all types of school. It is, nevertheless, true that certain variables were more consistent in their general effect than others, and reached significance a greater number of times. On these criteria we were able to isolate those aspects of school environment which appeared to be associated with high attainment in all types of school, irrespective of initial ability. Our most unequivocal finding is that teacher training is important. The variable *number of untrained teachers* operated negatively with attainment in all types of school, at all ages, for sixteen-plus external examinations and for all school subjects except mathematics and science. Seven of its partial correlations reached a level of significance of at least 5%. Teacher qualifications were found to be most importantly associated with attainment in the secondary modern schools, where all the negative associations for all subject areas at all ages were significant. *Graduate teachers* were found to be positively connected with good sixteen-plus results in all types of school, and in the secondary modern schools there was a significant relationship with second and third year school attainment. That these two variables did not produce significant results in the selective school analyses is because these schools are more homogeneous in their proportions of graduate and untrained teachers, and the variables here have very little discriminatory power.

The next most consistent variable was *opportunities to acquire formal status.* This operated negatively in all types of school, at all ages, for all school subjects except social sciences and non-academic subjects, and seven of the negative partial correlations reached significance. It appears that the provision of a large number of pupil offices and positions of responsibility is associated with low attainment.

We found that homework, poor social atmosphere, good school equipment, large school size, good specialist rooms, good quality building, good first impression, poorer provision for individual welfare and a higher proportion of teachers under the age of thirty were associated with high attainment in that they operated consistently in direction of effect in each of the first three years in all types of school, even though they are more specifically related to particular school subjects. It would also appear that our pupils have done better, on the whole, in unstreamed schools—as *streaming by ability* produced negative partial correlations in all school types, for all subjects, at all ages, and the connection was significant for the social sciences. Where a school is streamed it appears that flexibility of movement between streams is associated with high attainment, as the variable *transfer between streams* operated positively in all types of school in the second and third years, and overall for mathematics, the sciences and social sciences, and three of the partial correlations were significant.

The variables *migration, streaming on entry, pupil/teacher ratio, sociability of pupils, number of informal parents' meetings* and *visits in school time,* where they were consistent in effect in all types of school, were more specific to a particular subject area or a particular age and always operated negatively in these instances. *Number of formal parents meetings,* on the other hand, was positively associated with attainment in the first three years and with English attainment, in all types of school. *Authoritarianism of headteacher* was positively associated with first year attainment and mathematics in all types of school, though not significantly. *Number of internal examinations per year* was positively related to second year attainment and science in all school types, and a longer teaching day with first year attainment and English. *Out-of-school activities* operated in a consistently positive direction in all school types for second year attainment and English. If, from these results, we were tentatively to construct a profile of a high achieving school which amalgamated all these aspects, we should have to say that it would be a large school with good equipment, good specialist rooms, producing a favourable first impression in an observer. There would be few untrained teachers and a small number of pupils per teacher. The emphasis on homework would be strong, and if streaming were applied at all it would be flexible and accommodating. The school day would be long, there would be many out-of-school activities and more than one internal examination per year. The headteacher would be inclined to authoritarianism and the pupils would not be described as noticeably sociable. Pupils would be unable to aspire to a wide range of positions giving them formal status in the school, and there would be no great provision for individual welfare. The general impression is one of orthodoxy and work-centredness, with considerable organizational effort along traditional lines.

As far as external examinations at sixteen-plus are concerned, the salient features of high achieving secondary schools appear to be good individual pupil records, coeducation, few school journeys and a good quality library, in all types of school.

Measured attainment is one aspect of school success. The decision to stay at school after the statutory leaving age is another. We have found that in schools of all types those with a higher proportion of pupils leaving at the age of fifteen are characteristically small in size, with little emphasis on homework, few internal examinations, few school journeys and out-of-school activities and many offices giving pupils formal status. The general impression is of small schools where little effort is made along formal organizational lines, with many jobs delegated to pupils.

We have discovered that a few of our variables operated in different directions in different types of school. Old buildings, absence of corporal punishment and the use of innovatory techniques were positively associated with all aspects of attainment in the grammar schools, and negatively in the technical high and secondary moderns. Young headteachers appeared to be associated with high attainment in the selective schools, and older heads in the secondary modern schools.

The school environment variables not already discussed—*size of class, teachers over age fifty, teacher turnover, male teachers, sex of school, subject setting, graduate headteacher, attitude to inquiry, quality of headteacher, school uniform, emphasis on external examinations, vocational guidance, voluntary school, number of teaching periods in one day, movement between lessons, prefect system, house system, merit mark system* and *availability of staff to parents*—were so inconsistent in their direction of effect over school types and subjects at different ages, that we cannot regard them as 'educational' predictors in any general sense so far as our sample is concerned. Several of them produced significant partial correlations for a specific school subject, at a particular age, in a single type of school, but—as we are concerned to find environment features which predict all types of attainment at all ages—we cannot include these in such a category.

The fourth aspect of eleven-plus selection is the effect of *type of school* as a single variable. This produced partial correlations little different from zero and variable in direction. We must conclude that differences in initial ability and related provision produced the differentials in attainment between types of school, and that no residual attainment effect could be attributed to prestige or the lack of it. We produced some evidence that the 'self-image' of schools may have affected the assessment of attainment, which suggests that school type may have subtle effects which are difficult to justify unless children are deliberately selected for the different kinds of ability thought appropriate in different kinds of institution. We suggested that mathematical ability was all important in the technical high schools and verbal ability highly important in the grammar schools, and that this may have resulted in certain talents having been overlooked and inadequately rewarded if they were not appropriate for a particular type of specialist education. There was further substantiation for this view in that there appeared to be associations between statutory leaving and poor mathematics attainment in the technical high schools, and between statutory leaving and poor verbal ability in the grammar schools. The fact that the most successful non-selective schools appeared to be those which emulated the selective schools in many characteristics, does suggest that what is good for some children may be good for all children, at least where academic achievement is concerned.

The factor analyses provided further support for the findings of the correlational studies, and made it plain that environment and initial ability are so crucially interrelated in the secondary schools that it is probably unrealistic to consider either aspect in isolation. Commonsense, however, tells us that the actual existence of schools is the most important factor in the production of measurable attainment. If pupils absented themselves from school permanently they would be unlikely to acquire the skills and knowledge required for measurement in examinations, internal or external. Though it may be unrealistic to discount initial ability in the study of examination results, this has been necessary in our investigation in order to try to isolate school characteristics and aspects of provision which were, in themselves, advantageous to achievement when examination results are accepted as the criterion of a school's success. The factors produced by our Varimax analyses which were relatively free of intake variance, but which contained small but specific amounts of educational variance, are the best pointers we have to the intrinsic value of aspects of provision and organization. The high loadings in these factors are very similar in aspect to the findings of our partial correlation analyses. Because they have rather unrealistically excluded the effects of intake, they can only provide hypotheses—rather than conclusive findings—as to which efforts in the secondary school are positively worth pursuing, and which owe their apparent success to imported ability in the first place. As a concrete example, we can look at the effects of wearing school uniform, which at first sight appeared to have a highly significant relationship with attainment. If, on this evidence, a non-selective school headteacher thought he could improve his pupils' attainment by insisting that they wear uniform, he would be wasting a good deal of time and effort. The relationship has been shown to be entirely due to the fact that pupils of high initial ability went to schools that insisted on uniform. In itself, the wearing of uniform had no effect whatsoever on attainment. If it were insisted upon for some other reason, of course this would be an entirely different matter.

Our sample of schools is small and specific to one urban area in the north of England. In a sense it is also historical in nature as the data we collected from the schools early in 1967 is no longer topical, since reorganization on comprehensive lines has altered many of our schools almost beyond recognition. The suggestions we have made as to the probable association of certain environment variables with attainment would have to be explored further with samples more representative of the total secondary school population before generalizations could be made. Our general findings that the orthodox schools with a work-centred ethos tend towards a higher level of attainment also require some qualification. We had no school in our sample that deviated from traditional norms to any marked degree, and the expected variance on school environment factors could have been only small. We are also aware that, by force of circumstance, in confining our attainment measures to those subjects which can be measured by examination, a rather narrow view has been taken of what schools may have been trying to achieve according to their own lights. We did find, for the whole sample of schools, that the high loadings for Factor X described—in their positive aspect—a school atmosphere redolent of pupil-centredness, pleasantness, care and concern, that had little to do with measured attainment but were associated with staying at school beyond the statutory leaving age. It is not possible to overlook that, had we been able to measure such intangibles as socialization, personality development or even happiness, they would probably have contributed a high percentage of variance to this factor. It would be possible to take the rather pessimistic view that a school must be either work-orientated or pupil-centred, and that both conditions cannot exist in the same institution. However, we cannot rule out that, as long as society gives its greatest rewards to academic success, such success will be a school's highest priority if it appears to be within the bounds of possibility.

9 Conclusions—the analysis of individuals

The analysis of individuals was based on 114 pupils from the 1544 children who were the subjects of the schools study. By means of correlations, average correlations, partial correlations and factor analysis, we endeavoured to isolate features in the environment and experience of these children which have been salient to high attainment in the secondary school, at different ages and in different subject areas. We also attempted, by chi-squared analyses, to discover the nature of the background to improvement and deterioration after the age of transfer.

Complex partial correlation analyses were made necessary by the obvious and expected lack of variance produced by the environment variables, and were specifically associated with attainment in the secondary school. The findings of the Plowden primary survey, involving the same individuals, showed quite clearly that at the age of transfer to secondary school environment and attainment were strongly and crucially related. It was not envisaged that the simple fact of transfer would break these environment-attainment links and produce very different patterns of interaction from those already demonstrated. As many of our secondary stage variables were the same or similar to those in the primary study, closely corresponding results could be expected, with secondary school attainment as the criterion of achievement. Our preliminary correlational analyses and the subsequent Varimax rotations confirmed our expectations. Out of the seventy-nine environment variables, forty-two correlated significantly with each of the eight age measures from seven-plus to sixteen-plus, a further seventeen correlated significantly with more that half of the age measures, seventeen with less than half, and three with none—*sex of child, family health* and *mother not working*. The heavy Factor I produced by the Varimax rotation accounted for 82% of the educational test variance and included the highest loadings for each of the educational tests from seven-plus to sixteen-plus, ranging from 0·712 for 7+ *arithmetic* to 0·953 for *total first year secondary attainment*. Forty-six of the seventy-nine environment variables produced major loadings in this factor, isolating those background attributes from which educational achievement in both primary and secondary school could not be regarded as independent.

Most of the environmental attributes included in our analyses had associations with attainment apparent when the child was aged seven and persisting in effect up to the age of sixteen-plus. This finding, in itself, is a vindication of the Plowden recommendations that attempts to ameliorate the adverse effects of certain home background factors must begin as early as possible in the child's life through the provision of nursery education and the formation of sound and consistent cooperation between home and school.

Our variables were clearly interdependent, and we were concerned to try to find the source of their mutual dependence. The presence in the first educational factor of the major loadings on all three parent-education variables led us to believe that parents' own educational experiences were a salient factor in the school attainment of their children and, as the highest of these three loadings was for *parents' 11+ selection* (higher than *parents' formal education level*), we concluded that parental ability was an underlying factor. The presence of a very high loading for the child's intelligence, measured by the administration of a picture test as early as age seven, also made it clear that parental ability is not unconnected with the level of child intelligence. Our partial correlation exercises, holding *parents' 11+ selection* and child's *7+ intelligence* constant in turn, demonstrated that many of the associations found between environment and overall attainment could have been accounted for by these single ability measures. However, these demonstrable associations between education and environment—reaching back not only to the child's first primary years, but also to the eleven-plus transfer test achievements of their parents—are not so deterministic as they first appear. Certainly, families do exist which are predisposed to the production of high-achieving children, as others seem to be predisposed to having children on whom the educational process will have little effect as far as school attainment is concerned. But we cannot say that, because these predispositions are natural, attempts to maximize the effects of education are unrealistic. We do know from our partial correlations that there are certain variables which, though related in some degree to parental ability or the initial ability of the children, nevertheless had a significant association with school attainment that could not be accounted for by these factors. There is no reason to suppose that similar variables had not affected the parents' own test results at eleven-plus, and that if we had been able to investigate these interactions, holding grandparents' intelligence constant, we should not have arrived at similar partial correlations which retained significance. These variables, which are relatively free of dependence on background ability and may or may not be genetic, are worth our closest scrutiny. They are the clearest indicators to those areas of parental attitude and family practice which should be amenable to modification with the object of improving attainment results and maximizing the ability to take full advantage of the educational system. They allow us to leave on one side, with a fair amount of confidence, the thorny problem of heredity, and examine features of the environment which, in themselves, are conducive to high attainment at any age from seven to sixteen.

Most importantly, we have shown that educational ambition—as exemplified by *preferred age of leaving*, *career qualifications desired*, *importance of school performance to child's future*, *earliness of leaving decision*, *nature of further education desired*, *occupational ambition of child* and *child's preference for extended schooling*—have significant associations with overall attainment not overwhelmingly concerned with parental ability or the child's initial ability. Certain aspects of family literacy—*nature of child's reading matter*, *duration of child's library membership*, *parents influenced child to join library*, *child likes reading at home* and *library membership of parents*—are, in themselves, significantly associated with overall attainment, irrespective of considerations of background ability. It is interesting that the parents of high achievers formulated their educational aspirations for their children very early in their children's lives—perhaps before the children were born or even conceived. Metaphorically speaking, certain of our parents 'put their children down for Eton' before any realistic assessment of potential was possible, and this phenomenon was not wholly the result of the parents' own educational experience or the brightness of their children. Educational aspiration and literacy are surely two areas of parental behaviour which might be influenced by schools, through parent-teacher links, or other local authority services. No parent should be allowed to remain unaware of the opportunities afforded by the educational system until the crucial decision about school leaving has to be made, or is made for them. There is no reason why even nursery or infant schools should not be propagandist in this sense, through the medium of parent-teacher meetings. And if parents are apprehensive about joining the local library or uninterested in reading as a leisure pursuit, might not the schools step in and operate lending schemes, with the help of the library services, for books to be loaned to parents either for their own enjoyment or to read to their children?

However, our main concern has been to examine the interaction of environment variables and aspects of the secondary school experience of our sample pupils. Most of the associations between environment and secondary school attainment could have been predicted by the eleven-plus selection test scores of our subsample but, because of the higher and more frequently significant correlations with secondary school tests, we concluded that many home background attributes increased in educational importance as the children advanced in years. Entry to sixth form was, not surprisingly, associated with high attainment in each of the first three secondary years, and with all school subjects except the non-academic. *Preferred age of leaving* had significant relationship with high attainment in all three years also, and specifically with mathematics and the sciences. *Amount of child's homework*, a school variable with overtones of parental awareness, was also related to high attainment in all years, and to English and non-academic subjects in particular. *Father from small family* is the clearest specifically 'secondary' attainment predictor. This was not highly related to any of the primary school test measures but, with initial ability held constant, it still retained significance in its association with each of the secondary year measures, and specifically with sciences and non-academic subjects. We have concluded that the attributes of fathers become increasingly important, and suggest that all attempts to involve fathers in the life of the secondary school would be very well worthwhile.

Occupational ambition of child is not highly associated with first year secondary attainment, but becomes significant in the second and third years, and is also particularly related to success in the sciences and non-academic subjects. Five variables declined in effect, being related to first year but not to third year attainment. These are—*child's preference for extended schooling*, *nature of child's reading matter*, *nature of child's hobbies and interests* and *nature of mother's reading* and *amount of mother's reading*. Respectively they have specific associations with sciences and non-academic subjects, English and social sciences, sciences and social sciences, social sciences, and sciences and social sciences. *Attendance* becomes increasingly important over the years and is specifically associated with high mathematics attainment, a similar result to that reported by Warburton (1964), whose hypothesis that high attendance would show beneficial effects chiefly in arithmetic was confirmed. *Interest taken by school in leaving decision* was specifically associated with science attainment only. Four variables had very specific relations with single subject areas—*influence of education on long-term plans* with mathematics, *school performance important to child's future* and *family involvement during long school holidays* with the social sciences, and perceived low *deference* demands with non-academic subjects. A further thirteen variables had specific association with attainment in a single secondary school year, but not more. In all there were thirty-three environment variables related significantly in their partial correlation to one or more aspects of secondary school attainment in the first three years. These are the variables which have not completed their effect before entry to secondary school but continue to operate as environmental forces. They suggest that although we have shown that remedial procedures must begin as early as possible in a child's life, it is not too late at secondary school stage to attempt the amelioration of adverse social factors.

When we looked at *16+ external examination* results as the criterion of attainment, environment at secondary level was shown to be even more important. Sixteen environment variables were significantly associated in their partial correlation to this measure of attainment, in addition to those shown to be salient to internal school assessments in the first three years, no doubt because of their relationship to the background factors associated with staying on at school after the statutory leaving age. These additional variables are concerned with the long-standing nature of leaving decisions and career plans, the nature of further education desired, the parents' library membership and the quality of books bought for the child, the cleanliness of the child and evidence of care, the nature of radio listening and family weekend activities, the willingness of parents to help in the teaching process, and their giving of systematic and specific help with school work. *Housing standard* is also important here, as is *mother from small family*.

The single social class variable of *father's occupation* was positively and significantly related to sixth-form entry only, as was *rateable value*. The variables for *material needs adequate* and *housing standard* operated negatively and significantly for leaving at the statutory leaving age. Thus, socio-economic measures clearly discriminated between the statutory leavers and the sixth-form entrants, even though they had been shown to have little relationship to attainment itself. The provision of equal educational opportunity for all has obviously not resulted in an equal or similar educational experience for the children of all social groups.

Adverse background factors bore more heavily on the statutory leavers, as forty environment variables operated negatively and significantly with this group. *Father's occupation* was not among these, and the correlations were dominated negatively by *father from small family*. The statutory leavers also saw their schools as being demanding in terms of orderliness and deference to superiors. The sixteen-year-old leavers differed from the statutory leavers in terms of the ambition variables, cleanliness, and selectivity of radio and television habits, and from the sixth-form entrants by virtue of the fact that the mothers of the latter group tended not to go out to work.

Perhaps the most intriguing of our findings was the relationship of the size of father's childhood family to the secondary school attainment and experience of his children, the age at which they leave school, and to other environment variables. Further research into this variable with larger and more representative samples is suggested, as we have the basis for a tentative hypothesis that the number of a man's siblings affects his relationships with his wife and children. The man from a large family appears to have negative attitudes to education, but his very negativeness is a dominating feature of the lifestyle of the family. It would not be possible from our findings to state that we have uncovered an 'Andy Capp' syndrome underlying the poor attainment of children, but this would certainly be worth exploring. The involvement in school affairs of fathers of low-achieving children would probably be the most difficult of all home-school efforts to organize, requiring tact and diplomacy of a very high order, but we suggest that it might be a fruitful though challenging activity. When we consider that both *father from small family* and *mother from small family* retained positive and significant associations with sixteen-plus external examinations, we were forced to the conclusion that size of family has an ongoing effect in succeeding generations, and that there is less conflict between the family image that man and wife separately bring to the marital situation in the homes producing high achieving children. Male domination is not undocumented as a feature of working class lifestyle, and shared responsibility as a feature of middle class life. The effect of these factors on educational attainment and the school experience of children requires further investigation in depth, in order to understand how underlying parental attitudes are manifested in effective family behaviour.

The rather meagre results which differentiated improvers from deteriorators in the high and low selection groups suggested that school variables had affected improvement in the selected group, and that parental interest and attitudes were the crucial determinants of improvement in the non-selected group. When we considered the few clear improvers as individuals—an admittedly extreme attenuation of our data—we concluded that care and concern of a very specific and individual nature on the part of both parents and teachers produced results which could not have been forecast from early attainment. Obvious specific talent and obvious specific need appear to have provoked wholly salutary responses for achievement from those in a position to help. Insight into less obvious needs and talents on the part of parents and teachers, and its translation into individual and specific advice and encouragement, might well still be the most effective means of improving educational standards. In spite of the few children involved, the case for individual educational counselling and guidance is not ruled out as a promising field of educational effectiveness. There is no reason why educational guidance at this personal level should be regarded as a secondary school province, as all our evidence points to the fact that remedial procedures to counteract adverse forces in the environment should begin as early as possible, and that there should be no break in continuity because transfer to secondary school has intervened.

A further point worth mentioning on the question of home-school cooperation is that pupils themselves are not reliable intermediaries. Only the sixth-form entrants were significantly fond of parent-teacher encounters and, when we examined our original data, we found that 15% of the subsample admitted that they did not always transmit messages from school to home. Lack of attendance at school functions cannot always be laid at the door of parental indifference, and a home visit by a teacher or teacher/social worker would seem to be a first essential in many cases.

10 Discussion of conclusions

None of the findings from either the school-based or individual-based study contradicts those produced for the Plowden survey when these same pupils were of primary school age. Factors in the home background are of major importance in the acquisition of educational attainment and, in a total view of education up to the age of leaving school, are even more important than the primary survey could have predicted. Our study of school environment showed clearly that home background is not only associated with the attainment a child brings to the secondary school, but also with aspects of secondary school provision and organization. A disadvantageous home background in early years leads to a disadvantageous school background in later years, and the adverse effects of both are thus compounded. This may no longer be the case in those areas of the Manchester secondary school system which are now run on comprehensive lines, as the differences between schools may have been to some extent evened out, but we have no hard evidence to support this suggestion.

Parental attitudes to the process of education, to school and to books have emerged—as in the primary school study—as of far greater importance than social class or occupational level as far as school attainment is concerned. However, whether a child takes full advantage of the school system in terms of length of schooling has been shown to be related to socio-economic factors. There is sufficient evidence that adverse environmental forces operate from the earliest ages up to the time the decision to leave school is made. Some of these adverse forces have completed their major effect by the age of transfer at eleven-plus, confirming that the provision of ameliorative social measures should begin as early as possible after birth. Other adverse forces continue to operate instrumentally against attainment increments in the secondary school, which suggests that it is never too late to attempt to involve parents in the education of their children. We also have tentative evidence that attitudes to education have an ongoing effect through succeeding generations, irrespective of considerations of abilities which may or may not be innate. Every possible means that might modify these adverse attitudes should be explored if any progress is to be made.

The study of schools showed that qualifications of teachers were significantly related to school attainment and, in particular, that teacher training was an asset in the non-selective schools. On the basis of our evidence we favour a trained, graduate teaching profession and, in view of the overwhelming effect of home background factors, we concur with the proposals outlined in the primary survey that teacher training should include studies of the effects of social environment on the children to be taught. Teacher/social workers—not necessarily attached to a particular school but to a particular group of children—to recognize cases of deprivation and stay with them throughout their school careers, encouraging cooperative action between schools, teachers, parents and children and all appropriate social agencies, would probably be the ideal solution. Any steps taken appropriate to this eventual goal would certainly increase our knowledge of the complex social and psychological interactions which underly parents' attitudes to education, to books, to culture and to the family unit itself. It is evident that the childhood of parents affects their parenthood and this, in turn, affects the childhood of their children. One of the factors involved is family size, of which the implications require further study.

A multivariate investigation such as this inevitably reveals the seamless nature of the garment under scrutiny, and there are many more variables, known and unknown, which might have been included. If all schools were identical in every respect then it would be possible with more clarity to isolate factors in the home background that produce differential educational results. Conversely, if all homes were identical, differentials in school effects could be calculated more accurately. Of course, neither contingency can ever apply because, even if physical conditions were equal, we are still dealing primarily with human beings—parents, children and teachers, whose individual personal constructs affect environment and are affected by environment in extremely subtle fashion. The situation is not completely hopeless. A start could be made by ensuring that, in school, all children enjoy an equal amount of those facilities and conditions that have been shown—however marginally—to be related to high attainment. This would certainly be the most desirable way of holding school variables constant in reality, and we could then begin with more certainty to unravel and describe the remaining threads in the 'seamless coat of many colours' that we call education.

Bibliography

Bloom, B. S. *Stability and Change in Human Characteristics*. John Wiley, New York, 1964.

Central Advisory Council for Education (England), *Children and their Primary Schools* [The Plowden Report]. HMSO, 1967.

Central Advisory Council for Education (England), *Half our Future*. [The Newsom Report] HMSO, 1963.

Griffin, A. 'The effects of secondary school organization on the development of intelligence, attainment in English and attitude to school'. M.Ed. thesis, University of Manchester, 1968 (unpublished).

Kemp, L. C. D. 'Environmental and other characteristics determining attainment in primary schools'. *British Journal of Educational Psychology*, **25**, pp. 67–77, 1955.

Mollenkopf, W. G. *A Study of Secondary School Characteristics Determining Attainment in Primary Schools* (Educational Testing Service Research Bulletin No. 6). ETS, Princeton, New Jersey, 1956.

Morris, J. M. *Standards and Progress in Reading*. National Foundation for Educational Research in England and Wales, 1966.

Newsom Report, see Central Advisory Council for Education (England), *Half our Future*.

Pace, C. R. and Stern, G. G. *A Criterion Study of College Environment*. Syracuse University Research Institute, Psychological Research Center, 1958.

Peaker, G. F. in *Children and their Primary Schools* [The Plowden Report]. Vol. 2, Appendix 4, 'The Regression Analyses of the National Survey', HMSO, 1967.

Plowden Report, see Central Advisory Council for Education (England), *Children and their Primary Schools*.

Warburton, F. W. in *Education and Environment*, ed. S. Wiseman. Chapter VI, Manchester University Press, 1964.

Wiseman, S. in *Children and their Primary Schools* [The Plowden Report]. Vol. 2, Appendix 9, 'The Manchester Survey', HMSO, 1967.

Wiseman, S. et al. 'Collins Secondary Guidance Programme'. University of Manchester (unpublished).

Appendices

E.E.F.—6

Appendix 1
Questionnaire to headteachers to establish attainment criteria

1 Do you hold internal examinations to assist you in the assessment of your pupils' attainment? ....

2 If your answer to question 1 is 'NO' and you have an alternative method of assessment, please describe...

3 If your answer to question 1 is 'YES', we should like to know how many internal examinations have been taken by *all present third year pupils* since they entered your school. Please indicate by ticking the appropriate boxes below.

	First year	Second year	Anticipated or taken in third year
On entry			
Christmas			
Easter			
Whitsun			
Midsummer			
Any other time Please state when			

4 It would be helpful if we could know the method of recording school examination marks in operation, so that we may decide the best method for collecting data. Please place a tick against any of the following which

apply in your case, and add any further methods which we may have overlooked.

(a) Individual record cards ....
(b) Carbon copies of individual report forms ....
(c) School mark registers ....
(d) Form teacher's records ....
(e) ....

5 In order to arrange for the scaling test for *all* present third year pupils we should be glad to know the total number of pupils at present in *all* third year forms. No. of present third year pupils........

6 In respect of present third year pupils please give the designations of the first, second and third year forms to which they could have been allocated, in descending order of ability. If forms are parallel please state.

First year forms	Second year forms	Third year forms
....	....	....
....	....	....
....	....	....
....	....	....

7 If there is any subject setting between streams or classes, please name the subjects to which this applies ....

8 In respect of present third year pupils we should be glad to have details of the examinations they took in their first, second and third years in the following terms:

(a) Were the same examination papers taken irrespective of stream or set and a standard system of marking adopted?
(b) Were separate papers prepared for each stream or set with different marking standards?
(c) Was there any overlapping of papers or marking standards between streams or sets?

First year..
Second year...
Third year ....

9 In order to isolate the school subjects in which all present third year pupils in all schools were examined in common, please place ticks in the appropriate boxes below. Please note that only those subjects taken by

	Year 1	Year 2	Year 3		Year 1	Year 2	Year 3
English (total mark)				Art			
(a) Language				Craft			
(b) Literature				Music			
(c) Essay				Needlework			
(d) Comprehension				Woodwork			
(e) Oral				Metalwork			
(f)				Housecraft			
(g)				Rural science			
				R.I.			
Mathematics (total mark)				P.E.			
(a) Arithmetic				Games			
(b) Mental arithmetic							
(c) Problem arithmetic				*Languages*			
(d) Mech. arithmetic				French			
(e) Algebra				Latin			
(f) Geometry				German			
(g)				Spanish			
(h)				Russian			
Combined sciences							
Physics							
Chemistry							
Biology							
History							
Geography							
Social studies							

all pupils in any one year (or subjects taken by all boys or all girls in mixed schools) should be marked. Please add any other subjects which we may have omitted, or any other aspect of school life which you consider to be important for which a mark or grade would be available.

Comments ....

10 In order to scale examination marks it will be necessary for us to take note of any movement of pupils between streams or sets. Your replies to the following questions will greatly assist us in planning our analysis of the various methods adopted.

Were the present *third year pupils* streamed or set according to ability

(a) in the first year? ....

(b) in the second year?.........

(c) in the third year?...........

Comments ....

....

....

Appendix 2 Questionnaire to headteachers for scoring objective school characteristic variables

A **Children**

1 Number of pupils on roll — March 1965 ....
March 1966 ....
March 1967 ....
2 Number of forms or classes — March 1967 ....
3 Percentage attendance in the school year 1965/66 ....
4 Number of children who have qualified for Special Schools of any description since September, 1964. Please enumerate by type of school...
5 Number of children at present in the school whose mother tongue is not English ....
6 Number of children at present in the care of the local authority ....
7 Number of children at present receiving free meals ....
8 Number of children at present receiving a grant for clothing ....
9 Number of children gaining selected places in the 11-plus examination (secondary modern schools only)
Intake 1964 ....
Intake 1965 ....
Intake 1966 ....

B **Staff** (including headteacher)

10 AGE DISTRIBUTION (Ages at January 1st, 1967)

	20–29 years	*30–49 years*	*Over 50 years*
Number of men	....	....	....
Number of women	....	....	....

11 TRAINING

	Trained	*Untrained*
Number of graduates	....	....
Number of non-graduates	....	....

12 Number of teachers who have been appointed to your staff since September, 1964 ....

C Organization

Number of single teaching periods in one day ....
Length of a single teaching period in minutes ....

D Building

Date of building of main structure of school ....

Comments ....
....

Appendix 3
Schedule completed at interview with headteachers

School...

No.	Variable		Rating
26	*Attitude to inquiry*		
	Cooperativeness—suspiciousness of H.T.		(Rating 1–3).........
27	*Quality of headteacher*		
	Sympathy with modern methods	....	
	Efficiency	....	
	Relations with staff	....	
	Relations with pupils	....	(Rating 1–5).........
28	*Innovation*		
	Teaching machines	....	
	Visual and aural aids	....	
	Nuffield projects	....	
	Newsom projects	....	
	Social work projects	....	
	Work practice schemes	....	
	Television (use of)	....	
	Radio (use of)	....	
	Modern maths apparatus	....	
	Other experimental projects	....	(Rating 1–5).........
29	*School uniform*		
	Does it exist?	....	
	Is it compulsory?	....	
	Percentage wearing	....	
	No. of clothing items involved	....	
	Rules about hair cut?	....	
	Rules about jewellery?	....	
	Rules about skirt length?	....	

No.	Variable		Rating
29	Rules about trouser width?	....	
	Methods of enforcement	....	
	Amount of pupil resentment to appearance rules	....	
	Importance attached to uniform as educational policy	....	
	Reasons for or against uniform	....	(Rating 1–5).........
30	*Emphasis on external examinations*		
	Is GCE O-level taken?	....	
	Is CSE taken?	....	
	Any other examinations?	....	
	Year exam preparation begins	....	
	Any intensive course for resits?	....	
	Are exams important incentive?	....	
	Are non-entrants depressed by inability to enter?	....	
	Preferred mode in CSE	....	
	How important are internal exam marks to promotion?	....	(Rating 1–5).........
31	*Homework*		
	Regular homework for all?	....	
	Who is exempted?	....	
	Supplied on request?	....	
	Facilities provided at school?	....	
	Average no. of hours per week	....	
	Does system work well?	....	
	Are home conditions a handicap?	....	(Rating 1–5).........
32	*Vocational guidance*		
	Is there a careers teacher with special responsibility?	....	
	Careers room?	....	
	Careers library?	....	
	Any careers conventions held?	....	
	Visiting careers lecturers?	....	
	Are parents involved?	....	
	Is full advantage taken of Youth Employment Service?	....	(Rating 1–5).........

No.	Variable		Rating
37	*Out-of-school activities*		
	No. of academic clubs	....	
	No. of hobbies clubs	....	
	School orchestra?	....	
	School choir?	....	
	Dramatic society	....	
	Youth club	....	
	No. of athletic clubs	....	
	Outdoor pursuit clubs	....	
	Cadet corps	....	
	Scouts and Guides	....	
	St John's/Red Cross	....	
	Duke of Edinburgh Award	....	
	Community and social work	....	
	Any others	....	(Rating 1–5).........
38	*School journeys*		
	Typical number in one year	....	
	No. of pupils involved	....	
	No. of staff involved	....	
	Duration (average)	....	
	Any in school time?	....	
	Restricted to UK?	....	(Rating 1–5).........
39	*School visits*		
	Many in school time?	....	
	No. of specific instances recalled over last year	....	
	Mainly cultural	....	
	Mainly vocational	....	
	Mainly social	....	(Rating 1–5).........
49	*Opportunities for pupils to acquire formal status*		
	Is there a head boy/girl?	....	
	How many prefects?	....	
	Are there house captains?	....	
	Are there games captains?	....	
	Are there form captains?	....	
	Range of prizes awarded	....	
	Honours board?	....	
	Any other offices?	....	(Rating 1–5).........

No.	Variable		Rating
50	*House system*		
	Is there a house system?	....	
	How are staff and pupils allocated?	....	
	....		
	House assemblies?	....	
	Frequency of meetings	....	
	Mainly for administration	....	
	Mainly social	....	
	Mainly sport/athletics	....	
	Inter-house competitions?	....	
	No. of officers	....	
	How are they elected?	....	(Rating 1–5)........
51	*Rewards*		
	Academic prizes?	....	
	Games prizes?	....	
	Games colours?	....	
	Merit mark system?	....	
	Demerits or order marks?	....	
	Rewards for attendance?	....	
	Rewards for punctuality?	....	
	Rewards for good behaviour?	....	
	Any other method?	....	(Rating 1–5)........
52	*Individual welfare*		
	Is there a member of staff responsible for pastoral care?	....	
	With a responsibility allowance?	....	
	Is full advantage taken of School Welfare Service?	....	
	Sick room?	....	
	How used?	....	(Rating 1–5)........
60	*Parents' meetings—formal*		
	P.T.A. or P.A.?	....	
	Initiation meeting for parents of new entrants?	....	
	No. of parents' meetings	....	
	Open day or evening?	....	
	Prize giving?	....	
	How many parents attend at dental or medical exams?	....	

No.	Variable		Rating
	How many parents attend interview with YEO?	....	
	Formal meeting to discuss subject options?	....	
	Formal meeting to discuss school leaving?	....	
	Any other formal meetings?	....	(Rating 1–5).........
61	*Parents' meetings—informal*		
	Parents invited to sports day?	....	
	Parents invited to plays?	....	
	Parents invited to services?	....	
	Parents invited to school outings and journeys?	....	
	Jumble sales/bazaars?	....	
	Dances, whist drives, etc.	....	(Rating 1–5).........
62	*Availability of teachers to parents*		
	Must parents make an appointment to see headteacher?	....	
	Are home visits made?	....	
	Who by?	....	
	What proportion of parents come for advice of their own accord?	....	
	Could a parent apply to see a particular teacher?	....	
	Would the head have to be present?	....	(Rating 1–5).........

N.B. The school variables covered by this schedule were assessed by means of ratings on evidence provided by headteachers during interviews with the research associates. In order to reduce subjectivity in rating, notes were made against each of the sub-items, where applicable. The sub-items helped to structure the interviews and were used as aides-memoires when reaching final rating decisions. Additional notes made on the schedule in Appendix 4, completed during tours of the schools, were also taken into account before arriving at final ratings in the case of certain variables.

Appendix 4
Schedule completed on school observation visit

School..

No. Variable

7 *Appearance of children*
Cleanliness ....
Evidence of care .... (Rating 1–5)........

8 *Sociability of children*
General liveliness ....
Attitude to observer .... (Rating 1–5).........

25 *Social atmosphere*
General atmosphere with emphasis on staff/pupil relationships
(Rating 1–5)........

26 *Attitude to inquiry*
Cooperativeness—suspiciousness of teachers (Rating 1–5)........

27 *Quality of headteacher*
Comments by teachers relating to efficiency,
attitude of HT, or conflict of ideas...................................
....

29 *School uniform*
Estimate proportion of children wearing uniform ....
Teachers' opinions of importance...................................

31 *Homework*
Teachers' opinions of efficiency of homework system.......................
Teachers' opinions of importance of homework...............................

No. Variable

36 *Corporal punishment*

Evidence of use ....
Teachers' comments about use ....
Pupils' comments about use .... (Rating 1–3)........

37 *Out-of-school activities*

Evidence of existence (notice-boards etc)
....

47 *Movement between lessons*

Teacher based ....
Form based .... (Score 1 or 2)...........

50 *House system*

Evidence of functioning (notices, colours, trophies, etc.)
....
Teachers' comments on whether flourishing or moribund.................

55 *First impression of school*

Cleanliness ....
Neatness ....
Decoration ....
Atmosphere .... (Rating 1–5)........

56 *Quality of building*

Provision and size of hall ....
Toilets ....
Spare classrooms ....
Specialist rooms ....
Traffic noise ....
Playing fields ....
Garden ....
Staff room(s) ....
Medical room ....
General outlook .... (Rating 1–5)........

57 *School equipment*

Quality of PE equipment ....
Art/craft materials ....
Quality of furniture ....
Science equipment ....
Teaching machines ....

No.	Variable		
	Language laboratories	....	
	Television sets	....	
	Radios	....	
	Musical instruments	....	
	Any special equipment?	....	(Rating 1–5).........
59	*Library*		
	Specially designed?	....	
	Makeshift?	....	
	None?	....	
	Space and arrangement	....	
	Provision of books	....	
	Cataloguing?	....	
	Equipment for covering books?	....	
	Hours of opening?	....	
	Home lending facilities?	....	
	Special allowance for library teacher?	....	
	General impression of usage	....	(Rating 1–5).........

N.B. The research associates used this schedule to structure their observations during visits to schools. Ratings were made on certain of the school variables by reference to these notes, e.g., variables 7 and 8 Appearance and Sociability of Children. Where a variable also appears on the Headteacher Schedule in Appendix 3, the notes made here were used in conjunction with those made in discussion with headteachers before a final rating was arrived at.

Appendix 5 List of variables—School analysis

Variable		Source	Basis	Distribution of raw scores (actual distribution for scales and ratings: range only for remainder)
1	Size of school	Headteacher	No. of pupils on roll—average of 3 years (1964–1967)	145–1419
2	Size of class	Head	No. of pupils on roll in March 1967 divided by the number of classes	15–34
3	Pupil/teacher ratio	Head	No. of pupils on roll in March 1967 divided by the number of teachers, including head.	12–24·6
4	Attendance	Head	Percentage attendance in school year 1965/66	76·5–96·0
5	Free meals	Head	Percentage of school roll in March 1967	0·6–27·6
6	Free clothing	Head	Percentage of school roll in March 1967	0·3–21·4
7	Appearance of pupils	Observer	5-point rating on cleanliness and evidence of care	3:10:16:19:5
8	Sociability of pupils	Observer	5-point rating on general liveliness and attitude to observer	1:4:18:22:8
9	Statutory leaving	Head	Percentage of sample pupils leaving school at age 15	0–100

	Variable	Source	Basis	Distribution of raw scores (actual distribution for scales and ratings: range only for remainder)
10	Leaving at age 16	Head	Percentage of sample pupils leaving school at age 16	0–77
11	Entry to sixth form	Head	Percentage of sample pupils entering sixth form	0–100
12	Migration	Pupil records	Percentage of age group not on school roll for whole of 3-year period (1964–1967)	0–48·1
13	Size of entry for external exams	Head	Percentage of sample pupils entered for external examinations—GCE O-level or CSE	0–100
14	Subject range in external exams	Head	No. of external exam subjects taken divided by the number of sample pupils entered	0–10
15	Teachers under age 30	Head	Percentage of staff including head, in March 1967	18·9–61·3
16	Teachers over age 50	Head	Percentage of staff including head, in March 1967	0–42·9
17	Graduate teachers	Head	Percentage of staff including head, in March 1967	0·5–93·5
18	Untrained teachers	Head	Percentage of staff including head, in March 1967	0–47·7

19	Teacher turnover	Head	No. of teachers appointed within 3 years as percentage of staff in March 1967	10–145·2
20	Male teachers	Head	Percentage of staff in March 1967 excluding head	0–100
21	Sex of school	Head	4-point scale: 1 girls only; 2 mixed with female head; 3 mixed with male head; 4 boys only	14:2:26:11
22	Graduate headteacher	Head	2-point scale: 1 non-graduate; 2 graduate	19:34
23	Age of headteacher	Head	Age in years in March 1967	41–65
24	Authoritarianism of headteacher	Observer	5-point rating on dominance and rigidity of headteacher's attitudes	6:14:13:10:10
25	Social atmosphere	Observer	5-point rating on warmth of head/staff/pupil relationships	2:5:16:23:7
26	Attitude to inquiry	Observer	3-point rating on attitude of head, and staff to inquiry (cooperative, v. suspicious)	9:16:28
27	Quality of headteacher	Observer	5-point rating on efficiency, relations with staff and pupils, and awareness of modern educational trends	1:8:20:18:6
28	Innovation	Observer	5-point rating on awareness and use of modern educational ideas, techniques and equipment	7:12:14:14:6
29	School uniform	Observer	5-point rating on extent and rigidity of enforcement of wearing of uniform	3:15:10:15:10
30	Emphasis on external examinations	Observer	5-point rating on importance of external examination results to raison d'être of school	3:12:10:15:13

Variable		Source	Basis	Distribution of raw scores (actual distribution for scales and ratings : range only for remainder)
31	Homework	Observer	5-point rating on amount, regularity and enforcement of homework	5:12:7:16:13
32	Vocational guidance	Observer	5-point rating on provision of staff and facilities over and above the services of the Youth Employment Service	3:17:13:17:3
33	Internal examinations	Head	No. of internal examinations held in 1 year	1–3
34	Type of school	Head	6-point scale : 1 unreorganized; 2 secondary modern; 3 comprehensive; 4 technical high; 5 maintained grammar, 6 direct grant grammar	1:29:2:9:9:3
35	Voluntary school	Head	2-point scale : 1 maintained non-religious; 2 voluntary (RC or CE)	38:15
36	Absence of corporal punishment	Head, pupils and observer	3-point scale : 1 frequently used; 2 seldom used; 3 never used	21:16:16
37	Out-of-school activities	Head, pupils and observer	5-point rating on number and range of school clubs and societies	6:7:19:16:5
38	School journeys	Head, pupils and observer	5-point rating on number, regularity and range of journeys at home and abroad	3:12:24:12:2
39	School visits	Head, pupils and observer	5-point rating on number, regularity and range of visits made during school time	6:8:16:18:5

40	Coeducation	Head	2-point rating: 1 single sex; 2 coeducational	24:29
41	Teaching periods	Head	No. of teaching periods in 1 school day	6–8
42	Length of school day	Head	4-point scale: 1 less than $4\frac{1}{2}$ hours; 2 $4\frac{1}{2}$–$4\frac{3}{4}$ hours; 3 $4\frac{3}{4}$–5 hours; 4 longer than 5 hours per day	3:30:11:9
43	Adequacy of pupil records	Observer	3-point rating on comprehensiveness, individuality and up-to-dateness of pupil records	8:12:33
44	Streaming at entry	Head	2-point scale: 1 no streaming in first year; 2 streamed on entry	17:36
45	Streaming by ability	Head	2-point scale: 1 no streaming by ability; 2 some streaming by ability	8:45
46	Extent of subject setting	Head	No. of subjects in which setting takes place across streams or forms	0–7
47	Movement between lessons	Head	2-point scale: 1 pupils move to teachers; 2 teachers move to pupils	36:17
48	Prefect system	Head	2-point scale: 1 no prefect system, 2 prefect system	8:45
49	Opportunities for pupils to acquire formal status	Head	5-point rating on number and range of offices which give pupils status in school e.g., form, house, games captains, etc.	2:13:17:19:2
50	House system	Head and observer	5-point rating on strength, liveliness and integration of house system (if any) into life of school	9:19:12:7:6
51	Merit mark system	Head	2-point scale: 1 no merit mark system; 2 merit mark system	18:35

Variable		Source	Basis	Distribution of raw scores (actual distribution for scales and ratings: range only for remainder)
52	Welfare	Head	5-point rating on provision of staff and facilities for dealing with problems of individual pupils	5:13:14:20:1
53	Extent of transfer between streams	Pupil records	Percentage of sample pupils demoted or promoted during 3 years 1964/67	0–100
54	Age of building	Head	No. of years from building of main structure to 1967	1–117
55	First impression of school	Observer	5-point rating on cleanliness, neatness, decoration and general atmosphere of buildings	6:7:16:20:4
56	Quality of building	Observer	5-point rating on provision and size of hall, toilets, spare classrooms, traffic noise, playing fields, staff rooms, medical rooms and general outlook	7:6:15:23:2
57	Provision of specialist rooms	Observer	5-point rating on adequacy of science laboratories, workshops, art rooms, housecraft rooms, etc.	4:7:13:25:4
58	School equipment	Observer	5-point rating on amount and quality of PE, games, art and craft, science equipment, etc.	4:9:23:12:5

59	Library	Observer	5-point rating on space and equipment available and uses to which put	1:3:24:24:1
60	Parents' meetings—formal	Head	5-point rating on frequency and regularity of formal parents' meetings	2:10:17:20:4
61	Parents' meetings—informal	Head	5-point rating on opportunities and facilities provided for parents to make informal contact with life of school	2:19:15:14:3
62	Availability of headteacher and staff to individual parents	Head	5-point rating on informality of appointment procedures and attitude of head to parents' visits	3:6:17:21:6
63	Verbal general ability 14+	Test	Mean score	3·4–32·0
64	Non-verbal general ability 14+	Test	Mean score	9·4–34·8
65	Verbal+non-verbal general ability	Tests	Mean score of summated marks	16·3–66·8
66	10+ total score	Tests	Mean of summated scores	451·2–764·8
67	10+ MH verbal reasoning	Test	Mean score	165·4–258·5
68	10+ MH English	Test	Mean score	81·5–132·0
69	10+ composition (Manchester)	Test	Mean score	79·3–127·2
70	10+ MH mathematics I	Test	Mean score	81·7–132·0
71	10+ MH mathematics II	Test	Mean score	76·6–134·8
72	First year secondary—English	Exams	Mean score of scaled marks	3·3–30·3
73	First year secondary—mathematics	Exams	Mean score of scaled marks	2·7–29·3
74	First year secondary—sciences	Exams	Mean score of scaled marks	3·8–31·8
75	First year secondary—social science	Exams	Mean score of scaled marks	3·2–29·0
76	First year secondary—non-academic	Exams	Mean score of scaled marks	4·0–33·5

Variable		Source	Basis	Distribution of raw scores (actual distribution for scales and ratings: range only for remainder)
77	First year secondary—total	Exams	Mean score of total of scaled marks	17·7–153·0
78	Second year secondary—English	Exams	Mean score of scaled marks	3·2–32·5
79	Second year secondary—mathematics	Exams	Mean score of scaled marks	2·8–32·3
80	Second year secondary—sciences	Exams	Mean score of scaled marks	3·1–28·2
81	Second year secondary—social science	Exams	Mean score of scaled marks	3·2–28·2
82	Second year secondary—non-academic	Exams	Mean score of scaled marks	3·7–34·7
83	Second year secondary—total	Exams	Mean score of total of scaled marks	16·9–155·0
84	Third year secondary—English	Exams	Mean score of scaled marks	3·4–32·2
85	Third year secondary—mathematics	Exams	Mean score of scaled marks	2·9–30·1
86	Third year secondary—sciences	Exams	Mean score of scaled marks	3·0–30·2
87	Third year secondary—social sciences	Exams	Mean score of scaled marks	2·6–29·5
88	Third year secondary—non-academic	Exams	Mean score of scaled marks	3·5–32·2
89	Third year secondary—total	Exams	Mean score of total of scaled marks	16·4–155·0
90	16+ external examinations	Exams	Mean points score—scaled GCE O-level and CSE results	0–40·2

Appendix 6 List of variables—Individual analysis

	Variable	Source	Basis		Distribution or range: highest coding given to category on right
1	Sex of child	Pupil	2-point scale:	1 boy	45:69
				2 girl	
2	Father's occupation	Plowden data	8-point scale:	1 unemployed	1:13:3:21:14:54:7:1
				2 RGO Class 5 unskilled	
				3 RGO Class 4 non-manual	
				4 RGO Class 4 manual semi-skilled	
				5 RGO Class 3 non-manual	
				6 RGO Class 3 manual skilled	
				7 RGO Class 2 managerial	
				8 RGO Class 1 professional	
3	Rateable value of house	Rating Office	9-point scale:	1 £19–29	15:11:9:27:17:18:7:6:4
				2 £30–39	
				3 £40–49	
				4 £50–59	
				5 £60–69	
				6 £70–79	
				7 £80–89	
				8 £90–99	
				9 £100+	

	Variable	Source	Basis		Distribution or range: highest coding given to category on right
4	Material needs adequate	Observer	2-point scale:	1 inadequate	12:102
				2 adequate	
5	Cleanliness of home	Observer	3-point scale:	1 much below satisfactory	7:5:102
				2 below satisfactory	
				3 satisfactory	
6	Housing standard	Observer	3-point scale:	1 poor	2:87:25
				2 tolerable	
				3 good	
7	Smallness of family	Parents	No. of children		11–1
8	Family health	Parents	2-point scale:	1 a member of family has had serious illness	29:85
				2 no serious illness in family	
9	Father from small family	Parents	5-point scale:	1 5 or more in family	36:36:11:22:9
				2 4 in family	
				3 3 in family	
				4 2 in family	
				5 only child	
10	Mother from small family	Parents	5-point scale:	1 5 or more in family	42:28:23:15:6
				2 4 in family	
				3 3 in family	
				4 2 in family	
				5 only child	

11	Mother not working	Parents	2-point scale: 1 mother works 2 mother does not work	79:35
12	Type of secondary school	Pupil	6-point scale: 1 unreorganized all ages 2 secondary modern 3 comprehensive 4 technical high 5 maintained grammar 6 direct grant grammar	2:73:8:16:12:3
13	Entered sixth form	Headteacher	2-point scale: 1 left before sixth form 2 entered sixth form	96:18
14	Left school at age 15	Headteacher	2-point scale: 1 stayed beyond statutory leaving age 2 left at statutory leaving age	56:58
15	Left school at age 16	Headteacher	2-point scale: 1 left at 15 or entered 6th form 2 left at age 16	76:38
16	Occupational ambition of child	Pupil	7-point scale: 1 RGO Class 5 2 RGO Class 4 non-manual 3 RGO Class 4 manual semi-skilled 4 RGO Class 3 non-manual 5 RGO Class 3 manual skilled 6 RGO Class 2 7 RGO Class 1	4:1:17:36:27:22:7
17	Cleanliness of child and evidence of care	Pupil	5-point rating on cleanliness, neatness, with no penalty for worn but clean clothing	3:10:31:44:26

	Variable	Source	Basis	Distribution or range: highest coding given to category on right
18	Child's outgoingness at interview	Observer	3-point scale: 1 shy 2 normally sociable 3 very outgoing	27:66:21
19	Preferred age of leaving—parents	Parents	5-point scale: 1 first opportunity 2 15–16 3 16+ 4 17+ 5 18+	54:31:10:14:5
20	Child's preference for extended schooling	Pupil	3-point scale: 1 wants statutory leaving 2 neutral 3 wants to stay longer	47:9:58
21	Earliness of leaving decision	Parents	5-point scale: 1 recent decision 2 after secondary entry 3 after junior entry 4 after infant entry 5 before school age	29:26:16:24:19
22	Influence of education on long-term plans	Parents	2-point scale: 1 no 2 yes	94:20
23	Type of further education desired	Parents	3-point scale: 1 none 2 vocational training 3 higher education	31:58:25

24	Career qualifications desired	Parents	4-point scale:	1 none 2 training or apprenticeship 3 professional or technical 4 highest professional	36:45:26:7
25	Earliness of career plans	Parents	3-point scale:	1 recent decision 2 during secondary school 3 at primary school or before	40:55:19
26	Interest taken by school in leaving decision	Pupil	6-point scale:	1 no action by school 2 general talk to leaving group 3 talk to individuals 4 meeting for parents 5 interviews with parents 6 discussion with parents and pupil	38:17:6:8:1:44
27	Parents' library membership	Parents	2-point scale:	1 neither parent in library 2 one or both member of library	80:34
28	Amount of mother's reading	Parents	5-point scale:	1 never reads 2 seldom reads 3 sometimes reads 4 frequently reads 5 reads regularly and continuously	8:53:23:21:9

Variable	Source	Basis	Distribution or range: highest coding given to category on right
29 Nature of mother's reading matter	Parents	6-point scale: 1 nothing 2 occasional newspaper 3 newspapers/women's magazines 4 moderate range of publications 5 wide range of books, etc. 6 extensive including non-fiction	4:47:31:25:7:0
30 Amount of father's reading	Parents	5-point scale: 1 never reads 2 seldom reads 3 sometimes reads 4 frequently reads 5 reads regularly and continuously	14:52:21:17:10
31 Nature of father's reading matter	Parents	6-point scale: 1 nothing 2 occasional newspaper 3 few newspapers and periodicals 4 moderate range of publications 5 wide range of books and publications 6 extensive including non-fiction	11:37:42:19:4:1

32	Duration of child's library membership	Parents	4-point scale: 1 not joined 2 during secondary school 3 during primary school 4 before old enough to have ticket	31:24:35:24
33	Parents influenced child to join library	Parents	3-point scale: 1 not applicable 2 other influences 3 parents wholly responsible	31:45:38
34	Child likes reading at home	Parents	3-point scale: 1 not at all 2 reads sometimes 3 very keen always	66:36:12
35	Nature of publications bought for child	Parents	3-point scale: 1 none 2 comics 3 magazines with more serious content	36:56:22
36	Nature of child's reading matter	Parents	4-point scale: 1 comics, pop magazines 2 modest range of periodicals 3 fiction, hobbies, newspapers 4 wide range of fiction/non-fiction	39:50:13:12
37	Nature of books bought for child	Parents	4-point scale: 1 none 2 annuals 3 light fiction 4 fiction/non-fiction on higher level	39:28:41:6
38	Provision for child to store own books	Parents	4-point scale: 1 none 2 general provision 3 shared provision 4 own provision	34:12:25:43

	Variable	Source	Basis	Distribution or range: highest coding given to category on right
39	Parents influence choice of books	Parents	2-point scale: 1 no influence 2 parents exert influence	83:31
40	Nature of radio listening	Parents	4-point scale: 1 none 2 pop music only 3 largely pop 4 selective	18:38:39:19
41	Selectivity of child's TV viewing	Parents	5-point rating from 1 anything to 5 small range of 'suitable' programmes	8:9:16:38:43
42	Nature of child's hobbies and interests	Parents	4-point rating from 1 'playing out' to 4 serious and long standing interests	11:49:31:23
43	Number of school clubs and societies joined	Pupil	No. of school clubs and societies joined during first 3 secondary school years	0–3
44	Involvement of child in parents' activities	Parents	4-point scale: 1 never involved 2 occasionally 3 fairly often 4 most of the time	75:13:13:13
45	Nature of family weekend activities	Parents	3-point scale: 1 none 2 shopping, visiting relations 3 educational outings	56:50:8
46	Family involvement during long school holidays	Parents	3-point scale: 1 none 2 days out 3 longer holidays	46:40:28

47	Parents' 11+ selection	Parents	3-point scale: 1 neither parent selected 2 one parent selected 3 both parents selected	62:36:17
48	Parents regret aspects of own education	Parents	4-point scale: 1 no regrets 2 some reservations 3 many reservations 4 very dissatisfied	14:65:14:21
49	Parents' further education involvement	Parents	4-point scale: 1 none 2 occasional night class or compulsory trade course 3 some examination work completed 4 longer course of high examination content	58:32:12:12
50	Amount of child's homework	Parents	5-point scale: 1 none 2 very little 3 some every week 4 nightly 1 hour 5 nightly 1 hour plus	19:27:22:20:26
51	Parents' knowledge of homework content	Parents	5-point rating from 1 not applicable to 5 very detailed knowledge	7:19:31:41:16
52	Parents' approval of homework	Parents	4-point rating from 1 not necessary to 4 highly desirable	18:39:50:7
53	Parents check homework	Parents	5-point rating from 1 never to 5 regularly	13:20:22:24:35

	Variable	Source	Basis	Distribution or range: highest coding given to category on right
54	Parents' formal education level	Parents	4-point scale: 1 basic only 2 selective secondary 3 O-level, apprenticeship 4 post O-level, advanced vocational	78:25:9:2
55	Parents chose secondary school on educational grounds	Parents	5-point rating from 1 no remembrance of choice to 5 educational factors closely considered	8:38:15:25:28
56	Father involved in choice of school	Parents	2-point scale: 1 father not involved 2 father involved	38:76
57	Parents want to assist in the teaching process	Parents	2-point scale: 1 no desire for involvement 2 involvement seen to be desirable	30:84
58	Parents' visit to secondary school before entry	Parents	3-point scale: 1 neither parent visited 2 one parent visited 3 both parents visited	34:33:47
59	School performance important to child's future	Parents	5-point rating from 1 not relevant to 5 very important	11:29:39:31:4
60	Parents' assessment of child's effort at school	Parents	4-point rating from 1 no effort made to 4 has worked very hard	27:19:41:27
61	Parents' knowledge of class position in individual subjects	Parents	5-point scale: 1 no idea 2 little idea	19:24:37:26:8

			3 some knowledge 4 fair knowledge 5 detailed knowledge	
62	Child talks about school	Parents	5-point scale: 1 never 2 seldom 3 sometimes 4 often 5 very often	12:22:22:36:22
63	Amount of family discussion on school progress	Parents	4-point scale: 1 none 2 infrequent 3 quite frequent 4 very frequent	34:31:43:6
64	Amount of parental discussion of school reports	Parents	5-point scale: 1 none 2 rarely discuss 3 sometimes discuss 4 usually discuss 5 always discuss	7:11:30:20:46
65	Nature of parental help with school work	Parents	5-point rating from 1 none to 5 detailed explanation of specific points	26:33:30:10:15
66	Parents ask about school	Pupil	3-point scale: 1 never 2 sometimes 3 frequently	28:40:46
67	Child likes parents and teachers to meet	Pupil	3-point scale: 1 not at all 2 doesn't mind 3 likes meetings	24:32:58
68	Involvement of child in school activities	Pupil	No. of school activities involved in, e.g. sports teams, choirs, orchestras	0–7

Variable	Source	Basis	Distribution or range: highest coding given to category on right
69 No history of truancy	Parents	3-point scale: 1 repeatedly played truant 2 yes rarely played truant 3 never played truant	2:14:98
70 No attendance problems	Parents	4-point scale: 1 always a problem 2 sometimes a problem 3 no problem 4 keen to attend	3:2:99:10
71 Attendance	Parents	6-point scale: 1 very poor 2 poor 3 fair 4 good 5 very good 6 excellent	7:6:5:14:49:33
72 Child has own room	Parents	2-point scale: 1 shared 2 own room	47:67
73 Child helps at home	Parents	3-point scale: 1 never helps 2 sometimes helps 3 regularly helps	11:59:44
74 Both parents control child	Parents	5-point rating from 1 left entirely to mother to 5 both parents always involved	26:32:19:21:16
75 Educational value of peer group influence	Parents	3-point scale: 1 a bad influence 2 neutral 3 a good influence	5:88:21

76	Affiliation	Pupil questionnaire	11-point scale: school provides opportunities for warm social relationships	0–10
77	Deference	Pupil questionnaire	11-point scale: insistence of school on deferential attitude to superiors	0–10
78	Order	Pupil questionnaire	11-point scale: neatness and orderliness of school	0–10
79	Primary headteacher's rating	Plowden data	5-point rating on overall benefit from primary education after making allowance for difference in general scholastic ability	3:24:42:37:8
80	7+ Picture Intelligence MH	Plowden date	Raw score	26–76
81	7+ Arithmetic (NFER)	Plowden data	Raw score	26–74
82	8+ Sentence Reading Test (NFER)	Plowden data	Raw score	24–76
83	8+ Mechanical Arithmetic (Manchester)	Plowden data	Raw score	24–76
84	8+ Problem Arithmetic (Manchester)	Plowden data	Raw score	29–76
85	9+ MH Junior Reasoning	Plowden data	Raw score	24–76
86	9+ MH Junior English	Plowden data	Raw score	24–76
87	10+ MH Verbal Reasoning	Plowden data	Raw score	30–76
88	10+ MH English	Plowden data	Raw score	32–76
89	10+ Composition (Manchester)	Plowden data	Raw score	30–81
90	10+ MH Mathematics I	Plowden data	Raw score	29–73
91	10+ MH Mathematics II	Plowden data	Raw score	31–74
92	10+ total	Plowden data	Average of total raw 10+ scores	34–74
93	14+ verbal general ability	Test	Scaled score	40–79

	Variable	Source	Basis	Distribution or range: highest coding given to category on right
94	14+ non-verbal general ability	Test	Scaled score	32–72
95	English secondary year 1	Examination	Scaled marks	39–82
96	Mathematics secondary year 1	Examination	Scaled marks	37–90
97	Sciences secondary year 1	Examination	Scaled marks	39–80
98	Social sciences secondary year 1	Examination	Scaled marks	39–86
99	Non-academic secondary year 1	Examination	Scaled marks	37–84
100	Total first year secondary attainment	Examinations	Average of scaled marks	37–86
101	English secondary year 2	Examination	Scaled marks	37–91
102	Mathematics secondary year 2	Examination	Scaled marks	37–92
103	Sciences secondary year 2	Examination	Scaled marks	36–86
104	Social sciences secondary year 2	Examination	Scaled marks	36–83
105	Non-academic secondary year 2	Examination	Scaled marks	37–80
106	Total secondary year 2 attainment	Examinations	Average of scaled marks	37–88
107	English secondary year 3	Examination	Scaled marks	39–86
108	Mathematics secondary year 3	Examination	Scaled marks	37–88
109	Sciences secondary year 3	Examination	Scaled marks	37–89
110	Social sciences secondary year 3	Examination	Scaled marks	37–91
111	Non-academic secondary year 3	Examination	Scaled marks	36–79
112	Total secondary year 3 attainment	Examinations	Average of scaled marks	37–90
113	16+ external examinations	Examinations	Scaled marks	44–76

Appendix 7
Interview and observation schedule followed at home visit

Anticipated variable	Basis	Score
2 Father's occupation	8-point scale:	
	1 unemployed	....
	2 RGO 5 unskilled	....
	3 RGO 4 non-manual	....
	4 RGO 4 manual semi-skilled	....
	5 RGO 3 non-manual	....
	6 RGO 3 manual skilled	....
	7 RGO 2 managerial	....
	8 RGO 1 professional	....
4 Material needs	2-point scale:	
	1 inadequate	....
	2 adequate	....
5 Cleanliness of home	3-point scale:	
	1 much below adequate	....
	2 below adequate	....
	3 adequate	....
6 Housing standard	3-point scale:	
	1 poor	....
	2 adequate	....
	3 good	....
7 Family size	Number of children in family	....
8 Family health	2-point scale:	
	1 A member of the family has had serious illness	....
	2 No member of the family has had serious illness	....

Anticipated variable	Basis	Score
9 Number of children in paternal family	5-point scale:	
	1 5 or over	....
	2 4	....
	3 3	....
	4 2	....
	5 only child	....
10 Number of children in maternal family	5-point scale:	
	1 5 or over	....
	2 4	....
	3 3	....
	4 2	....
	5 only child	....
11 Does mother go out to work?	2-point scale:	
	1 mother works	....
	2 mother does not work	....
19 At what age would you like X to leave school?	5-point scale:	
	1 first opportunity	....
	2 15–16	....
	3 16+	....
	4 17+	....
	5 18+	....
21 When did you come to this decision?	5-point scale:	
	1 recent decision	....
	2 after secondary entry	....
	3 after junior entry	....
	4 after infant entry	....
	5 before school age	....
22 Has your feeling for the importance of X's schooling influenced the family's long-term plans?	2-point scale:	
	1 no	....
	2 yes	....
23 What type of further education do you hope is available to X?	3-point scale:	
	1 none	
	2 vocational training	....
	3 higher education	....
24 What kind of career qualifications do you hope X's schooling will lead to?	4-point scale:	
	1 none	....
	2 training or apprenticeship	....
	3 professional or technical	....
	4 highest professional	....

Anticipated variable	Basis	Score
25 How long have you had these plans?	3-point scale:	
	1 recent	....
	2 during secondary school	....
	3 during primary school or before	....
What is X hoping to do when he/she leaves school?	4-point scale:	
	1 don't know	....
	2 general idea	....
	3 some plans	....
	4 specific ambition	....
Have you any specific plans for X to continue with further education	4-point scale:	
	1 no	....
	2 undecided	....
	3 yes—unformulated	....
	4 yes—detailed	....
Has any other member of the extended family been able to help X to think about and prepare for the future?	2-point scale:	
	1 no	....
	2 yes	....
Nature of relationship if YES..		
27 Does either of you belong to a library?	2-point scale:	
	1 neither	....
	2 one or both	....
28 How often does mother read when she gets a chance to relax?	6-point scale:	
	1 never	....
	2 seldom	....
	3 sometimes	....
	4 frequently	....
	5 regularly and continuously	....
	6 extensive including non-fiction	....
29 What kind of things does mother like to read when she gets the chance?	5-point scale:	
	1 nothing	....
	2 occasional newspaper	....
	3 newspapers/women's magazines	....
	4 moderate range of publications	....
	5 wide range books and publications	....

Anticipated variable	Basis	Score
30 How often does father read during his spare time?	5-point scale:	
	1 never	....
	2 seldom	....
	3 sometimes	....
	4 frequently	....
	5 regularly and continuously	....
31 What kind of things does father like to read when he gets the chance?	6-point scale:	
	1 nothing	....
	2 occasional newspaper	....
	3 few newspapers and periodicals	....
	4 moderate range of publications	....
	5 wide range of books and publications	....
	6 extensive including non-fiction	....
Does X belong to the public library?	2-point scale:	
	1 no	....
	2 yes	....
32 How long has X been a member?	4-point scale:	
	1 not joined	....
	2 during secondary	....
	3 during primary	....
	4 before old enough to have ticket	....
33 Do you think X joined the library because of your influence?	3-point scale:	
	1 not applicable	....
	2 other influences	....
	3 wholly responsible	....
34 Is X a keen reader?	3-point scale:	
	1 not at all	....
	2 reads sometimes	....
	3 very keen always	....
35 Do you buy any publications for X on a regular basis?	3-point scale:	
	1 none	....
	2 comics	....
	3 magazines with more serious content	....

Anticipated variable	Basis	Score
36 What kind of material is X particularly interested in reading?	4-point scale:	
	1 comics, pop magazines	....
	2 modest range of periodicals	....
	3 fiction, hobbies, newspapers	....
	4 wide range of fiction and non-fiction	....
37 What kind of books have you bought for X in recent years?	4-point scale:	
	1 none	....
	2 annuals	....
	3 light fiction	....
	4 fiction/non-fiction on higher level	....
Do you take any periodicals regularly?	3-point scale:	
	1 none	....
	2 newspaper only	....
	3 newspapers and magazines	....
Does X like to read the paper?	3-point scale:	
	1 no	....
	2 sports column only	....
	3 wider interest	....
Do you ever discuss news items with X?	3-point scale:	
	1 never	....
	2 occasionally	....
	3 frequently	....
38 Has X somewhere at home where he can keep his books?	4-point scale:	
	1 no	....
	2 general provision	....
	3 shared provision	....
	4 own provision	....
39 Have you ever tried to influence X's choice of books?	2-point scale:	
	1 no	....
	2 yes	....
Did you ever play word games with X?	3-point scale:	
	1 never	....
	2 sometimes	....
	3 frequently	....

	Anticipated variable	Basis	Score
	Is the wireless used much?	3-point scale:	
		1 rarely	....
		2 quite often	....
		3 most of the time	....
40	What kind of radio programmes do you listen to?	4-point scale:	
		1 none	....
		2 pop music only	....
		3 largely pop	....
		4 selective	....
	Has any radio programme led to a family discussion?	2-point scale:	
		1 no	....
		2 yes	....
	Would you say X watches a lot of television?	3-point scale:	
		1 too much	....
		2 fair amount	....
		3 very little	....
41	What kind of programmes does X watch most?	5-point rating ranging from 'anything' to small range of 'suitable' programmes	....
	Do you ever stop X watching something you consider unsuitable?	3-point scale:	
		1 no	....
		2 has been known	....
		3 very often	....
	Does the family leave you with any time of your own for activities outside the home?	2-point scale:	
		1 no	....
		2 yes	....
44	Does X ever join you in these activities?	4-point scale:	
		1 never	....
		2 occasionally	....
		3 fairly often	....
		4 most of the time	....
42	What kind of hobbies and interests does X have?	4-point rating from 1 'playing out' to 4 serious and long-standing	....

Anticipated variable	Basis	Score
45 Have you any favourite weekend pastimes in which all the family join?	3-point scale:	
	1 none	....
	2 shopping, visiting relations	....
	3 educational outings	....
Is all the family together daily?	4-point scale:	
	1 never	....
	2 only occasionally	....
	3 for some meals	....
	4 often	....
46 Does the family take holidays together away from home?	3-point scale:	
	1 none	....
	2 days out	....
	3 longer periods	....
Does X belong to a youth movement or club?	2-point scale:	
	1 no	....
	2 yes	....
Has X any pen-friends or other regular correspondents?	2-point scale:	
	1 no	....
	2 yes	....
47 Did either mother or father pass the 11+ examination for a selected place?	3-point scale:	
	1 neither	....
	2 one	....
	3 both	....
48 Has either mother or father any regrets about aspects of their own schooling?	4-point scale:	
	1 none at all	....
	2 some reservations	....
	3 many reservations	....
	4 very dissatisfied	....
49 Has either mother or father been involved in any further education after leaving school?	4-point scale:	
	1 none	....
	2 occasional night-class or compulsory trade course	....
	3 some examination work completed	....
	4 longer course of high examination content	....

Anticipated variable	Basis	Score
54 What was the highest level of education obtained by either father or mother?	4-point scale:	
	1 basic only	....
	2 selective secondary	....
	3 O-level, apprenticeship etc.	....
	4 post O-level, advanced vocational	....
50 How much homework does X have?	5-point scale:	
	1 none	....
	2 very little	....
	3 some every week	....
	4 nightly 1 hour	....
	5 nightly 1 hour plus	....
51 What subjects does X have for homework?	5-point rating from 1 not applicable to 5 very detailed knowledge	....
52 Do you think homework is a good thing?	4-point rating from 1 not necessary to 4 highly desirable	....
53 Do you ever check to see if X has done his homework properly?	5-point rating from 1 not applicable to 5 regularly	....
Have you ever made X do homework over again to improve it?	4-point scale:	
	1 not applicable	....
	2 never	....
	3 sometimes	....
	4 often	....
Have you ever asked the teachers for work X could do at home?	2-point scale:	
	1 no	....
	2 yes	....
Do you think X gets too much homework?	3-point scale:	
	1 not applicable	....
	2 yes	....
	3 no	....
Does X ever bring printed subject books home from school?	3-point scale:	
	1 don't know	....
	2 never	....
	3 yes	....

Anticipated variable	Basis	Score
Can you describe any of them?	4-point rating from 1 not applicable to 4 detailed knowledge of several	....
55 What made you choose X's secondary school out of those made available?	5-point rating from 1 no remembrance of choice to 5 educational factors closely considered	....
Did you get your first choice?	3-point rating:	
	1 don't know	....
	2 no	....
	3 yes	....
Would you now have preferred X to have gone to a different school?	2-point scale:	
	1 no	....
	2 yes	....
56 Did father have any feelings about which secondary school X should go to?	2-point scale:	
	1 father not involved	....
	2 father involved	....
57 Do you think teaching should be left entirely to teachers or would you like to be involved?	2-point scale:	
	1 no wish to be involved	....
	2 involvement seen to be desirable	....
58 Were father and mother able to visit X's secondary school before he/she went there?	3-point scale:	
	1 neither visited	....
	2 one parent visited	....
	3 both parents visited	....
What was your first impression of the school?	4-point scale:	
	1 not applicable	....
	2 poor	....
	3 satisfactory	....
	4 good	....
Did you have any other ways of knowing what the school was like?	2-point scale:	
	1 no	
	2 yes	....
Was your school visit useful?	3-point scale:	
	1 not applicable	....
	2 no	....
	3 yes	....

Anticipated variable	Basis	Score
How many times have you talked to X's headteacher since he went to this school?	4-point scale:	
	1 never	....
	2 once	....
	3 a few times	....
	4 many times	....
Are you happy about the arrangements at X's school for seeing the head or other teachers?	2-point scale:	
	1 no	....
	2 yes	....
What do you feel about the way the teachers control the children?	3-point scale:	
	1 too strict	....
	2 about right	....
	3 too soft	....
Would you say that X was treated fairly on the whole at school?	3-point scale:	
	1 don't know	....
	2 no	....
	3 yes	....
How often have you needed to complain at school?	3-point scale:	
	1 frequently	....
	2 once	....
	3 never	....
Do you feel you would be welcome to arrive at X's school to see someone without arranging it beforehand?	2-point scale:	
	1 no	....
	2 yes	....
When did you last speak to one of X's class teachers?	5-point scale:	
	1 never	....
	2 don't remember	....
	3 first year	....
	4 second year	....
	5 recently	....
59 How important is X's school performance likely to be for his future?	5-point rating from 1 not relevant to 5 crucially important	....
60 Would you say that X was trying hard at school?	4-point rating from 1 no effort made to 4 working hard	....

Anticipated variable	Basis	Score
Has X done better at school than you hoped?	2-point scale:	
	1 no	....
	2 yes	....
61 Can you remember where X comes in the class for any of his/her subjects?	5-point scale:	
	1 no idea	....
	2 little idea	....
	3 some knowledge	....
	4 fair knowledge	....
	5 detailed knowledge	....
What are X's best and weakest subjects?	3-point scale:	
	1 no idea	....
	2 uncertain	....
	3 specific answer	....
Are there any basic subjects with which X has difficulty?	3-point scale:	
	1 no idea	....
	2 uncertain	....
	3 specific answer	....
62 How often does X talk about how or what he/she is doing at school?	5-point scale:	
	1 never	
	2 seldom	....
	3 sometimes	....
	4 often	....
	5 very often	....
Are there any other ways whereby you find out what X is doing at school?	2-point scale:	
	1 no	....
	2 yes	....
63 Do you ever discuss progress with him/her?	4-point scale:	
	1 never	....
	2 infrequently	....
	3 quite often	....
	4 very often	....
How often does X bring home a report from school?	2-point scale:	
	1 don't know	....
	2 specific answer	....
64 Do mother and father discuss X's report when it comes?	5-point scale:	....
	1 never	....
	2 rarely	....
	3 sometimes	....
	4 usually	....
	5 always	....

Anticipated variable	Basis	Score
Do you think school reports are helpful to you?	2-point scale:	
	1 no	....
	2 yes	....
Does X ever ask you to help with school work?	4-point scale:	
	1 never	....
	2 rarely	....
	3 sometimes	....
	4 often	....
65 In what ways have you been able to help X most?	5-point rating from 1 none to 5 detailed explanations of specific points	....
Do you feel you have to spend too much time helping with school work?	2-point rating:	
	1 no	....
	2 yes	....
Can you think of any other ways you have been able to help and encourage X's school work?	2-point rating:	
	1 no	....
	2 yes	....
75 Do you feel that X's friends are a bad or good influence so far as school work is concerned?	3-point rating:	
	1 bad influence	....
	2 neutral	....
	3 good influence	....
71 How would you describe X's attendance at school?	6-point scale:	
	1 very poor	....
	2 poor	....
	3 fair	....
	4 good	....
	5 very good	....
	6 excellent	....
Is X's school very strict about attendance?	3-point scale:	
	1 no	....
	2 yes	....
	3 very	....
70 Have you ever had any difficulty in getting X to go to school?	4-point scale:	
	1 always a problem	....
	2 sometimes	....
	3 no problem	....
	4 keen to attend	....

Anticipated variable	Basis	Score
Would you say that X welcomes an excuse to stay away from school?	2-point scale:	
	1 yes	....
	2 no	....
69 Do you know if X has ever played truant?	3-point scale:	
	1 repeatedly	....
	2 yes rarely	....
	3 never	....
Did mother have a job outside home before X went to school?	2-point scale:	
	1 yes	....
	2 no	....
72 Where does X sleep?	2-point scale:	
	1 shared	....
	2 own room	....
Does X have a desk or table to himself where he can work?	2-point scale:	
	1 no	....
	2 yes	....
73 Does X help at home?	3-point scale:	
	1 never	....
	2 sometimes	....
	3 regularly	....
Does X persevere until a job is properly done?	4-point scale:	....
	1 never	....
	2 rarely	....
	3 usually	....
	4 always	....
74 Does father play a big part in controlling the children, or is it mainly mother's job?	5-point rating from 1 left entirely to mother to 5 both parents always involved	....
Would you say X had been a difficult child?	4-point scale:	
	1 very	....
	2 not really	....
	3 hardly ever	....
	4 never	....
Are there any adults in your circle of family and friends that X may have heard about who could be regarded as an example of achievement?	3-point scale:	
	1 no	....
	2 yes	....
	3 yes—educationally	....

Anticipated variable	Basis	Score
Does X's school have many events of a more social nature to which you are invited?	3-point scale:	
	1 don't know	....
	2 no	....
	3 yes	....
Do either or both of you try to attend?	4-point scale:	
	1 neither/never	....
	2 sometimes one	....
	3 sometimes both	....
	4 frequently both	....
Is there a parents' association at X's school?	2-point scale:	
	1 no	....
	2 yes	....
Would you say that mother usually deals with school matters, or is father able to take an equal interest?	3-point scale:	
	1 always mother	....
	2 sometimes both	....
	3 always both	....
Can you remember if you have ever tried to influence X's choice of friends?	3-point scale:	
	1 never	....
	2 recently	....
	3 always	....
Do you think it is a good idea for the government to raise the school leaving age to 16?	2-point scale:	
	1 no	....
	2 yes	....
Have you, on the whole, been satisfied with the education X has received so far?	2-point scale:	
	1 no	....
	2 yes	....

NB Items left unnumbered were not included in the final analyses because of their low relationship with all aspects of attainment.

Appendix 8
Interview and observation schedule—individual pupils

Surname	Code No.	
Christian names	Sex Boy (1) Girl	1 2
Address		
Telephone No.		
School (12)	Unreorganized Secondary modern Comprehensive Technical high Maintained grammar Direct grant grammar	1 2 3 4 5 6
Date of birth	Age...........Yrs...........Months	
11-plus selection	Not entered Not selected Selected place Technical high Grammar	1 2 3 4 5
Whether secondary school attended was first, second or third choice	Third choice Second choice First choice	1 2 3
Statutory leaving date Born on or before 1 Feb 1953 Born on or before 1 Sept 1953	 Easter 1968 Midsummer 1968	 1 2

Wearing school uniform	No		1
	Yes		2
Cleanliness and evidence of care	5-point rating		1
			2
			3
			4
(17)			5
Interview behaviour	Shy		1
	Normally sociable		2
(18)	Very outgoing		3
Do you intend to leave school at Easter/Midsummer this year? (Enter statutory leaving date)	Staying beyond statutory leaving date	No	1
		Don't know	2
		Yes	3
(a) Are you glad you are leaving school at Easter/Midsummer?	Wants to leave at statutory leaving date	Yes	1
		Neutral	2
	(20)	No	3
Why? .... Why not?			
(b) Are your parents glad you are leaving school then?	Parents want statutory leaving	Yes	1
		Neutral	2
Why? .... Why not?		No	3
Are you staying on at school for an extra term, until 16+ or longer?	Anticipated length of extended schooling	none	1
		extra term	2
		16+	3
		longer	4
(a) Are you glad you are staying on?	Wants to stay at school	no	1
		neutral	2
Why? .... Why not?		yes	3
(b) Are your parents glad you are staying on?	Parents want extended schooling	no	1
		neutral	2
Why? .... Why not?		yes	3

When was it decided that you should leave at 15/stay on longer?	Age of leaving decision	Not decided yet This year In the third year In the second year In the first year At primary school Before that	1 2 3 4 5 6 7
Did the school help you to make up your mind? How?	Involvement of school in leaving decision (26)	No action by school General talk to leaving group about possibilities Talk to individuals Meeting for parents Interviews with parents Discussion with parents and pupil	1 2 3 4 5 6
If everybody had to leave school at the same age, what age would be best? Why?................................	(20)	Before 15 15 16 17 18	1 2 3 4 5
What job would you like to do when you finish your education? .... Why?................................	Occupational RGO ambition (16)	Class 5 Class 4 nm Class 4 mss Class 3 nm Class 3 ms Class 2 Class 1	1 2 3 4 5 6 7
When you go home from school, do your parents ask you what you have been doing that day?	Parents ask about school (66)	never sometimes often	1 2 3
Do you tell your parents what goes on at school even if they don't ask?	Pupil talks about school	never sometimes often	1 2 3

Do your parents like to come to school events such as plays, concerts, exhibitions, carol services, etc.?	Parents' liking for school events	no not much neutral yes very much	1 2 3 4 5
Do you tell your parents if there is something going on at school which they can attend?	Pupil passes on information about school events	never usually always	1 2 3
Do you like your parents and teachers getting together for a chat?	Pupils likes parents and teachers to meet (67)	no neutral yes	1 2 3
Do your parents discuss your school reports with you?	School reports discussed	never sometimes always	1 2 3
Did you do much homework in the first 3 years in the secondary school?	Homework	none some–irregular some–regular nightly	1 2 3 4
Do your parents think that homework is a good thing?	Parents' attitude to homework	no neutral yes	1 2 3
Did you enjoy your first 3 years in the secondary school? Why?.............................. Why not?	Pupil likes school	not at all not very much on the whole very much	1 2 3 4
What was your favourite subject? Or subjects? Why?..............................	Favourite subject	non-academic mixed academic	1 2 3
Were there any subjects you disliked? Why?..............................	Disliked subjects	academic mixed non-academic	1 2 3

Which subjects were you best at?	Best subjects	non-academic mixed academic	1 2 3
Which were your weakest subjects?	Weak subjects	academic mixed non-academic	1 2 3
Which subjects, if any, did you improve in the most?	Opinion of improvement	none one named several named	1 2 3
Are you going to sit for any external examinations at 16+?	External examinations	no yes (ask next question)	1 2
Which external examinations do you think you might take?	Examination ambition	none CSE GCE O-level GCE A-level	1 2 3 4
How many of these activities have you taken part in at secondary school? Sports teams.........Plays......... Choir...............Concerts...... Any others...........................	Involvement in school activities (68)	Rate No.	
Have you ever joined a school club or society at secondary school. Which ones?.........................	School clubs and societies (43)	Rate No.	
Have you ever been away on holiday with a school party? Where to?...........................	School journeys	never once twice more	1 2 3 4
Have you ever had a paid job outside school? What kind?........................	Paid job	no yes	1 2

Is there any aspect of secondary school you think ought to be changed?

....

NB Bracketed numbers refer to variable numbers in Appendix 6. Items left unnumbered were not included in the final analyses because of their low relationship with all aspects of attainment.

Appendix 9
Schools characteristics inventory completed by pupils

Instructions: Read the question carefully. If you think the statement is true for your secondary school, put a ring round 'T' for true on the scoring sheet. If you think the statement is not true for your school put a ring round 'F' for false.

1 Teachers here are very interested in our ideas and opinions about school affairs.
2 You soon get to know who does well in exams.
3 Marks are read out in class so that everybody knows who got the high and low marks.
4 If a pupil had an idea for a school club or society, he/she would be encouraged to get it going.
5 When you have been here a year you know exactly what the rest of your school career will be like.
6 Most lessons are well planned.
7 Pupils are often expected to work on their own at problems the teachers know they can't solve.
8 The pupils in the older forms don't have to obey as many rules as the rest of the school.
9 Lessons would be a lot more exciting if we could join in more.
10 Teachers would not dream of inviting pupils to their homes.
11 If a pupil sat at a different desk one day, the teachers would notice and pass a remark.
12 Pupils get really excited at school games matches.
13 Teachers here are genuinely concerned with pupils' feelings.
14 A lot of pupils like chess, crosswords, brainteasers and other such puzzles.

---

15 You have to get permission to do anything around here.
16 You can usually get through exams even if you don't work very hard during the year.
17 In PE, everybody has to do the same exercises no matter how good or bad he is at them.
18 There is a lot of school spirit and everybody sticks up for the school.
19 Courses, subjects, timetables and books frequently change from year to year.
20 Teachers never really explain what we can get out of lessons and why they are important.
21 When we think a teacher's decision is unfair, we try to get it changed.

22 Teachers go out of their way to make sure that we address them with due respect.
23 Pupils put a lot of energy into everything they do—in class and out.
24 A lot of pupils go right through the school without the head knowing them by name.
25 Many teachers get upset if pupils report to class a little late.
26 There is not much support by pupils for the big school events.
27 Outside class most teachers are friendly and find time to chat with us.
28 Pupils never get together in their own time to talk about things they have learned at school.

---

29 The staff always take note of our parents' wishes before they decide something about our school careers.
30 Most teachers are strict about homework.
31 Once you have made a mistake it is hard to live it down in this school.
32 It is easy to make friends here because of all the things going on for everybody to join in.
33 Many pupils have lived abroad or in different parts of the country.
34 The pupils who did not do well in a test would really try hard to do better next time.
35 Teachers do not encourage us to speak up freely and openly in class.
36 If your opinion differs from that of the teacher, you keep quiet about it.
37 We are often so busy that the bell at the end of a lesson comes as a surprise.
38 We hardly ever send the teachers cards or presents on special occasions.
39 Many teachers make pupils do work over again to make it neater.
40 There are not many dances, parties or other social activities.
41 The pupil who tries to help is liable to be regarded as a fuss-pot.
42 Debates and discussions on serious subjects are not held very often.

---

43 Teachers very often make you feel like a little child.
44 You can get good marks just by being popular and bluffing a bit.
45 You don't have much choice in the subjects you can take.
46 Not many pupils stay after school for different activities or sports.
47 This school has the same activities every year.
48 Most school clubs and societies are properly organized.
49 Pupils do not hesitate to voice their complaints.
50 We always wait for teacher's permission before speaking in class.
51 There are so many things to do here you are busy all the time.
52 We often run errands or do other personal services for the head and teachers.
53 At this school the motto seems to be—'a place for everything and everything in its place'.
54 Having a good time comes first with most pupils here.

55 The teachers see themselves as guides to show you how to learn, and don't just pass on facts.
56 There is not much point in just learning notes by heart and then writing them out again in an exam.

---

57 Pupils sometimes have to take the blame for things whether they did them or not.
58 There is a lot of emphasis on passing external examinations for the glory of the school.
59 Pupils have to get up in class and read or recite no matter how embarrassed they might be.
60 It would be nice to have an old pupils' association.
61 New ideas are always being tried out here.
62 Most teachers give clear instructions so that everybody knows what to do.
63 Pupils grumble about this school rule or that, but they never take any active steps to put things right.
64 Teachers sometimes call each other by their first names when pupils can hear.
65 Teachers here seem to be very interested in what they are doing.
66 There does not seem to be much interest here in doing things to help others, such as collecting money or food for the needy.
67 The average blackboard still has bits of yesterday's lessons on it.
68 The school is always buzzing with new jokes, funny stories and sayings.
69 Many teachers seem to be under the impression that pupils know a lot more than they actually do.
70 Most lessons follow the same pattern of listening to the teacher for a bit and then writing something.

---

71 Most teachers don't make you feel as though you are wasting their time.
72 School examinations really test how much you have learned.
73 Teachers often ask the pupils personal questions.
74 The school games teams get really good support from the rest of the school.
75 Most pupils act pretty much alike.
76 Many teachers seem to be more interested in their subject than in the pupils.
77 Pupils tend to behave badly for the teachers who try to be strict.
78 Most teachers don't mind if we disagree with them in a class discussion.
79 It's possible to get so wrapped up in what you are doing, you forget everything going on around you.
80 Pupils try in all sorts of ways to be friendly, especially to newcomers.
81 The school buildings and grounds often look a little untidy.
82 Everyone has a lot of fun at this school.

83 Most teachers are not interested in a pupil's personal problems.
84 Most teachers only tell you what you could read for yourself in a book.

---

85 On the whole those in charge are very patient with us.
86 Most pupils expect to go on with their education after they leave school.
87 If a pupil does something a teacher does not like, he/she is always asked to explain why.
88 Most pupils would not stay after school for any kind of activity.
89 The teachers seem to be changing all the time.
90 If special equipment is needed for a lesson it is always ready when wanted.
91 Everyone prefers the easy teachers and tries to avoid the tough ones.
92 We sometimes call the teachers by their first names or nicknames when we talk about them.
93 Teachers put a lot of energy and enthusiasm into their lessons.
94 When they collect money or things for charities at school, we always try hard to get as much as possible.
95 Pupils move the desks around to suit the way they want to sit.
96 It is easy to get a group together to play a game or go out with out of school time.
97 One nice thing about this school is the personal interest they take in us.
98 Most of the teachers are very interesting about their own subject.

---

99 If you get into trouble with one teacher, the other teachers soon know about it.
100 The only prizes they give here are connected with work and examinations.
101 If a pupil were only good at one thing everybody would go all out to help him develop it to the full.
102 Most pupils keep the same set of friends in school time and outside school time.
103 The school is especially proud of its history and traditions.
104 Most pupils have no regular plans for study and play.
105 No one gets pushed around at this school without fighting back.
106 The teachers, not the pupils, move around from class to class.
107 Lessons are pretty boring.
108 Many of the teachers are very interested in charities and schemes to help other people outside school.
109 Nobody, not even the teachers, pays much attention to the rules for moving about the school.
110 On the whole pupils here just come to school, get through lessons and then go home again, and not much else.
111 The teachers mostly go out of their way to help you.
112 There is a lot of interest here in learning for its own sake, not just for getting good marks in exams.

---

113 Pupils do not argue with teachers, they just admit they are wrong.
114 After-school projects in such things as science, history etc., would not be very popular.
115 A pupil could stay on at school as long as he liked, even if he were not very brilliant at a lot of subjects.
116 There are a lot of group projects on which you can work with your friends, in and out of school.
117 Most of the teachers have lived in or around Manchester all their lives.
118 It is hard to revise for exams because pupils hardly ever know what they will be tested on.
119 The headteacher is always willing to listen to pupils' grievances.
120 We hardly ever make fun of the teachers when we talk among ourselves.
121 In class we have some very lively and intense discussions.
122 When someone is off sick for a while his friends always let him know that he is missed.
123 Classrooms are always kept very clean and tidy.
124 You have to work hard in your own time because there's so much fooling about during the day.
125 Pupils seem to get plenty of help from school in choosing a job.
126 The school library is well used for private study.

---

127 A lot of pupils in this school are always trying to curry favour with the teachers.
128 You can only get on in this school by getting good marks for work.
129 If you slackened off in a subject for a week or two the teacher would soon let you know about it.
130 There are lots of open days, exhibitions, plays, etc., and everybody can help with them.
131 You never know what's going to happen next at this school.
132 Most teachers give very clear and useful notes.
133 There's not much squabbling and arguing among pupils.
134 Pupils can feel free to disagree with teachers without worrying about it.
135 Teachers could make us work a lot harder than we do.
136 Pupils in this school have a reputation for friendliness.
137 Pupils keep in lines when moving about the school, or when out on a visit.
138 You are liable to be a bit of a social outcast if you let the rest of the class know how much work you have actually done.
139 The teachers try hard to make sure that you take the right subjects to help you in your future career.
140 You have to think clearly and carefully when writing essays, or the teachers here will not give you a good mark.

Appendix 9 Scoring sheet

1	T	F	15	T	F	29	T	F	43	T	F	57	T	F	71	T	F	85	T	F	99	T	F	113	T	F	127	T	F		Abasement
2	T	F	16	T	F	30	T	F	44	T	F	58	T	F	72	T	F	86	T	F	100	T	F	114	T	F	128	T	F		Achievement
3	T	F	17	T	F	31	T	F	45	T	F	59	T	F	73	T	F	87	T	F	101	T	F	115	T	F	129	T	F		Adaptiveness
4	T	F	18	T	F	32	T	F	46	T	F	60	T	F	74	T	F	88	T	F	102	T	F	116	T	F	130	T	F		Affiliation (76)
5	T	F	19	T	F	33	T	F	47	T	F	61	T	F	75	T	F	89	T	F	103	T	F	117	T	F	131	T	F		Change
6	T	F	20	T	F	34	T	F	48	T	F	62	T	F	76	T	F	90	T	F	104	T	F	118	T	F	132	T	F		Conjunctivity
7	T	F	21	T	F	35	T	F	49	T	F	63	T	F	77	T	F	91	T	F	105	T	F	119	T	F	133	T	F		Counteraction
8	T	F	22	T	F	36	T	F	50	T	F	64	T	F	78	T	F	92	T	F	106	T	F	120	T	F	134	T	F		Deference (77)
9	T	F	23	T	F	37	T	F	51	T	F	65	T	F	79	T	F	93	T	F	107	T	F	121	T	F	135	T	F		Energy
10	T	F	24	T	F	38	T	F	52	T	F	66	T	F	80	T	F	94	T	F	108	T	F	122	T	F	136	T	F		Nurturance
11	T	F	25	T	F	39	T	F	53	T	F	67	T	F	81	T	F	95	T	F	109	T	F	123	T	F	137	T	F		Order (78)
12	T	F	26	T	F	40	T	F	54	T	F	68	T	F	82	T	F	96	T	F	110	T	F	124	T	F	138	T	F		Play
13	T	F	27	T	F	41	T	F	55	T	F	69	T	F	83	T	F	97	T	F	111	T	F	125	T	F	139	T	F		Succourance
14	T	F	28	T	F	42	T	F	56	T	F	70	T	F	84	T	F	98	T	F	112	T	F	126	T	F	140	T	F		Understanding

NB Bracketed numbers refer to variable numbers in Appendix 6.
Items left unnumbered were not included in the final analyses because of their low relationship with all aspects of attainment.